Improving Quality in American Higher Education

Richard Arum

Josipa Roksa

Amanda Cook

Improving Quality in American Higher Education

Learning Outcomes and Assessments for the 21st Century

JB JOSSEY-BASS™

A Wiley Brand

Copyright © 2016 by John Wiley & Sons, Inc. All rights reserved.

Published by Jossey-Bass

A Wiley Brand

One Montgomery Street, Suite 1000, San Francisco, CA 94104-4594—www.josseybass
.com

Jossey-Bass books and products are available through most bookstores. To contact
Jossey-Bass directly call our Customer Care Department within the U.S. at 800-956-7739,
outside the U.S. at 317-572-3986, or fax 317-572-4002.

Wiley publishes in a variety of print and electronic formats and by print-on-demand.
Some material included with standard print versions of this book may not be included
in e-books or in print-on-demand. If this book refers to media such as a CD or DVD that
is not included in the version you purchased, you may download this material at http://
booksupport.wiley.com. For more information about Wiley products, visit www.wiley.com.

Library of Congress Cataloging-in-Publication Data available at:

ISBN 978-1-119-26850-5 Hardback

ISBN 978-1-119-26852-9 ePDF

ISBN 978-1-119-26851-2 ePUB

Cover Design: Wiley

Cover Images: © John Giustina/Getty Images, Inc.

Printed in the United States of America

FIRST EDITION

HB Printing   10 9 8 7 6 5 4 3 2 1

Contents

Acknowledgments

This volume emerges from a large-scale collaborative effort organized by the Social Science Research Council (SSRC) and supported by a large number of individuals and institutions from across the country. Our colleagues at the SSRC provided support for this initiative at multiple levels: Ira Katznelson, Mary McDonnell and Ron Kassimir, as leadership at the Council, embraced the importance of the work from its initial stages and provided guidance and unwavering support throughout; Amanda Cook not only contributed to the project conceptually, but administratively oversaw the initiative during her time at the Council; additional assistance was provided by Abby Larson in initial phases of the project and most ably by Eleanor Blair during the final production of white papers and this volume.

A vital complement to the SSRC's role in this project was the steadfast intellectual and organizational support of a great many disciplinary associations and other organizations. In particular, we are deeply grateful to leadership at the following organizations for partnering with us and providing constructive feedback and input on the work: the American Economic Association, the American Historical Association, the American Sociological Association, the Association to Advance Collegiate Schools of Business, the National Communication Association, the National Institute for Learning Outcomes Assessment, the Stanford History Education

Group, the Society for the Advancement of Biology Education Research, and the Educational Testing Service.

Another essential factor behind the success of this endeavor was the support of both the Bill & Melinda Gates Foundation and the Teagle Foundation, who not only provided generous financial support, but also served as valuable thought partners throughout. We are particularly grateful to the following foundation officers: Dan Greenstein, Patrick Methvin, Jason Palmer, Jim Ptaszynski, and Stacey Clawson from the Gates Foundation; and Judith Shapiro, Loni Bordoloi Pazich, Richard L. Morrill, Annie W. Bezbatchenko from the Teagle Foundation.

At Jossey-Bass, the project benefited from editorial guidance and support from Marjorie McAneny, Shauna Robinson, Prithviraj Kamaraj, and Kristi Bennett. We are also grateful to some of the leading voices in higher education learning and assessment—Charles Blaich, Peter Ewell, Natasha Jankowski, George Kuh, Carol Geary Schneider, and Kathleen Wise—who were willing to contribute critical commentary on the work. We've included their voices in this volume, which reflects our belief that for an initiative of this character to be successful, it must be open to criticism and committed to iteration over the years to come.

Most of all, we owe our deepest gratitude to the faculty members from the six disciplines who came together to respond to the historic challenge we are facing in higher education. We are deeply indebted to the faculty who contributed their time and ideas to the Measuring College Learning panels, to their colleagues who they consulted and who offered constructive feedback, and most of all to the coauthors of the chapters to follow.

About the Editors

Richard Arum is professor of sociology and education at New York University and director of the Education Research Program at the Social Science Research Council.

Josipa Roksa is associate professor of sociology and education at the University of Virginia.

Amanda Cook is assistant director of the Education Research Program at the Social Science Research Council.

About the Contributors

Sam Allgood is Edwin J. Faulkner Professor of Economics at the University of Nebraska, Lincoln.

Amanda Bayer is professor of economics at Swarthmore College.

Sara Beckman is senior lecturer and Earl F. Cheit Faculty Fellow in the Haas School of Business at the University of California, Berkeley.

Steven Beebe is Regents' and University Distinguished Professor of Communication Studies at Texas State University.

Charles Blaich is director of the Center of Inquiry and the Higher Education Data Sharing Consortium at Wabash College.

Lendol Calder is professor of history at Augustana College.

William Carbonaro is associate professor of sociology at the University of Notre Dame.

Clarissa Dirks is professor of biology at The Evergreen State College.

Peter Ewell is president of the National Center for Higher Education Management Systems.

Susan Ferguson is professor of sociology at Grinnell College.

Natasha Jankowski is associate director of the National Institute for Learning Outcomes Assessment at the University of Illinois and Indiana University.

Ira Katznelson is Ruggles Professor of Political Science and History at Columbia University and president of the Social Science Research Council.

Nancy Kidd is executive director of the National Communication Association.

Jennifer Knight is associate professor of molecular, cellular, and developmental biology at the University of Colorado, Boulder.

George Kuh is director of the National Institute for Learning Outcomes Assessment, adjunct research professor of education policy at the University of Illinois, and Chancellor's Professor of Higher Education Emeritus at Indiana University.

W. Bradford Mello is associate professor of communication at Saint Xavier University.

Jeff Nesteruk is professor of legal studies in the Department of Business, Organizations, and Society at Franklin and Marshall College.

Trevor Parry-Giles is director of academic and professional affairs at the National Communication Association and professor of communication at the University of Maryland.

Carol Geary Schneider is president of the Association of American Colleges and Universities.

Tracy Steffes is associate professor of education and history at Brown University.

Kathleen Wise is associate director of the Center of Inquiry and director of the Teagle Assessment Scholar Program at Wabash College.

Foreword

Ira Katznelson

We live in an age of metrics. With measurement everywhere, critical questions concern not whether, but how to gauge and evaluate. All the more reason to celebrate the pioneering approach to pedagogical achievement represented in this stimulating volume.

The Social Science Research Council is especially pleased to host the ambitious Measuring College Learning Project that has been guided by Richard Arum, Josipa Roksa, and Amanda Cook because its core principles and methodology resonate so richly with the history and objectives of the SSRC. Founding in 1923, the Council was fashioned by then young learned societies in Anthropology, Economics, History, Political Science, Psychology, Sociology, and Statistics. Their intellectual leaders sought to deepen the craft of social science by crossing intellectual boundaries while respecting the individual vectors of each subject of study. They wished to galvanize social scientists to work on crucial public issues, including education. They also aimed to build the capacity of students and scholars to learn and conduct inquiry about the human condition.

What the founders did not do was focus on pedagogy or on assessing how undergraduates were acquiring knowledge. Notwithstanding, each of their principal aspirations only could be achieved if buttressed by high-quality teaching and learning. Then as now, none of the Council's primary objectives can be secured without inspiring young adults to thoughtfully understand and deploy the work of systematic social knowledge. This capacity also provides a foundation for democratic citizenship in which members of the society are called on to thoughtfully judge key aspects of social life and public affairs.

By way of a compelling corrective, the past decade has witnessed a major effort by the SSRC to engage with and evaluate the results of collegiate instruction. The Council's program on higher education has originated powerful research concerned with what students actually learn in college, and with how their experiences project into adulthood. Based on rich data and incisive analysis, *Academically Adrift* revealed limits on learning and pressed colleges and universities to become more focused on goals and processes. That book's successor, *Aspiring Adults Adrift*, revealed profound challenges for the cohort of students studied in the earlier volume as that group left the shelter of the university for the world of more independent adulthood.

What the current work detailed below adds is a powerful insistence that meaningful assessments of learning outcomes depend on a small number of key decisions and judgments too rarely made. This approach to measuring outcomes revolves around the insight that faculty intentions not only motivate how education best proceeds, subject by subject, but how learning's achievements are refracted through competencies and concepts that educators believe to be essential for their fields of study.

At a time when too many standards impose artificial and mechanical criteria that fail to measure rigorously and thoughtfully, this project's diversity of fields, respect for the distinctiveness of different types of learning, and commitment to more incisive and precise measurements that move beyond too-simple efforts at accountability show that it is possible to advance learning by combining understanding with clarity about objectives, means, and results.

Both the overview and the treatments of learning in the six disciplines this book considers are not intended to be dispositive. Rather, they convene a way of working that necessarily varies across subjects and across institutions and student communities. The issues dealt with in these essays go to the heart of defining what faculty instructors believe to be indispensable knowledge. They are bound to be controversial in both substance and method. As such, they should be read as a robust invitation to a wide variety of persons concerned with higher education to think hard, in fresh ways, about the ambitions, tools, and consequences of what we do as educators.

We are in the midst of a public conversation about the price, value, and effects of college-level pedagogy. Much of this talk has been based on uneven information, sporadic impressions, and limited analyses that are based on measures about cost, rates of completion, factual retention, and post-college job market experiences. These dominant approaches are not adequate. What we lack and urgently require are supple and knowledge-focused ways to appraise how those aspects of subjects that teachers and researchers believe to be fundamental to critical thought are conveyed and received. It is with passion for this set of challenges that the Measuring College Learning Project has begun to make important gains.

Much remains to be accomplished. The kinds of appraisals recommended here require new instruments, buy-ins by persons and organizations, effective persuasion and dissemination, and understanding of the utility of faculty- and discipline-based appraisals. In all, the success of this venture has large implications for the future of social knowledge and the character of civic life.

Improving Quality in American Higher Education

Defining and Assessing Learning in Higher Education

Josipa Roksa
University of Virginia

Richard Arum
SSRC and New York University

Amanda Cook
SSRC

This contribution presents an overview of the Measuring College Learning (MCL) project, a faculty-led effort coordinated by the Social Science Research Council in collaboration with a set of national disciplinary associations to articulate essential learning outcomes and develop improved measures of undergraduate-level student learning in six academic disciplines. It begins with a description of the motivating forces behind the project, which include a desire to bring faculty voices and a focus on student learning to the fore of discussions about the desired outcomes of higher education. Next, it describes the core principles of the MCL project, its goals and activities, and lessons learned from progress on the project to date. It concludes with a summary of the six discipline-specific contributions that follow and some general recommendations for the future of assessment in higher education.

Introduction

The value of higher education is no longer taken for granted. Headlines asking, "Is college worth it?" pepper popular newspapers and public opinion surveys (see Davidson 2011; McArdle 2012; Williams 2012). Although the public regards higher education as important, the majority also questions whether it provides students with good value for the money invested.[1] Social science research documents the labor market value of college education—on average, college graduates fare better on a number of dimensions, from avoiding unemployment to having higher paying jobs (Hout 2012)—but questions remain about whether higher education could do more to prepare students to transition into life after college.

Policymakers, too, are asking questions about the value of college. In recent years they have subjected higher education to increasing levels of scrutiny and calls for accountability. Although accountability has been part of the state policy conversations since the early 1980s (Ewell 1994), recent trends of rising tuition, the economic challenges brought forth by the Great Recession, low and declining graduation rates, and indications that college students may not be developing crucial 21st-century skills such as critical thinking and problem solving have raised accountability concerns to a new level, including getting the attention of the federal government.[2] The Spellings Commission, a U.S. Department of Education

---

[1] A recent Pew survey reported that 57 percent of Americans believe that the higher education system in the United States fails to provide students with good value for the money they and their families spend (Taylor et al. 2011).

[2] For evidence regarding declining graduations rates, see, for example, Astin and Osegura (2005) and Bound, Lovenheim, and Turner (2010). For evidence regarding limited development of general collegiate skills such as critical thinking, see, for example, Arum and Roksa (2011, 2014a).

taskforce on the future of postsecondary education, recommended implementing "serious accountability measures" in higher education, including creating a "consumer-friendly information database" (U.S. Department of Education 2006, 21–22). These recommendations were used to develop the College Scorecard and a proposed, but subsequently abandoned, federal college ratings plan.[3]

Higher education leaders have been quick to critique these kinds of external accountability measures. There is indeed reason to be cautious about the College Scorecard, the now abandoned ratings plan, and other external accountability measures, especially given the lessons learned regarding the pitfalls of accountability in K–12 education. Critiquing proposed endeavors, however, falls short of offering a vision for the future of higher education. Rather than making their own case for higher education, today's leaders have often focused on defending it based on the terms advanced by policymakers, which typically means engaging in debates about externally proposed metrics, such as cost, wages, or loan default rates. The National Governors Association, for example, recently reduced higher education to primarily one metric: preparing students for high-paying, high-demand jobs (Sparks and Waits 2011).

Clearly, higher education can help to support students' labor market aspirations, but it offers much more than workforce training. At its best, college prepares students for participation in a democratic society and provides enriching contexts for personal growth and development. Even when it comes to professional development,

---

[3] For the College Scorecard, see https://www.whitehouse.gov/issues/ education/higher-education/college-score-card; for the college ratings system, see https://www.whitehouse.gov/the-press-office/2013/08/22/fact-sheet-president-s-plan-make-college-more-affordable-better-hargain . The federal college ratings plan, proposed in 2013, was abandoned in June 2015 (http://chronicle.com/article/Education-Department-Now-Plans/231137/). For some examples of responses to the proposed college ratings system, see Field (2014) and Blumenstyk (2014).

it would be shortsighted to focus narrowly on providing training for short-term gains. Rather, colleges should develop in students a passion for learning and discovery and help students develop higher order skills and attitudes that will foster long-term professional success. After all, surveys of employers repeatedly highlight the need for broader competencies such as critical thinking and problem solving and not job-specific skills (AAC&U 2008; NRC 2012). Higher order skills are necessary in a globalized world that is experiencing rapid technological change, where many tasks and challenges that graduates are likely to face in their personal, civic, and professional lives may not yet exist.

The absence of a more expansive vision of higher education in policy debates has various roots. Given the complexity of what higher education institutions aim to offer, there is a great deal of normative disagreement around desirable outcomes (Arum and Roksa 2014b). But perhaps more notable than this disagreement is the fact that faculty voices are often largely absent from conversations about the outcomes that higher education should accomplish. Without faculty voices, policy debates are overlooking what should arguably be the core function of higher education: student learning.

But even if faculty were a larger part of the discussion, they would find it difficult today to identify high-quality, comparable measures to demonstrate what students were actually learning. Measuring graduation rates and early-career earnings, though not without challenges, is much easier than measuring student learning, given the absence of agreed upon measures. A few high-quality measures of generic competencies like critical thinking have been developed in recent decades, but the development of discipline-specific[4] (i.e., major-specific, domain-specific, or field-specific) measures lags substantially behind. Many of the currently available discipline-specific

---

[4] We use the term *discipline* in this paper interchangeably with *field*, *domain*, and *subject*, although some scholars prefer to use the term more restrictively (see Abbott 2001).

measures focus on content knowledge or lower levels of abstraction, outcomes not compatible with faculty goals. This lack of high-quality discipline-specific measures is a significant problem, especially in light of the fact that many faculty and students place a great deal of value on discipline-specific teaching and learning.[5]

Engaging in conversations about the outcomes of higher education, and in particular placing *faculty* and *learning outcomes* at the center of these conversations, is not easy. Nonetheless, we believe strongly that faculty have a crucial role to play in defining appropriate outcomes for higher education and in facilitating the development of tools that will accurately measure those outcomes. The fact that conversations about higher education outcomes and how to measure them are fraught with difficulties makes it that much more important for higher education faculty to contribute, and indeed, lead the way, especially when it comes to defining and measuring what students should be learning.

Faculty care deeply about what students are learning. They spend a substantial portion of their professional lives thinking about what students should learn, organizing classroom activities to facilitate learning, and assessing what students have learned in their courses. Beyond assessment in their individual courses, faculty care about what students are learning in their major, what they are learning outside of their major, and how well they can apply that learning to life beyond college. Being able to assess what students are learning is central to understanding what students know and are able to do. It is also central to understanding how to improve instruction in the future. Assessment can provide insights into which pedagogical practices and curricular structures are best

---

[5] Indeed, as others have pointed out, "most postsecondary faculty have strong disciplinary identities, and view themselves as teaching particular content, and not 'generic' thinking and reasoning skills" (Pallas 2011, 215). Similarly, most undergraduates' academic identities are tightly linked to their major field(s) of study (Pitt and Tepper 2012).

poised to accomplish the goals faculty set for their students. Assessment can thus be beneficial for helping faculty and departments engage in evidence-based instructional improvement efforts.

Being able to clearly articulate and demonstrate what students are learning can have benefits beyond the classroom and specific departments. At the system level, improved assessments could make it possible to craft larger scale, learning-centered transfer articulation agreements, something that could save students and institutions time and money and increase college completion rates. At the labor market level, students could use improved assessments to demonstrate their competencies to employers, or employers could use them as a way to identify talented and capable candidates from across a variety of institution types.

The Measuring College Learning (MCL) project has aimed to provide a platform for faculty to engage in national conversations about student learning and assessment. Over the past two-plus years, faculty participants in the project have thought long and hard about the essential 21st-century competencies, conceptual knowledge, and practices that students in their disciplines should develop in college. Each of MCL's six discipline-specific faculty panels produced a white paper that clearly articulates a set of learning outcomes[6] for students in their discipline, providing

---

[6] In the teaching, learning, and assessment literature, there is some level of debate over the distinctions between various learning-related terms, such as *learning objective* and *learning outcome*. Some scholars argue that learning objective should be used to refer to *desired* learning, whereas learning outcome should be used to refer to *actual* learning. Others prefer to use the term learning outcome to refer to both desired and actual learning because it is thought to reflect a more student-centered orientation to education—it emphasizes results over targets. Many feel that it is also simpler to use a single term instead of two very similar terms. In the MCL project, most faculty panelists expressed a moderate preference for the single-term approach. In general, this preference is reflected in the six MCL white papers.

a roadmap for departmental and disciplinary conversations about what undergraduate-level students should be expected to learn. Moreover, the white papers put forth disciplinary principles for learning outcomes assessment, illuminating the characteristics of assessments needed to capture the complex knowledge and skills that are at the heart of learning in higher education. This book, a compilation of the six MCL white papers, is a unique opportunity to hear faculty voices as they engage in the difficult work of defining and measuring learning outcomes in their disciplines.

Core Principles of the Measuring College Learning Project

Aiming to counter the absence of faculty voices from public debates about higher education outcomes, the first principle of the MCL project is this:

> Faculty should be at the forefront of defining and measuring undergraduate-level learning outcomes.

Bringing faculty together to engage in these kinds of efforts is crucial not only to help avoid the narrow focus on outcomes over which colleges have only limited control (e.g., early post-graduation wages) but also to steer the conversation to the core of higher education: teaching and learning.

With the centrality of faculty comes a focus on students, which leads to the second core principle of MCL:

> Students from all backgrounds and institutions should be given a fair opportunity to demonstrate their knowledge and skills.

Many social scientists and policymakers subscribe to the idea that higher education helps to enhance individuals' knowledge and skills (i.e., human capital) (Becker 2009). However, today's students are limited in their ability to demonstrate their human capital when it matters most. For example, many students and recent graduates find it difficult to convey adequately what they know and are able to do to prospective employers. Indeed, decades of course diversification and grade inflation have given rise to a situation where employers rarely ask to see college transcripts, leaving students with little verifiable and transferable evidence of their learning.[7] To give another example, many students encounter significant obstacles when attempting to transfer course credits from one institution to another. Colleges and universities themselves demonstrate skepticism of student transcripts, often challenging and limiting credit transfer based on course titles and grades from other institutions. Regardless of their backgrounds or institutions attended, we believe that students should have opportunities to demonstrate what they know and are able to do when transferring from one academic institution to another or when attempting to transition into the labor force. Designing measures that can be used for multiple purposes—institutional improvement, credit transfer, and demonstration of knowledge and competency—is very challenging, but the benefits to doing so outweigh the costs. Indeed, when students understand that an assessment could benefit them directly, they are more likely to be motivated to do their best, thus providing the most accurate indication of their knowledge and skills.

Recognizing the complexity of knowledge and competencies developed in higher education leads to the third core principle of MCL:

> Any single measure of student learning should be a part
> of a larger holistic assessment plan.

---

[7] Just over a third (37 percent) of recent college graduates reported that employers asked to see their transcripts (Arum and Roksa 2014a, 74).

Even focusing exclusively on academic learning produces a long list of concepts and competencies that students should be expected to acquire in higher education, including a range of generic competencies, discipline-specific concepts, and civic and intercultural competencies. No single instrument can capture all of these outcomes, and even within specific domains different instruments may capture different dimensions of learning. Thus, to ensure that students are developing across a number of important domains and that assessments reflect the true complexity of learning, a variety of instruments are needed. The assessment tools that may be developed based on the insights of the MCL project need to be supplemented with other assessment strategies, including the evaluation of authentic student work through the use of grading rubrics, such as the Association of American Colleges and Universities' VALUE rubrics, which are currently being piloted by institutions across the country.[8]

Using a variety of instruments can also facilitate a focus on institutional improvement. Different institutions may emphasize different dimensions of student learning, and a single institution may emphasize different dimensions at different points in time. Defining and measuring an array of learning outcomes allows for a virtuous cycle of improvement: Initial measurement provides an indication of where students are, thus illuminating to faculty which areas need attention. As departments and programs change their curricula and instructional practices to improve outcomes, follow-up assessments can provide evidence of improvement or suggest other areas in need of attention.

This focus on improvement leads to MCL's fourth core principle:

> Institutions should use assessment tools on a voluntary basis.

---

[8] For more information on the VALUE rubrics and the recent multistate pilot project, see https://www.aacu.org/value/rubrics.

Externally imposed accountability is undesirable and would likely be counterproductive (see Arum and Roksa 2011, 2014a). The complexity of higher education, including the diversity of goals and institutional types, makes it likely that external accountability would not be effective or productive in terms of improving student outcomes (see also Roksa 2015).

The final principle of the MCL project is this:

> Measures of student learning should be rigorous and high quality and should yield data that allow for comparisons over time and across institutions.

A growing number of institutions and higher education agencies are working internally to assess and improve student outcomes. Many are also creating coalitions and consortia that involve sharing data on student outcomes.[9] Through these voluntary collaborations, institutions aim to learn from each other about best practices and effective ways of improving student learning. Instruments developed to assess student learning outcomes need to facilitate these conversations and support continuous engagement in institutional improvement.

Goals and Activities

The MCL project began in 2013 under the auspices of the Social Science Research Council as an opportunity to engage faculty in conversations about student learning outcomes and assessment in

---

[9] Not all institutional collaborations measure student learning (e.g., Western Interstate Commission for Higher Education), but some do (e.g., Higher Education Data Sharing Consortium and the New England Consortium on Assessment and Student Learning).

their disciplines. Over the course of two-plus years, panels of faculty from six academic disciplines—biology, business, communication, economics, history, and sociology—engaged in a series of forward-thinking and consensus-driven discussions about their priorities for student learning and their vision for the future of learning outcomes assessment. The six MCL disciplines were chosen to represent the intellectual diversity of the higher education system, from the traditional arts and science fields to the professional fields. Collectively, they account for over 35 percent of the bachelor's degrees that are granted each year in the United States.[10]

Each MCL faculty panel brought together ten to fifteen individuals, selected on the basis of their dedication to undergraduate education and their expertise in defining and measuring learning outcomes. Table 1.1 provides a complete list of MCL faculty panelists. During the selection process, we worked closely with the disciplinary associations or their equivalents in each of the six disciplines to identify a group of faculty who met these criteria. Working closely with the disciplinary associations and related entities during the selection process and throughout the project has been critical to the success of our efforts because they have an unparalleled understanding of the state of their fields and faculty leadership in specific domains.

We strove to ensure that each MCL panel was representative of a wide range of institutional types, geographic locations, and subfields. In the end, most of the panelists hailed from four-year institutions, but some of them were community college faculty members and disciplinary association leaders. Notably, the majority

---

[10] This figure was calculated using Tables 313 and 364 of NCES's *2012 Digest of Education Statistics* (Snyder and Dillow 2013). The individual disciplines break down as follows: business (21.3 percent); biological and biomedical sciences (5.2 percent); communication, journalism, and related programs (4.9 percent); history (2.0 percent); sociology (1.7 percent); and economics (1.7 percent).

Table 1.1 MCL Faculty Panelists

Discipline	Name	Institutional Affiliation
Biology	Cynthia Bauerle	Howard Hughes Medical Institute
	Sara Brownell	Arizona State University
	Clarissa Dirks*	The Evergreen State College
	Chris Kaiser	Massachusetts Institute of Technology
	Jennifer Knight*	University of Colorado, Boulder
	Susan Singer	National Science Foundation
	Michelle Smith	University of Maine
	Nancy Songer	Drexel University
	Gordon Uno	University of Oklahoma
	William Wood	University of Colorado, Boulder
	Robin Wright	University of Minnesota
Business	Sara Beckman*	University of California, Berkeley
	Thomas Calderon	University of Akron
	Lynn Doran	Georgetown University
	Anne Greenhalgh	University of Pennsylvania
	Doug Guthrie	George Washington University / Apple, Inc.
	Kathleen Krentler	San Diego State University
	Kathy Lund Dean	Gustavus Adolphus College
	Jeff Nesteruk*	Franklin & Marshall College
	Claire Preisser	The Aspen Institute
	Robert Reid	Association to Advance Collegiate Schools of Business
	Paige Reidy Soffen	The Aspen Institute
	Scott Romeika	University of Pennsylvania
	William Sullivan	Wabash College
	Karen Tarnoff	East Tennessee State University
	Lynn Wooten	University of Michigan, Ann Arbor

Discipline	Name	Institutional Affiliation
Communication	Walid Afifi	University of Iowa
	Timothy Barney	University of Richmond
	Steven Beebe*	Texas State University
	Pat Ganer	Cypress College
	Nancy Kidd*	National Communication Association
	Joseph Mazer	Clemson University
	W. Bradford Mello*	Saint Xavier University
	Kevin Meyer	Illinois State University
	Trevor Parry-Giles*	National Communication Association
	Ken Sereno	University of Southern California
Economics	Sam Allgood*	University of Nebraska, Lincoln
	Amanda Bayer*	Swarthmore College
	Stephen Buckles	Vanderbilt University
	Charles Clotfelter	Duke University
	Melissa Famulari	University of California, San Diego
	Rae Jean Goodman	United States Naval Academy
	Mark Maier	Glendale Community College
	KimMarie McGoldrick	University of Richmond
	John Siegfried	Vanderbilt University
	William Walstad	University of Nebraska, Lincoln
	Michael Watts	Purdue University
History	Julia Brookins	American Historical Association
	Lendol Calder*	Augustana College
	Elaine Carey	St. John's University
	James Grossman	American Historical Association
	Anne Hyde	Colorado College
	Norm Jones	University of Utah
	Kenneth Pomeranz	University of Chicago
	Nancy Quam-Wickham	California State University, Long Beach
	Tracy Steffes*	Brown University
	Maris Vinovskis	University of Michigan, Ann Arbor
	Emily Swafford	American Historical Association

(continued)

Table 1.1 (Continued)

Discipline	Name	Institutional Affiliation
Sociology	Jeanne Ballantine	Wright State University
	William Carbonaro*	University of Notre Dame
	Paula England	New York University
	Susan Ferguson*	Grinnell College
	Sally Hillsman	American Sociological Association
	Katherine McClelland	Franklin & Marshall College
	Matthew McKeever	Mount Holyoke College
	Aaron Pallas	Columbia University
	Richard Pitt	Vanderbilt University
	Margaret Weigers Vitullo	American Sociological Association
	Theodore Wagenaar	Miami University
	Sarah Willie-LeBreton	Swarthmore College

*White paper coauthors

of panelists have been or currently are involved in other faculty-led efforts to articulate and measure learning outcomes. This deep familiarity with related efforts greatly contributed to the project, ensuring that it built on and productively extended previous and ongoing endeavors.

Each of the MCL panels drew on a multitude of prior and ongoing initiatives related to student learning and assessment. For example, the biology panel benefited from decades of important efforts to improve the quality of biology education, including a recent American Association for the Advancement of Science (AAAS) report, *Vision and Change in Undergraduate Biology Education: A Call to Action* (2011). To give another example, the history and communication panels relied on ongoing national efforts to articulate learning outcomes for their disciplines through Tuning.[11] All six panels also benefited from insights about learning outcomes and measurement put forth by organizations such as the Association of American Colleges and Universities (AAC&U) and the National Institute for Learning Outcomes Assessment (NILOA).[12]

MCL panelists worked to pull together and synthesize insights from decades of prior work, but they also strove to be uniquely forward-thinking in their efforts. One of the key ways MCL differs from other efforts is in how it articulates learning outcomes. Following an example set by the discipline of biology, faculty in each of the MCL disciplines have organized their top priorities for student learning into a set of *essential concepts* (i.e., complex ideas, theoretical understandings, and ways of thinking central to the discipline) and *essential competencies* (i.e., disciplinary practices and skills necessary to engage effectively in the discipline). Broadly speaking, essential concepts and competencies are *ideas* and *practices* that faculty believe are fundamental to the discipline, valuable to students, and worth emphasizing given limited time and resources. The essential concepts and competencies articulated in the MCL white papers should not be seen as fixed, universal, or comprehensive. Rather, they aim to be reasonable and productive frameworks that can orient departmental and disciplinary discussions about learning, assessment, and institutional improvement.

The MCL panels have focused on articulating a limited number of essential concepts and competencies, as opposed to a comprehensive set of learning outcomes, for a couple of reasons. First, given that MCL strives to inform evaluation and program design

---

[11] For information on Tuning, see http://www.luminafoundation.org/dqp-and-tuning.

[12] For AAC&U LEAP Initiative, see https://www.aacu.org/leap, and for NILOA endeavors see http://www.learningoutcomeassessment.org/NILOAResources.html.

efforts nationwide, it is important to emphasize concepts and competencies that resonate with as many faculty as possible, regardless of subfield or institution type. Second, keeping in mind that the goal of MCL is to provide resources to support improved measurement of learning outcomes, articulating a relatively manageable number of concepts and competencies makes it less daunting for faculty to think about incorporating them into their deliberations and assessment efforts.

The other notable way MCL differs from prior endeavors is by engaging faculty in conversations about assessment. MCL panels not only articulated learning outcomes but also aimed to identify key principles of assessment in their disciplines by investigating the following questions: What kinds of discipline-specific assessment resources are currently available, and how are they being used? To what extent do existing resources meet faculty members', students', and other stakeholders' needs? Do they align with the concepts and competencies the panel has identified? Looking to the future, what kinds of assessment tools should be built for—and by—the discipline, and how should they be used? In the end, each of the MCL faculty panels has articulated a series of principles for assessment, illuminating the qualities that assessments need in order to capture the concepts and competencies that faculty, students, and others value. These principles move the assessment conversation in each of the MCL disciplines forward in important ways, highlighting a clear path forward for faculty, disciplinary associations, and assessment designers.

What We Have Learned: Lessons from MCL

The first thing we learned, which may come as a surprise to audiences both inside and outside academia, is that faculty, to a large extent, readily agree on what students should learn in higher education. In particular, when focusing on their own disciplines—on what students should learn in their majors—there is a substantial amount of agreement.[13] This surfaced early on in the MCL project and in other endeavors such as Tuning. It may be difficult to list everything students should know and be able to do, but when faculty are asked to focus on essential elements they are quite ready, willing, and able to define priorities for student learning in their disciplines.

Across all six MCL disciplines, faculty have emphasized the importance of moving beyond learning content for content's sake (i.e., memorization and regurgitation). To be sure, content is crucial, but not in the form of facts that can be memorized. Rather, content matters insofar as it serves as a building block for more complex forms of thinking. Indeed, faculty are eager to move beyond the basic levels of Bloom's taxonomy, including remembering and simple forms of understanding, where many current assessments in higher education reside.[14] They are focused on getting students to apply, analyze, and evaluate from their disciplinary perspectives. By the time students graduate, faculty also believe that students should be able to operate at the highest level of Bloom's taxonomy—to create—often in the form of asking and answering research questions, even if only in relatively rudimentary forms.

In moving beyond content knowledge, faculty in each discipline have been able to identify a set of essential concepts and competencies. This conceptualization of learning outcomes as existing at the intersection of concepts (what students know and understand) and competencies (what students are able to do) draws extensively from the *Vision and Change* document produced by faculty in biology (AAAS 2011). Given the focus of each discipline on selecting a limited number of concepts and competencies,

---

[13] There is also agreement with respect to generic competencies with faculty being almost unanimous on the importance of critical thinking (Bok 2006).

[14] On Bloom's taxonomy and recent revisions, see the 2002 Special Issue: Revising Bloom's Taxonomy, *Theory Into Practice* 41, no. 4.

the concepts identified at times reflect more general topic areas or themes. In most cases, more specific concepts can be said to underlie these broader topics or themes. At their core, the essential concepts that faculty have articulated aim to capture theoretical understandings and ways of thinking. Competencies, on the other hand, reflect the ways of doing the discipline, or the skills necessary to engage effectively in the discipline. Collectively, concepts and competencies reflect the habits of mind and practices that are characteristic of the discipline. Although the faculty panels were not explicitly asked to address values, the concepts and competencies identified in many ways reflect disciplinary values by revealing what faculty in the discipline believe is valuable and important. With regard to values in the more traditional sense (i.e., civic engagement and ethical reasoning), some disciplines explicitly included these in their definitions of discipline-specific learning outcomes.

The six disciplines participating in the MCL project varied in the extent to which they had engaged in organized efforts to define learning outcomes before MCL. Each of the disciplinary white papers in this volume describes prior efforts and the ways the MCL project builds on and extends those endeavors. Variation observed across disciplines—in terms of whether and how faculty have engaged in organized discussions about learning outcomes— in part reflects the activities of disciplinary associations or their equivalents. Some disciplines, such as biology, do not have one overarching disciplinary association and are divided into many associations representing different subdisciplines. Robust National Science Foundation (NSF) funding, along with the establishment of faculty-led groups like the Society for the Advancement of Biology Education Research (SABER), however, have helped to propel biology as a discipline into extensive discussions of student learning. Economists, on the other hand, have a disciplinary association, the American Economic Association (AEA), which as a whole has been less engaged in questions surrounding learning;

instead, this conversation has been largely confined to the AEA's Committee on Economic Education. Other disciplines, such as history, sociology, and communication, have national associations— the American Historical Association, the American Sociological Association, and the National Communication Association—that have recently been very active in organizing conversations regarding student learning outcomes.

Despite vastly different starting points, resources, and institutional structures, all of the MCL disciplines were able to identify essential concepts and competencies, define them precisely, and offer concrete examples of desired outcomes. Even when faculty did not have many endeavors preceding MCL to use as building blocks, they were able to coalesce rather quickly around key learning outcomes in their respective disciplines. The amount of consensus and the level of detail provided in the respective white papers speak to the extent of thinking about student learning that has been occurring in higher education, often under the radar. Indeed, we have found that faculty are quite reflective and thoughtful about student learning outcomes, even if this does not always get mentioned or recognized at their institutions or mobilized and articulated through larger national endeavors.

One of the challenges we anticipated and worked on throughout is the overlap between discipline-specific and generic competencies. Given a number of already existing endeavors and measures aimed at capturing generic competencies, we urged the MCL panels to focus on discipline-specific knowledge and ways of thinking. The concepts that emerged through the MCL project are clearly discipline specific, but the competencies, although embedded in the disciplines, tend to resonate with other, often generic ones like critical thinking, analytical writing, quantitative reasoning, and problem solving.

Scholars of teaching, learning, and assessment have long been engaged in conversations about the extent to which certain higher order skills, such as critical thinking, are generic and can be measured in the absence of specific domains. Lee Shulman (2004a, 2004b), for example, is well known for emphasizing the importance of disciplinary knowledge. Liu, Frankel, and Roohr (2014) offer a compelling review of the debate, considering a range of perspectives, from those who see critical thinking as truly generic and thus possible to teach outside of the context of a specific discipline to those who argue that critical thinking is a domain-specific skill that cannot be automatically transferred from one domain to another.

Notwithstanding this debate, college-level courses are, by and large, discipline specific. This means that students, to the extent that they are developing broader skills such as analysis, writing, and critical thinking, are developing them in discipline-specific contexts. Learning how to think critically, write analytically, and problem solve in the disciplines is crucial, not only because it will enable students to be skilled disciplinary actors but also because it will give them a foundation that can then potentially be transferred to a range of other domains. Whether and how this transfer across domains can occur requires careful attention and is a worthy topic for further research (Koenig 2011). The contribution of the MCL project to this debate is to illuminate the connections between generic and discipline-specific competencies and to highlight how disciplinary ways of thinking align with broader concerns about developing students' ability to analyze, integrate, and problem solve.

All major efforts to articulate student learning outcomes agree about the importance of developing both discipline-specific and more generic competencies that could potentially be transferred across domains of knowledge. For example, both AAC&U's Liberal Learning and America's Promise (LEAP) and Lumina Foundation's Degree Qualifications Profile (DQP) include a category for subject-specific knowledge (referred to as "knowledge of human cultures and the physical and natural world" in LEAP and "specialized knowledge" in the DQP). MCL's essential concepts in each discipline aim to provide specific guidance regarding the knowledge students should acquire in each discipline (Table 1.2).

Table 1.2 Essential Concepts and Competencies from the Six MCL Disciplines

Discipline	Essential Concepts	Essential Competencies
Biology	• Evolution • Information Flow • Structure & Function • Pathways & Transformations of Matter and Energy • Systems	• Model • Apply Quantitative Reasoning • Engage in Argument from Evidence • Engage in Scientific Inquiry & Experimental Design • Analyze & Evaluate Data • Appreciate & Apply the Interdisciplinary Nature of Science
Business	• Business in Society • Globalization • Strategy • System Dynamics • Consumer Engagement • Transparency, Disclosure, & Metrics	• Select from and Deploy Diverse Thinking Skills (critical and analytical thinking, integrative thinking, systemic thinking, design thinking) • Exercise Ethical Judgment • Demonstrate Informational & Technological Literacy • Management, Teaming, and Cross-cultural Competence

(continued)

Table 1.2 *(Continued)*

Discipline	Essential Concepts	Essential Competencies
Communication	• Social Construction • Relationality • Strategy • Symbolism • Adaptability	• Engage in Communication Inquiry • Create Messages Appropriate to the Audience, Purpose, & Context • Critically Analyze Messages • Demonstrate Self-efficacy • Apply Ethical Communication Principles & Practices • Utilize Communication to Embrace Difference • Influence Public Discourse
Economics	• Individual Decision Making • Markets & Other Interactions • The Aggregate Economy • Role of Government & Other Institutions	• Apply the Scientific Process to Economic Phenomena • Analyze & Evaluate Behavior & Outcomes Using Economic Concepts & Models • Use Quantitative Approaches in Economics • Think Critically About Economic Methods & Their Application • Communicate Economic Ideas in Diverse Collaborations

Discipline	Essential Concepts	Essential Competencies
History	• History as an Interpretive Account • The Relationship of Past & Present • Historical Evidence • Complex Causality • Significance	• Evaluate Historical Accounts • Interpret Primary Sources • Apply Chronological Reasoning • Contextualize • Construct Acceptable Historical Accounts
Sociology	• The Sociological Eye • Social Structure • Socialization • Stratification • Social Change & Social Reproduction	• Apply Sociological Theories to Understand Social Phenomena • Critically Evaluate Explanations of Human Behavior & Social Phenomena • Apply Scientific Principles to Understand the Social World • Evaluate the Quality of Social Scientific Methods & Data • Rigorously Analyze Social Scientific Data • Use Sociological Knowledge to Inform Policy Debates & Promote Public Understanding

Moreover, the competencies developed across the MCL disciplines align with many other dimensions of LEAP and the DQP. For example, both of these national frameworks note the importance of developing intellectual skills, which include categories such as inquiry and analysis as well as critical thinking. All the MCL faculty panels placed a strong emphasis on those skills. The modes of thinking are defined in disciplinary ways (whether scientific inquiry in biology or analyzing and interpreting documents in history) but embody broader conceptualizations. Indeed, one could consider many of the competencies identified by the MCL panels as discipline-specific representations of the more generic competencies identified in LEAP and the DQP.

Finally, the purposeful design of the MCL project, with the intention of identifying both concepts and competencies and considering how they are related, aligns with LEAP and the DQP's emphasis on integrated thinking. The business faculty panel has gone the furthest in clearly and convincingly articulating the importance of integrated thinking. But faculty in all of the MCL disciplines have emphasized the importance of teaching students how to integrate and apply knowledge, whether it means integrating what one has learned across different courses and subdisciplines or applying theoretical knowledge to substantive concerns.

These insights from the MCL project are also highly relevant for designing assessments of student learning. To think of generic skills as simply generic can be limiting. If it is true that skills developed in a particular context do not easily transfer to other contexts, then it follows that a poor result on a generic skills assessment could indicate one of two things: a lack of a particular set of higher order skills or a lack of transfer. Not being able to distinguish between these two factors limits educators' ability to interpret assessment results and act on them in productive ways. Therefore, developing assessments that can measure higher order complex thinking skills in a range of disciplinary contexts, along with those abstracted from those contexts, is crucial. Doing so will allow scholars to examine the validity of the arguments regarding skills transfer and to provide valuable guidance for instruction.

In addition to the challenge of thinking about the distinction (or lack thereof) between generic and discipline-specific skills, we encountered another challenge that we did not anticipate at the start of the project. We began with the idea that each discipline would define learning outcomes for both the major and the introductory course. This was in part done for methodological reasons: so that learning gains could be measured from the beginning to the end of an introductory course and from the beginning to the end of the major. We also wanted to improve our understanding of the relationship between the introduction to the discipline and the study of the discipline in the major. We were curious about the extent to which those learning outcomes would be similar or different. In other words, we wanted to know the extent to which the introductory course was a microcosm of the discipline as a whole.

We learned quickly that defining learning outcomes for the introductory course is quite challenging in many disciplines. In some disciplines, such as history, a single, stand-alone introductory course typically does not exist; students interested in exploring the discipline or potentially majoring in it are able to choose from an array of different courses. In other disciplines, such as communication, one of the most common introductory courses—public speaking—provides students with important skills but sometimes offers an incomplete picture of the discipline as a whole. Even in the disciplines that have a designated introductory course, such as sociology, the course is not always required before students can take other courses in the discipline. Economics and biology stand out in that the majority of departments have course sequences that must be taken at the beginning of the major and that clearly define the fundamental knowledge on which much of the subsequent learning builds.

This variation in introductory courses reflects in part the differential structures of the disciplines and their relationships to general education. However, it also reflects in part a lack of intentionality in curriculum design in higher education. Although curriculum maps and backwards design techniques have gained some traction recently, relatively few departments articulate explicitly how courses fit together into a coherent whole (Wiggins and McTighe 1998). Accreditation agencies have begun to require that institutions define and measure learning outcomes, but this push has rarely translated into a serious evaluation of the curriculum or an alignment of courses with stated goals.

When there is a lack of intentionality around curriculum design and course sequencing, it can be quite difficult for faculty to foster the gradual, intentional development of students' knowledge and competencies. Indeed, in many disciplines and departments across the country, instructors in certain courses, especially upper-division electives, are unable to assume that students entering the course have any specific knowledge or skills. Often unrestricted by prerequisite requirements, these courses are likely to include students with extensive knowledge and skills and also those who are taking their first course in the discipline. At the department level, clearly defining a set of shared learning outcomes for the introductory course and the major can serve as a useful starting point for conversations about curriculum structure and the extent to which different courses can be sequenced and organized to scaffold student learning.

The final crucial lesson learned from the MCL project is the dire need for better assessments of learning outcomes in higher education. Faculty from across the higher education landscape are explicitly moving away from surface content knowledge and are instead emphasizing the importance of being able to perform more complex tasks: from analyzing and evaluating information to applying knowledge to new circumstances and even to creating knowledge by asking questions and following disciplinary practices to answer them. These kinds of learning outcomes require new types of assessments that go beyond measuring surface-level content knowledge via multiple-choice questions. Some organizations, such as AAC&U and NILOA, have started to develop and disseminate signature assignment templates and grading rubrics that can help faculty measure these types of meaningful outcomes at the student, classroom, and department level. AAC&U is also exploring the feasibility of using signature assignments and rubrics as a way of generating valid and reliable data at the institutional and cross-institutional levels.

In addition to these signature assignments and rubrics, we believe that there is a need to update, improve on, and in some cases fundamentally transform discipline-specific standardized assessments. Many existing standardized tools, because they were developed decades ago, are misaligned with contemporary priorities for student learning, not to mention being out of step with modern assessment technology. Still, some departments use these tools to gather data on student learning for the purposes of self-improvement or accreditation, or to comply with institutional or state-level assessment requirements. However, many faculty, including those who use existing tools, are frustrated by them because they fail to generate useful information about the extent to which students are developing the kinds of deep conceptual understandings and competencies that they, their students, and other key stakeholders value. Since most of these tools were developed, the technology of assessment has advanced in such a way that it is now possible to design standardized (i.e., psychometrically valid and reliable) instruments that measure the kinds of complex understandings and skills that are critical to success in the 21st century. If developed, these tools would be a valuable resource for faculty and departments with an interest in evidence-based instructional improvement.

The data generated by these new-and-improved standardized tools would be distinct from and complementary to the data generated by signature assignment assessment tools like the VALUE rubrics in a number of ways. Perhaps most importantly, standardized assessment tools could gather data on a larger number of discrete learning outcomes than a typical signature assignment, thus providing a broader and in some ways finer-grained sense of what students know and are able to do. Generally speaking, they would also be less time-consuming to administer and score than other assessment strategies. Furthermore, if departments were interested in comparing their students' performance with that of students at other institutions, these new standardized tools would offer a valid and reliable means for making such comparisons. Finally, because they would be developed for broad use, rather than a specific course or department, it would be possible for the developers of the assessments to invest the necessary resources toward constructing the highest quality questions and incorporating the latest advances in assessment technology. An economics assessment, for instance, could include an open-ended data analysis simulation that allowed the test taker to analyze and interpret real data. To give another example, a history assessment could feature a digital archive of documents that the test taker was prompted to sift through and interpret. Advances in assessment technology, such as adaptive testing technology, can also facilitate premeasurement–postmeasurement efforts. Standardized instruments should never be seen as the "end all, be all" of assessment tools, but if they are appropriately designed and deployed, they can play an important role in helping to improve student learning outcomes in higher education.

Volume Overview

The remainder of this volume consists of six MCL white papers and a series of commentary essays from higher education thought leaders. Each paper is the product of more than two years of in-depth discussion with disciplinary colleagues and extensive engagement with prior efforts in the discipline. The papers were written and revised several times over the course of two years as the authors aimed to synthesize panel discussions and to respond to specific feedback from their colleagues. Wherever possible, the white papers represent the consensus viewpoint of the panels. It should be noted, however, that there was not always uniform agreement within each panel and that the ideas presented in these pieces should be seen as inherently subject to ongoing change and development.

Each of the discipline-specific white papers follows a similar structure. They begin with a comprehensive overview of prior efforts to articulate learning outcomes in the discipline. Building on these efforts and the MCL panels' insights, each paper articulates a 21st-century framework for undergraduate-level learning in the discipline, also known as a framework of essential concepts and competencies. Finally, the papers take stock of existing learning outcomes assessments and present a forward-thinking, discipline-specific vision for the future of assessment. They address common concerns head-on and offer compelling reasons for why faculty should find productive ways to engage with assessment not only in their own classrooms but also in their departments and beyond.

This volume includes white papers from the following disciplines (and authors): history (Lendol Calder and Tracy Steffes); economics (Sam Allgood and Amanda Bayer); sociology (Susan Ferguson and William Carbonaro); communication (Nancy Kidd, Trevor Parry-Giles, Steven Beebe, and W. Bradford Mello); biology (Clarissa Dirks and Jenny Knight); and business (Jeffrey Nesteruk and Sara Beckman). In lieu of a traditional concluding chapter, the book closes with a series of short reflective essays on the MCL project by thought leaders in the field of teaching, learning, and assessment in higher education: Peter Ewell (National Center for Higher Education Management Systems); Natasha Jankowski and George Kuh (NILOA); Carol Geary Schneider (AAC&U); and Charles Blaich and Kathleen Wise (Center of Inquiry at Wabash College).

The Future of Higher Education Assessment

As the pressures for accountability and the need for improved learning outcomes assessment in higher education have continued to mount, the MCL project has engaged faculty and their disciplinary associations in an effort to generate proactive responses, and in so doing it has revealed an acute absence of appropriate discipline-specific assessment tools. Some disciplines have very little available in terms of standardized and validated assessments and often rely on homegrown, ever-changing assessments developed by individual departments for accreditation purposes. In other disciplines, available assessments are not appropriate for measuring complex thinking, higher order skills, or habits of mind. Even if colleges and universities were eager to embrace assessment, they would face a dearth of available tools.

This issue was brought to the fore recently by the events at Purdue University. Mitch Daniels, the recently appointed university president, embraced the need for assessment of student learning outcomes and asked the faculty to formulate a plan for how they could assess critical thinking and other skills that students develop during college. After two years, the faculty had not come up with a plan and asked for more time, leading to a clash with Daniels (Flaherty 2015). Although this situation has many complexities and some faculty may have been resistant to assessment, it is important to note that faculty had very little to work with, especially when it comes to assessing the domain-specific concepts and competencies that are at the core of their work as educators and experts in particular fields.

Even in less contentious situations, institutions that voluntarily join forces to examine student outcomes face an absence of domain-specific tools. In the Voluntary Institutional Metrics Project, a collective endeavor of eighteen colleges and universities supported by the Bill and Melinda Gates Foundation, the institutions aimed to develop a holistic framework for assessing college performance across five different dimensions, including student learning. However, the endeavor faltered on how to measure student learning, finding a lack of tools to assess domain-specific learning outcomes. The initial report from the project concluded that "there is a clear need for a focused effort to overcome the lack of comparative assessments of learning outcomes at the program (major/discipline) level. When joined with existing assessments of learning at the core skills level, such assessments would provide a basis for the use of learning outcomes to inform policy decision-making" (HCM Strategists 2013, 22).

Faculty involved in the MCL project have demonstrated that it is possible to reach a general consensus about priorities for student learning in specific disciplines. This effort and the accompanying white papers provide keen insights into essential student learning outcomes in each discipline. As such, departments can use the white papers to review curricula, align courses with disciplinary learning outcomes, and intentionally develop course sequences that can gradually and effectively build students' disciplinary understandings and competencies. The concepts and competencies proposed by the MCL project are neither fixed nor all-encompassing. As departments use the MCL learning outcomes frameworks in their own reflections about curriculum and student learning, they will inevitably need to supplement and refine these frameworks in a way that aligns with their unique program goals and institutional missions. The process of developing learning outcomes and assessments is always an iterative one; the MCL project offers one such iteration and anticipates more in the future.

The MCL project to date has focused a great deal of attention on the articulation of essential concepts and competencies for undergraduate-level learning in six disciplines. One of the next steps for the project is to foster the development of appropriate assessment tools that can capture these essential concepts and competencies in a way that aligns with each discipline's unique priorities. These 21st-century assessments cannot be reductionist instruments that simply identify students' recollection of course material. Instead, they need to measure complex skills and disciplinary habits of mind. This requires more complex and more innovate item types and assessment structures than have been common to date.

Each white paper offers specific insights about key principles for developing assessments as well as a range of possibilities for various forms of assessments that would align with those principles.

As much as faculty engagement has been crucial at this first phase of the process—in defining concepts and competencies—faculty need to engage a broader set of stakeholders in their efforts going forward. If assessments are built and pilot tested, faculty will need to be prominent in the conversations throughout the process of tool development, piloting, and interpretation of the pilot data, but so too will other voices, such as students and representatives from the employer community (e.g., leaders from the private, public, and nonprofit sectors). Notwithstanding the importance of broader engagement with stakeholders, we believe that faculty, as educators, should continue to assume the primary responsibility for driving and leading efforts in this area. Disciplinary associations can provide a powerful vehicle for this continuous form of faculty engagement. This will require bold leadership, from mobilizing faculty across institutions to engage collectively in this endeavor to working through the complexities of instrument design. The inherent appeal of easy administration, easy grading, and high reliability of multiple-choice assessments (and resulting lower cost) can be hard to resist. Developing more complex assessments will require substantial investments of time and financial resources. Disciplinary associations will need to stay firm in protecting and advancing their faculty members' vision for assessments that can capture complex 21st-century skills.

Higher education is at a crossroads. Policy and public pressure to demonstrate value shows no signs of abating. The choice is either to continue to resist those efforts and critique inappropriate outcomes and measures or to engage with the challenges and provide an alternative answer, one that refocuses the conversation on student learning. In this introduction, and throughout the discipline-specific white papers in this volume, we make the case for the latter. Higher education first and foremost *educates*. Educating students is the purview of the faculty, which places them at the center of conversations about what students ought to learn and how that learning should be assessed. It is thus imperative that faculty and their disciplinary associations make their voices heard. It has been our goal in this work to change the conversation and to offer pragmatic paths forward for improving student learning outcomes in higher education.

References

Abbott, Andrew. 2001. *Chaos of Disciplines*. Chicago: University of Chicago Press.

American Association for the Advancement of Science (AAAS). 2011. *Vision and Change in Undergraduate Biology Education: A Call to Action*. Washington, DC: AAAS Press.

Association of American Colleges and Universities (AAC&U). 2008. *How Should Colleges Assess and Improve Student Learning? Employers' Views on the Accountability Challenge*. Washington, DC: AAC&U.

Anderson, Lorin, Ed. 2002. "Special Issue: Revising Bloom's Taxonomy." *Theory into Practice* 41, no. 4: 210-267.

Arum, Richard, and Josipa Roksa. 2011. *Academically Adrift: Limited Learning on College Campuses*. Chicago: University of Chicago Press.

Arum, Richard, and Josipa Roksa. 2014a. *Aspiring Adults Adrift: Tentative Transitions of College Graduates*. Chicago: University of Chicago Press.

Arum, Richard, and Josipa Roksa. 2014b. "Measuring College Performance." In *Remaking College: Broad-Access Higher Education for a New Era*, edited by Mitchell Stevens and Michael Kirst, 169–189. Stanford, CA: Stanford University Press.

Astin, Alexander W., and Leticia Osegura. 2005. *Degree Attainment Rates at American Colleges and Universities (Revised)*. Los Angeles: Higher Education Research Institute, UCLA.

Becker, Gary. 2009 [1964]. *Human Capital: A Theoretical and Empirical Analysis, with Special Reference to Education*. Chicago: University of Chicago Press.

Blumenstyk, Goldie. 2014. "ACE Report Reiterates Opposition to Proposed College-Ratings Plan." *Chronicle of Higher Education*, March 19. http://chronicle.com/blogs/bottomline/ace-report-reiterates-opposition-to-proposed-college-ratings-plan/.

Blumenstyk, Goldie. 2015. "Education Department Now Plans a College-Ratings System Minus the Ratings." *Chronicle of Higher Education*, June 25. http://chronicle.com/article/Education-Department-Now-Plans/231137/.

Bok, Derek. 2006. *Our Underachieving Colleges: A Candid Look at How Much Students Learn and Why They Should Be Learning More.* Princeton, NJ: Princeton University Press.

Bound, John, Michael F. Lovenheim, and Sarah Turner. 2010. "Why Have College Completion Rates Declined? An Analysis of Changing Student Preparation and Collegiate Resources." *American Economic Journal: Applied Economics* 2, no. 3: 129–157.

Davidson, Adam. 2011. "The Dwindling Power of a College Degree." *New York Times*, November 23. http://www.nytimes.com/2011/11/27/magazine/changing-rules-for-success.html.

Ewell, Peter T. 1994. "Developing Statewide Performance Indicators for Higher Education: Policy Themes and Variations." In *Charting Higher Education Accountability: A Sourcebook on State-Level Performance Indicators*, edited by Sandra S. Ruppert, 147–166. Denver, CO: Education Commission of the States.

Field, Kelly. 2014. "Student-Aid Leaders Call for Alternatives to Obama's College-Rating System." *Chronicle of Higher Education*, July 1. http://chronicle.com/article/Student-Aid-Leaders-Call-for/147455/.

Flaherty, Colleen. 2015. "Test Anxiety." *Inside Higher Ed*, January 28. https://www.insidehighered.com/news/2015/01/28/purdues-president-and-faculty-clash-over-student-learning-assessment.

HCM Strategists. 2013. *A Better Higher Education Data and Information Framework for Informing Policy*, a report on the Voluntary Institutional Metrics Project. Washington, DC: HCM Strategists.

Hout, Michael. 2012. "Social and Economic Returns to Higher Education in the United States." *Annual Review of Sociology* 38: 379–400.

Koenig, Judith Anderson, Ed. 2011. *Assessing Twenty-First Century Skills: Summary of a Workshop*. Washington, DC: National Academies Press.

Liu, Ou Lydia, Lois Frankel, and Katrina Crotts Roohr. 2014. "Assessing Critical Thinking in Higher Education: Current State and Directions for Next-Generation Assessment." *ETS Research Report Series*, no. 1: 1–23.

Lumina Foundation. n.d. "DQP and Tuning." http://www. luminafoundation.org/dqp-and-tuning.

McArdle, Megan. 2012. "Is College a Lousy Investment?" *Newsweek*, September 9. http://www.thedailybeast.com/newsweek/2012/09/09/megan-mcardle-on-the-coming-burst-of-the-college-bubble.html.

National Research Council (NRC). 2012. *Education for Life and Work: Developing Transferable Knowledge and Skills in the Twenty-First Century*. Washington DC: National Academies Press.

Pallas, Aaron. 2011. "Assessing the Future of Higher Education." *Society* 48: 213-215.

Pitt, Richard N., and Steven Tepper. 2012. *Double Majors: Influences, Identities, and Impacts*. New York: Teagle Foundation.

Roksa, Josipa. 2015. "Gradations or Extremes: Another Look at the College Ratings." *Change Magazine*, March/April.

Shulman, Lee S. 2004a. *Teaching as Community Property: Essays on Higher Education*. San Francisco: Jossey Bass.

Shulman, Lee S. 2004b. *The Wisdom of Practice: Essays on Learning, Teaching, and Learning to Teach*. San Francisco: Jossey Bass.

Snyder, Thomas D., and Sally A. Dillow. 2013. "Digest of Education Statistics, 2012. NCES 2014–015." Washington, DC: National Center for Education Statistics.

Sparks, Erin, and Mary Jo Waits. 2011. "Degrees for What Jobs? Raising Expectations for Universities and Colleges in a Global Economy." Washington, DC: NGA Center for Best Practices.

Taylor, Paul, Kim Parker, Richard Fry, D'Vera Cohn, Wendy Wang, Gabriel Velasco, and Daniel Dockterman. 2011. "Is College Worth It?: College Presidents, Public Assess Value, Quality and Mission of Higher Education." Washington, DC: Pew Research Center.

U.S. Department of Education. 2006. *A Test of Leadership: Charting the Future of U.S. Higher Education*. Washington, DC: U.S. Department of Education.

The White House. N.d. "College Scorecard." https://www.whitehouse.gov/issues/education/higher-education/college-score-card.

Wiggins, Grant P., and Jay McTighe. 1998. *Understanding by Design*. Alexandria, VA: Association for Supervision and Curriculum Development.

Williams, Alex. 2012. "Saying No to College." *New York Times*, November 30. http://www.nytimes.com/2012/12/02/fashion/saying-no-to-college.html?smid=pl-share.

2

Measuring College Learning in History

Lendol Calder
Augustana College

Tracy Steffes
Brown University

This contribution advances a case for why historians must come together not only to articulate the value of historical study but also to demonstrate its value with evidence. The authors argue that today's students should develop a deep understanding of history as an interpretive account, the relationship of past and present, historical evidence, complex causality, and historical significance. In addition to mastering these essential concepts, today's history undergraduates should learn how to evaluate historical accounts, interpret primary sources, apply chronological reasoning, contextualize, and construct acceptable historical accounts. Following their in-depth discussion of learning outcomes, the authors review existing history assessments in K–12 and higher education. These include well-known tests like the Advanced Placement history tests and newer tools such as the Stanford History Education Group's Beyond the Bubble assessments. The authors conclude with a vision for the future of assessment in the discipline of history.

Introduction

In 2004, Richard Rothstein published an article in the *Journal of American History* titled "We Are Not Ready to Assess History Performance." A former national education columnist for the *New York Times*, now a respected education analyst for the Economic Policy Institute, Rothstein argued confidently that large-scale, standardized history assessment is impossible. It cannot be done, Rothstein concluded, for the simple reason that no public consensus exists about what history students should learn. Some want history instruction to foster American national identity with stories of heroes and triumphs. Others want to prepare the young to fight for social justice by learning about the power structures that benefit some while oppressing others. Still others want to foster civic and cultural literacy. To be meaningful, large-scale assessments must be aligned with accepted objectives for learning. If Americans do not agree on the outcomes for history education, Rothstein's conclusion follows: "This renders standardized assessment impossible" (2004, 1390).

Since 2004, periodic public controversies over history instruction show that Americans continue to disagree about its aims, especially the key goals, content, and narratives to teach in K–12 schools. For example, in 2014, when the College Board released a revised curriculum framework for Advanced Placement (AP) U.S. history, the new framework garnered praise from the American Historical Association (AHA) and the Organization of American Historians (OAH). But conservatives denounced the new course for being insufficiently celebratory about the nation's past and radically revisionist. The new AP framework was censured by school boards, threatened with defunding by a handful of state legislatures, and described by Republican presidential candidate Ben Carson as so "'anti-American' that most people completing the course will be ready to sign up for ISIS" (Lerner 2015).

Implicit in such critiques of revisionist history is a belief shared by many Americans—perhaps most—that history is what really happened, that is, a single, so-called right story of settled truths. In Florida this view is written into state law. A 2006 statute to raise historical literacy requires the state's public school history teachers to limit themselves to the "teaching of facts," stipulating that "American history shall be viewed as factual, not constructed . . . and shall be defined as the creation of a new nation based largely on the universal principles stated in the Declaration of Independence" (Florida K-20 Education Code 2015, 1003.42). On this view of the matter, it follows that achievement in history is to be measured by students' ability to remember and reproduce an authorized, unchanging canon of important facts and stories.

Yet for most college history faculty, history is all about interpretation. Historians are likely to agree with R. G. Collingwood, author of the canonical *Idea of History*, that "nothing capable of being learnt by heart, nothing capable of being memorized, is history" (1939, 75). Historians think of history not as settled truths about the past but as a sense-making activity, always and inescapably interpretative. History is a constructed explanation made from fragmentary evidence that is always incomplete and subject to revision. Constructing these narratives, historians draw from a discipline situated at the intersection of humanities and social science, with a distinctive set of ideas and practices that guides how we interpret and use evidence, weigh and evaluate plausible explanations, and think about the past in relation to the present. Thus, to historians, popular notions about history teaching largely misunderstand what is most valuable and meaningful about history as a discipline and misrepresent the goals of history teaching and learning, especially at the college level.

Returning to Rothstein's point, it is true that historians and the public do not see eye to eye about outcomes for history education. But the *we* in Rothstein's conclusion that "we are not ready to assess history performance" refers to the adult stakeholders of

K–12 education: parents, teachers, lawmakers, and policymakers. If we turn from the K–12 scene to higher education, different conclusions about assessment in history become possible and, we argue, necessary.

At the college level, historians disagree among themselves about certain aspects of history teaching and learning, such as how to balance breadth and depth, for example, and whether to require the study of any particular histories. But for the most part college history instructors share commitments to a disciplinary set of norms and assumptions that structure our goals and approach to teaching. In the past two decades, historians and others who have studied these disciplinary norms have documented a considerable amount of agreement among historians when compared with discussions about K–12 history education. Nearly all the scholarship and faculty-led efforts to articulate history learning outcomes assume that college students should learn about history *as a discipline*, with emphasis on the habits of mind of historical thinking. Historical thinking honed through disciplined study of the past offers many benefits for students. It fosters critical thinking and analysis skills that are useful for work, citizenship, and individual efficacy. History offers a critical perspective on the present and satisfies a natural longing most people have to situate themselves in a larger context and stream of time. A historical consciousness fosters perspective taking and empathy, and, because it requires students to wrestle with the limits of knowledge, historical thinking is a training ground for solving problems when definitive answers are elusive.

Still, despite the agreement among college history faculty about the goals and purposes of history instruction framed around disciplinary norms, few have stepped forward to challenge Rothstein's conclusion that standardized assessment is impossible. This is not surprising. As experts in the discipline, many of us have developed assessments tailored to individual courses that evaluate the learning outcomes we care most about. We have faith that the accumulation of experiences across history classes produces the student learning we desire (as it did for most of us). We value our autonomy and may view standardized assessment tools as a threat to it. Furthermore, news headlines given to K–12 testing regimes and burgeoning conversations about standardized assessment in higher education do not inspire enthusiasm for new assessment tools. Many faculty worry, not without reason, that the push for assessment will saddle faculty with irksome measures poorly designed to capture meaningful student learning or, at worst, measures that degrade history teaching and learning.

We share these concerns. No one wants ill-advised assessment regimes imported into higher education. No one wants to see a single-minded, narrow emphasis on quantifying value. No one desires deeply flawed metrics being used to compare institutions and individuals. Nevertheless, we believe it would be a serious mistake to let dissatisfaction with existing assessment lead historians to eschew all forms of evaluation or to refuse to engage in conversations about how to measure learning. In light of trends already reshaping higher education, we argue that cynicism about assessment is dangerous for the history profession. If historians do not come to the table for conversations about assessment, decisions will be made without us. The risk we take in opposing all forms of assessment is letting policymakers or external authorities impose on us tests that are far less valid and useful than ones we might have designed ourselves.

As historians, we live in a moment of declining history enrollments, popular attacks on the humanities, and growing demands that a college education have practical utility and demonstrable economic benefits. Decades of rapidly escalating costs for higher education have brought growing scrutiny from external stakeholders. With a majority of Americans believing that higher education in the United States is not providing students good value for their tuition dollars and an even larger majority—75 percent—saying college is too expensive to afford, policymakers and the public are pressing colleges and universities, and fields of study within them, to demonstrate their value (Taylor et al. 2011). Responding to this pressure, Mitch Daniels of Purdue University asked faculty to develop metrics to better measure learning outcomes (Flaherty 2015). The situation at Indiana is a sanguine version of a future awaiting the rest of us; other presidents may not seek faculty input. In an environment like the present, a rigid opposition to assessment is not an option.

If historians should not reject standardized assessment out of hand, neither should we view history assessment as simply a defensive move. In its worst forms, cynicism about assessment is indistinguishable from anti-intellectualism about history teaching and learning. As one tool in a larger assessment toolbox, a rigorously developed standardized instrument designed by historians could help us gather important evidence about student learning according to the criteria that we as historians deem most important for the discipline. It could help us to make more informed decisions about our teaching and curriculum and to explore with more evidence and precision what our students are learning. It could also help us make a stronger case to external audiences including students, university administrators and accreditors, employers, and policymakers about the value of history by helping to *demonstrate* the transferable knowledge, skills, and habits of mind history majors carry with them into the world and the ways historical study empowers them as citizens, workers, and individuals. A standardized assessment for college-level history could perhaps alter public perceptions about what history is for. The effort is worth making because now, as never before, the gulf in understanding about history between disciplinary experts and much of the public matters.

Historians today face a momentous opportunity to articulate clearly and persuasively the value of historical study for college students, most of whom will not pursue graduate study or careers in the historical professions. The AHA, through its Tuning Project, has begun this work already, supporting history departments across the nation to articulate the learning outcomes of a history major and communicate its value to students, employers, and policymakers. Our aim in this white paper is to advance this conversation already occurring within the discipline and to take it a step further. We want to explore how we can move from asserting the value of historical study to demonstrating it with evidence. Our conclusions reflect the perspective of disciplinary experts—historians and college history faculty—about what it means to be good at history and how we can measure student performance on tasks requiring a historical eye.

We begin by surveying the development over time of efforts to define essential disciplinary concepts, competencies, and habits of mind. We use these past and current conversations, along with insights and feedback from the diverse members of the Measuring College Learning (MCL) in History faculty panel, to construct a list of *essential concepts and competencies* that can serve as the basis of assessment in history.[1] This list is meant not to be comprehensive or exhaustive but rather to identify a focused set of essential concepts and competencies that have broad agreement within the discipline as fundamental, important, and valuable goals for history majors. We do not say these are the only things worth assessing in history or that this should be the only assessment—there should always be multiple measures—but this provides one way to assess important, fundamental, and valuable historical learning outcomes. After defining and justifying these concepts and competencies, we discuss current methods of history assessment and

---

[1] In addition to the white paper authors, the history faculty panel included Julia Brookins (American Historical Association); Elaine Carey (St. John's University); James Grossman (American Historical Association); Anne Hyde (Colorado College); Norm Jones (University of Utah); Kenneth Pomeranz (University of Chicago); Nancy Quam-Wickham (California State University, Long Beach); Maris Vinovskis (University of Michigan); and Emily Swafford (American Historical Association).

propose some ideas for what an assessment framed around these essential concepts and competencies might look like. We end by considering potential uses for a standardized history assessment tool and suggesting ways that the profession can engage in conversations that will extend our collective vision of the possible in the realm of valid, useful history assessment.

By itself, the idea of assessment is not difficult for historians. In our courses, we tie assessment organically to teaching as an act of historical inquiry into learning: all assessment is, in essence, a historical argument about something (learning) that happened. This white paper explores how we might do this at the level of the history major. All historians believe passionately in the value of our discipline. Now more than ever we need to communicate this value with tools that capture useful information about student learning.

A History of History Learning Outcomes

College history teachers have only recently adopted the terminology of *learning outcomes*. However, efforts to specify what history students should know, do, and value are not new at all but span back over a century with contributions from a number of disciplinary perspectives. Philosophers, historians, history educators, and recently cognitive scientists have applied themselves to the problem of defining historical understanding and best practices for history education. Today these braided conversations inform newly invigorated efforts of history faculty to theorize history learning outcomes and how we know whether students meet them. Using very broad strokes, we document here how thinking about the nature and purposes of history has been shaped over time by larger developments in the history profession and in K–16 education.

One important body of work affecting ideas about history teaching is that produced by philosophical reflection on the nature and meaning of historical consciousness. Exemplars include explorations written more than a half century ago by R. G. Collingwood, Marc Bloch, and Edward H. Carr, books that have the status of classic works today (Bloch 1953; Carr 1961; Collingwood 1946). Their reflections on the theory and practice of history have recently been supplemented by efforts to define what is distinctive and valuable about the discipline of history and defend the historian's craft from postmodern theories on one hand and social science critiques on the other (Evans 2000; Gaddis 2004). Of course, interpretative debates within the field have been many, varied, and at times vociferous. The magnitude of the quarrels is described by Keith Jenkins:

> Would you like to follow Hegel or Marx or Dilthey or Weber or Popper or Hempel or Aron or Collingwood or Dray or Oakeshott or Danto or Gallie or Walsh or Atkinson or Leff or Hexter? Would you care to go along with modern empiricists, feminists, the Annales School, neo-Marxists, new-stylists, econometricians, structuralists or post-structuralists, or . . . Marwick . . ., to name but twenty-five possibilities? And this is a short list! (Jenkins 1991, 18)

These interpretative debates involve substantial disagreements about what questions to ask, which voices and phenomena to prioritize, and which kinds of explanations are most persuasive. If philosophical reflection upon historical consciousness and methodology were all one had to go on for delineating history learning outcomes, we might conclude that consensus on disciplinary goals and methods is unattainable.

However, a second body of literature offers grounds for hope. History primers—that is, books, articles, and handbooks written for or about the training of history students—suggest that, notwithstanding their different schools and ideologies, historians share conceptual reference points that, once identified, offer clear markers to delineate competence in history. By identifying and demystifying the key intellectual "moves" and understandings common to expert historians, primers aim to foster student learning in history courses. What are the concepts and competencies said to be the common property of most historians and important enough to teach to undergraduates?

The short answer is that our understanding of these key moves has changed over time. For example, historians have long debated what outcomes realistically can be expected in the introductory college course. The nature and extent of this debate, and what it reveals about college faculty's expectations for history learning, are described by Joel Sipress and David Voelker in a 2011 essay examining how introductory courses became surveys of broad historical knowledge. According to Sipress and Voelker, the educational goals and methods defining the traditional introductory history course were settled over a century ago when coverage of historical information was made the goal of the introductory course and cultural literacy the chief learning outcome. Coverage and cultural literacy did not go unchallenged. Sipress and Voelker document moments in every generation of historians when reformers criticized the coverage model. For example, at the December 1897 meeting of the AHA, when historians debated whether or not primary source materials had a place in introductory courses, the University of Nebraska's Fred M. Fling argued for making source work "the staple of historical instruction" (Sipress and Voelker 2011, 1054). The following year, a Committee of Seven appointed by the AHA to study the issue agreed with Fling, contending "that the accumulation of facts is not the sole, or perhaps not the leading, purpose of studying history" (Sipress and Voelker 2011, 1054). Yet the recitation of authoritative knowledge continued to be the goal of a coverage-oriented history teaching that retained its dominance through the 20th century and persists today. Sipress and Voelker argue this was the case because the psychology of the coverage model was reinforced by historically contingent trends shaping higher education, including assumptions about (a) learning (e.g., early 20th-century behaviorism and its attic theory of cognition in which the mind must be stocked with facts before one can learn to think about them); (b) the purpose of history (e.g., the view, popular after WWI, that the primary burden of history instruction was the formation of citizens who would be safe for democracy, or know the right things); and (c) general education (e.g., the view after WWII that democracy was threatened by deficiencies in what students knew about Western and American civilization) (Sipress and Voelker 2011).

In recent decades, new challenges to the coverage model are undermining its hegemony and suggesting different outcomes for history education. An explosion of historical knowledge and subfields makes coverage more than ever an impossible objective. Even more damaging are the rejection of behaviorism in cognitive science and reforms in K–12 education that turned the attention of educators from teaching to learning. After A Nation at Risk (1983) warned the country was facing an educational crisis wrought by a "rising tide of mediocrity," education reformers embarked on a wide range of efforts to raise educational standards, frame ambitious curriculum content and student performance standards, and assess students' and schools' progress toward meeting those goals (National Commission on Excellence in Education 1983). Many supporters viewed standards-based reform as an equity effort, since it focused attention on whether students were learning and pressured schools to ensure that they did. Since the No Child Left Behind Act in 2001, this pressure on schools has become the dominant attribute of federal policy, a pressure that manifests itself through a high-stakes testing regime that issues escalating school sanctions based on test performance in the name of accountability. This testing has spurred strong and growing resistance because of its equity implications, negative impacts on teaching and learning, and simplistic equation of test scores on low-level standardized tests with school quality.

The backlash against this testing threatens to undermine assessment more generally, despite the conviction of many education reformers that appropriate assessments, tied meaningfully to curriculum, can help to enhance quality and equality in education by focusing attention on student learning.

In history, the Bradley Commission on History in Schools, which included over a dozen eminent historians along with teachers and writers, stepped into this national reform conversation about curriculum goals and standards. It articulated a rationale for studying history in schools, core themes and narratives to emphasize regardless of content, and elements of historical thinking. The Bradley Commission's *Building a History Curriculum* (1989) influenced the National Standards for History undertaken a few years later as part of an effort to develop voluntary national standards in core school subjects. After becoming embroiled in mid-1990s culture wars over what students should know and whether the standards were sufficiently celebratory of the nation's past and European tradition, the effort to create national standards was abandoned. In the rancorous debate about what content students should know, some of the innovations of the effort were buried, especially its emphasis on analytic thinking and skill-building activities to make history come alive in the classroom. However, these innovative efforts continued and gained ground in state-level curriculum standards reform, educational scholarship and teacher education, and some large-scale assessments like NAEP and the Advanced Placement history examinations.

For the most part, college history faculty members stand aloof from these changes and discussions. Yet as Sipress and Voelker relate, seeds of reform planted in the 1990s now promise to deliver the long-sought goal of pedagogical reformers: the end of the coverage model. One source of change was innovative theories and practices percolating up from K–12 history education, often endorsed by historians active in the preparation of future school history teachers. Another was the Carnegie Foundation's sponsorship in 1999–2000 of a cadre of historians to jump-start the scholarship of teaching and learning (SoTL) in history. Early on, history SoTL specialists realized that one of the most important tasks in front of them was replacing the coverage model's understanding of what it means to be proficient at history—which unintentionally reinforced public misperceptions of history as important things that happened—with new understandings of expertise based on how historians think and tuned to how people learn. To the early SoTL scholars, this was interesting intellectual work on its own terms, benefiting students and historians alike (Calder, Cutler, and Kelly 2002; Pace 2004). Only later, as calls for accountability in higher education grew louder, did it occur to anyone that there might be other uses for specifying expertise in history and designing valid assessments, such as defending history's value in a liberal arts curriculum.

In the last two decades, then, numerous workbooks, guides, and articles by SoTL scholars have defined and argued for the core concepts and skills that should be at the center of history teaching. On this question agreement in the literature of history primers is not perfect, but it is substantial. Conal Furay and Michael Salevouris's *The Methods and Skills of History: A Practical Guide* (1988) proposes five core elements of historical-mindedness: sensitivity to how other times and places differ from our own; awareness of basic continuities in human affairs over time; ability to note and explain significant changes; sensitivity to multiple causation; and awareness that all written history is reconstruction that inadequately reflects the past as it really happened. Thomas Holt (1995) identifies two characteristics of historical-mindedness every college student should master: analytic questioning and the ability to synthesize narratives. Lendol Calder (2006) recommends six core cognitive habits be taught to beginning students of history: questioning; contextualizing; sourcing; using evidence; recognizing multiple perspectives; and recognizing limits to what one knows. And Thomas Andrews and Flannery Burke (2007) put the power of alliteration to work with "the Five Cs of Historical Thinking": change, context, causality, contingency, and complexity.[2] The authors of these and other history primers concede that their chosen concepts and competencies reflect personal judgments and are neither comprehensive nor uncontroversial. In terms of reception, there seems to be little objection to specific items on the lists, just disagreements about the priority given to certain outcomes and questions about what level of undergraduate education they are best suited for. The many lists of core components of historical expertise define and prioritize the elements of historical thinking in different ways. But the most notable aspect of recent primers and handbooks is their unanimity on an important point: *that the main goal of history instruction should be historical thinking.* None frame student learning goals in terms of cultural literacy, historical knowledge, or specific content.

Pushing this conversation forward has been the work of cognitive scientists, particularly Sam Wineburg, on the mental processes that define historical expertise. As a doctoral student studying cognitive psychology at Stanford in the 1990s, Wineburg became intrigued by the elusive qualities of historical mindedness. Everything he read on this by historians, philosophers, and teachers came from introspective self-reporting, but he knew from research on expertise in other professions that a wide gap exists between what disciplinary experts say they do and what they actually do. Expert habits of mind are often invisible to the highly trained; they may forget there was a time when they did not know how to do what they have learned to do so well. To map the cognitive processes historians deploy, Wineburg used research protocols called think-alouds in which subjects are trained to think out loud while completing a task so that researchers can record and analyze their

---

[2] Allen Mikaelian, editor of the AHA's *Perspectives in History*, reports that Andrews and Burke's "Five Cs" essay is the most accessed article on the AHA Web archive. See *Perspectives on History* 52 (April 2014): 37.

introspections. Wineburg compared think-alouds conducted with historians to think-alouds with non-historians to learn how expert thinking differs from lay thinking. His empirical investigations showed that in history, experts and novices do not differ merely in *what* they know but, more crucially, in *how* they think. In particular, Wineburg stressed the ways expert historians source, corroborate, and contextualize evidence and the way they think about historical knowledge using concepts of significance, periodization, and narrative (Wineburg 2001).

Wineburg is but one of a number of cognitive psychologists who offer important insights into the mental operations of expert historians and clarify the often unstated expectations teachers hold for students. In a review of this literature in 2006, James Voss and Jennifer Wiley note that, compared with other fields, historians deal primarily with ill-structured problems that are not amenable to mathematics, formal logic, or repeatable experimentation. This leaves historians without common subject-matter knowledge and with more heterogeneity in the constraints they place on thinking. Nevertheless, like the authors of history primers, they found commonalities emerging in the literature. Voss and Wiley identified three interrelated tasks (historians obtain information, historians construct narratives, and historians make inferences and solve problems) and ten characteristics of history experts (CHEs). They report, for example, that as part of obtaining information, historians use sourcing heuristics to improve the structure of ill-structured problems, including corroboration, sourcing, contextualization, identifying absent evidence, and generating subtexts that illuminate the intentions of the author and thereby assist with the interpretation of sources. In constructing narratives, historians "provide rationales, explanations, elaborations, or speculations" in expository form and recognize the plausibility of alternative accounts (Voss and Wiley 2006, 575).

Ongoing work by cognitive scientists has made significant contributions to what we know about historical thinking and history learning goals. Many of the CHEs found by Voss and Wiley echo lists found in historians' reflections on the discipline. Some of the differences are interesting, though. For example, they do not include recognizing contingency, a concept that many historians claim is crucial for explaining historical change. It remains to be seen through further research whether this is because historians do not actually work the concept the way we think we do or whether researchers have not adequately identified and mapped this cognitive move. In any case, cognitive scientists' precise, fine-grained unpacking of what it means to think like a historian is useful for framing and prioritizing learning outcomes in history. The influence of this literature on the development of history teaching materials and assessments is immense and growing.

In the context of standards-based reform and the so-called turn from teaching to learning, in the last two decades various parties have made notable efforts to engage more college faculty in discussions of learning outcomes for history students (Barr and Tagg 1995). Two of these efforts, the Quality in Undergraduate Education (QUE) project and the AHA's Tuning Project, show how much attitudes of history faculty members have changed in a short amount of time.

QUE, the first major national effort to articulate learning outcomes in selected disciplines, began in 1997 and ran until 2004. Sponsored by the Education Trust Inc., the National Association of Systems Heads, and Georgia State University, QUE funded faculty from twenty-one institutions in four states and five disciplines (including history) to meet twice a year in national workshops and periodically in local clusters. Using the lever of learning outcomes, QUE aimed to focus faculty attention on improving student learning by shifting attention away from what teachers say in lectures to what students were expected to know and do at various points in a history degree program. Organizers saw QUE as a professional development project that would disseminate pedagogical innovations like student learning outcomes, backwards course design, rubrics for evaluating student work, and course-mapping tools for program improvement. However, the results disappointed expectations. Buy-in by faculty members and departments was mixed, with many history faculty members unwilling to concede that traditional teacher and content-centered pedagogies fail to generate higher level thinking. The learning outcomes produced by participating institutions varied greatly in quality; few saw the light of day as published models. The project that organizers and funders hoped would spark a revolution in higher education quietly died when its funding ended.

The story of the AHA Tuning Project, launched less than a decade later and funded by the Lumina Foundation, could not be more different.[3] Initially conceived to be a three-year project, it brings historians together to spell out the central skills, habits of mind, and understandings of the field of history in postsecondary education. Borrowing a model employed in European higher education, Tuning is a collaborative process in which participants define the core disciplinary elements of historical training and then harmonize, or tune, these goals in ways that are appropriate for their own institution's mission. Like QUE, Tuning does not aspire to standardize history curricula. Rather, it offers a process for departments to develop their own goals and curriculum while benefiting from conversation with others engaged in the same task. Unlike QUE, and critical for its success, Tuning has the AHA's authority behind it, making it a project led by historians for historians. Tuners have worked enthusiastically and productively in a collaborative process to create a Discipline Core Statement outlining what history students should know, do, and value. Whereas with QUE the identification of learning outcomes was merely the first step in a larger process of top-to-bottom reform of teaching and learning in the discipline, Tuning thus far restricts its scope to identifying learning outcomes. But in a crucial way Tuning is

---

[3] Coauthor Lendol Calder participated in both initiatives.

more ambitious than QUE, wanting to express history's core outcomes in ways that communicate the significance and value of a history degree to external audiences, including employers, policymakers, and students. Thus, departments engaged in Tuning are responsible for devising a "degree specifications profile" describing historical training at their institution and outlining core areas of competency expected of graduates from their program. The profiles released thus far draw from and adapt the Discipline Core statement, showing considerable overlap with concepts and competencies found in history primers (AHA, "About Tuning").

The surprisingly positive response to the original call for Tuners led the AHA to solicit applications for a second phase of the Tuning project. In January 2015, an even larger group of participants than the original sixty began working on their own degree specification profiles.

The success of Tuning shows how much has changed within the last decade. These changes likely reflect both developments within the profession—such as growing awareness of scholarship by historians on teaching and learning—and significant external pressures on history departments making them more receptive to defining learning outcomes with precision and transparency. Facing declining enrollments and pressure from administrators, accreditors, and policymakers to demonstrate the value of a history degree, more historians and departments have become engaged in conversations about defining and measuring student learning.

The AHA Tuning project indicates that there is considerable interest in the profession for the work of defining history learning outcomes. We believe the time may be right to carry this conversation to another level. It is one thing to theorize what it means to be good at history. It is another matter to consider how we might know whether students are achieving the goals we set for them. The interest and participation of over one hundred history departments in Tuning so far demonstrates strong interest among historians for thinking about what it means to be good at history and how one becomes so, especially when that effort is led by historians. Now that Tuners have put substantial time and effort into defining history learning goals for their departments and worked to adapt their curriculums to achieve them, they will want to find meaningful ways to evaluate whether their efforts have improved student learning. This should make Tuners a receptive audience for tools that can help guide them in further program revisions. More than that, we expect Tuners to be participants and leaders in efforts to develop more authentic assessments of student learning in history.

Essential Concepts and Competencies for the History Major

History primers, cognitive scientists, and the AHA Tuning Project have articulated comprehensive lists of student learning outcomes for history majors. We build on and advance this conversation by identifying a focused set of *essential concepts and competencies* that history faculty see as fundamental to the discipline, important enough to emphasize given limited time and resources, and valuable to students' lives. Focusing on a smaller number of outcomes enables more careful attention to how these core disciplinary goals can be learned, including more rigorous, targeted, and meaningful assessment. Moreover, framing these learning outcomes as *concepts* and *competencies* encourages historians to distinguish carefully between abilities and the conceptual understandings students must have to exercise those abilities.

In selecting these essential concepts and competencies, we looked for patterns of agreement in primers, cognitive science research, and current Tuning efforts. We relied on the input of the diverse historians in the MCL faculty panel, engaging with them in an iterative process of list making, feedback, winnowing, and further revision. Searching for areas of consensus in the field, we aimed to pinpoint *essential* outcomes, not a comprehensive list of markers defining expertise in history. Consequently, our list likely leaves off concepts and competencies that individuals or departments deem important. In that event, they can and should articulate these additional outcomes and develop methods of assessment for them.

Perhaps the most obvious omission from our list is historical content knowledge. Clearly, historians value factual information about the past and consider subject matter literacy an important goal in their teaching. Furthermore, historical thinking requires content to function; historical concepts and competencies cannot be developed or practiced in a vacuum. The problem with including content knowledge as a goal for assessment is the question of *which* knowledge to test. Although histories of the United States and Europe once held privileged places in the curriculum of most colleges and universities, many departments no longer require immersion in these subjects. Instead, they encourage concentrations in other geographic areas and exploration of new thematic fields and faculty specializations. Thus, any attempt to build a test on a particular national history or to privilege particular regions or periods likely would meet with significant controversy. Furthermore, it is the conviction of many historians that no particular history *ought* to be privileged because historical thinking, the ultimate purpose of undergraduate history instruction, can be fostered in sustained study of any historical content. Within our MCL group we had passionate debates about content, specifically whether one's national history should have a privileged place. With no consensus possible and remembering that we were not attempting to be comprehensive, we decided to exclude any specific subject knowledge from the essential concepts and competencies.

Concepts

Having reviewed what others before us have said in the ongoing conversation about history learning outcomes, we find the following concepts are most essential for specifying what undergraduate history students should know at the completion of a course of study.

History as an Interpretative Account

Students must understand that history is not simply what happened in the past unmediated by human sense-making. Rather, it is an interpretative account of the past constructed through a disciplined process of problem solving and supported by evidence that survives. Because we cannot apprehend the past through applications of mathematics, formal logic, or controlled experimentation, in historical accounts problem solving is usually verbal, with conclusions presented in the form of a narrative or an analytic argument developed in relation to particular questions, forms of evidence, and existing interpretations. Students must understand that when historians construct accounts their goal is not to reach a universal standard of validity or correctness as in the case of logical and mathematical proofs. Rather, the object is to convince an audience that an account of the past is highly acceptable. Evaluation of historical accounts occurs by examining the acceptability of the information provided as evidence, the extent to which the information supports the account, and the quality of counterarguments or alternative positions that may be offered. Both accounts and evaluations of accounts are influenced by historians' own beliefs, theoretical orientations, and other factors. Resting on interpretive accounts, it is the nature of historical knowledge to have relatively less certainty and more heterogeneity in how questions are answered than knowledge in some other disciplinary domains. This also means that historical knowledge is not fixed for all time. Rather, we can expect historical knowledge to be mutable. Historical knowledge is constantly being revised as new evidence comes to light and new generations ask different questions and attend to different constraints on our ability to know the past.

The Relationship of Past and Present

Students must understand the complex relationship between past and present. Acceptable sense making of the past walks a balance between two states of mind: familiarity and strangeness. Often, we are motivated to study the past when we become aware that the world we live in today is a product of past events and developments that continue to shape contemporary life. This is the *presentness of the past*. But since nothing in time stands still, the passage of time makes strange what once seemed ordinary. Therefore, historians also emphasize the *pastness of the past*, that is, recognition of the differences that separate our own time from the past. Being mindful that the past is a foreign country cautions us to not assume we have an intuitive understanding of historical actors, projecting our own values and assumptions onto people of different times and places. Instead, recognizing the pastness of the past directs historians to understand people of the past by contextualizing their actions: what they were trying to accomplish; the nature of their beliefs, attitudes, and knowledge; the culturally and historically situated assumptions that guided thought and action. Situating people, events, and sources within the context of their time is a primary mission of historical sense making. Furthermore, examining the past gives a sense of the abnormal present; in other words, it helps to destabilize what we might take for granted in the present and help us view the present moment with critical perspective. Mediating between the pastness of the past and the presentness of the past gives people with a historical perspective a reflective self-awareness that actively searches for the plausibility of beliefs and actions different from their own.

Historical Evidence

Students must understand that the acceptability of historical accounts depends a great deal on how evidence is used to support claims about the past. Sources of evidence are categorized as either *primary* or *secondary*. Primary sources are the raw materials for the study of the past originating from the time under study. Secondary sources are interpretive accounts of the past that historians use to generate new questions, corroborate conclusions, and test interpretations. Students should understand that the classification of a source depends on its use for a particular historical question. For example, a historical account of ancient Rome written during the 1950s would be a secondary source if the historical question is about ancient Rome and the source is used to ground an interpretation, or it could be a primary source if one is asking a historical question about the intellectual climate affecting historians in the 1950s. Students should understand the nature, potential, and limits of both kinds of evidence. In particular, students should know that primary sources come in diverse forms, represent diverse perspectives, and have distinct strengths and limitations as evidence about the past. They will avoid the misconception that primary sources are exact, unproblematic reflections of the past. Critically, students must understand that reading primary sources for evidence demands a different approach than reading them for information. Acceptable interpretations of the past require that primary source evidence be examined both for content and its unwitting testimony, that is, what the source says without directly saying it. This requires asking questions about their provenance and historical contexts and using the answers to constrain interpretations of the evidence.

Complex Causality

Students must understand that in contrast to disciplines that seek to isolate factors and reduce explanations to singular causes, history understands change over time to be complex and interconnected. Considerations include not only human agency but also structural, environmental, and other factors that play a role in stimulating, shaping, and resisting change. Thus, historical accounts are multiple and layered, avoiding monocausal explanations and reductionist thinking. They distinguish significant from insignificant causes and proximate from long-term, enabling conditions. Causes put forward to explain an event (and the priority of causes) may differ based on the scale of the history and the approaches of the historian.

Significance

Students must understand what makes something historically significant. Since the past is everything that happened before now, including everything that humans anywhere have thought, said, and done, no history can include all of the past. Therefore, the concept of significance is used to make choices about what subjects are worth remembering and constructing accounts about, what is worth including in an account, and what can be left out. Peter Seixas defines historical significance as "the valuing criterion through which the historian assesses which pieces of the entire possible corpus of the past can fit together into a meaningful and coherent story that is worthwhile" (Seixas 1994, 281). Historians generally regard something as significant if (a) it affects change or continuity with meaningful consequences, for many people, over a long period of time or if (b) it is revealing, leading us to understand other subjects in history and contemporary life in new ways, or was important at some stage in history within the collective memory of a group or groups.

Competencies

Basing our judgment on a review of the history and literature on history learning outcomes, we recommend the following competencies as most essential for specifying what undergraduate history students should be able to do at the completion of a course of study.

Evaluate Historical Accounts

Students must recognize historical explanations in their most common forms: narrative, exposition, causal model, and analogy.

They should be able to identify an author's interpretation and critically scrutinize the evidence and analysis used to support it. In addition, they should be able to critically evaluate, compare, and synthesize historical accounts.

Interpret Primary Sources

Students must be able to analyze and interpret information drawn from primary sources, drawing on specialized subject knowledge and concepts of historical thinking. More specifically, they should be able to distinguish primary from secondary sources; assess the credibility of sources and make judgments about their usefulness and limitations as evidence about the past; consider how the historical context in which information was originally created, accessed, and distributed affects its message; and address questions of genre, content, audience, perspective, and purpose to generate subtexts that illuminate the intentions of the author.

Apply Chronological Reasoning

Students must take account of the role of time, sequencing, and periodization in historical narratives. In particular, students should demonstrate sensitivity to complex causation, with an ability to distinguish between proximate and ultimate causes; with a discerning eye for continuity and change over time; and with the ability to formulate and evaluate historical periods and turning points as heuristic devices for making sense of the past, recognizing the artificiality of periods and turning points and the ways they favor one narrative, theme, region, or group over others.

Contextualize

Students must demonstrate the ability to place an event, actor, or primary source within the context of its time in order to interpret its meaning and significance. Rather than assume timeless, psychologized notions of why people behaved as they did in the past or that people of the past were similar or identical to ourselves, with the same beliefs, attitudes, instincts, and motivations, students must be able to appreciate the particular policies, institutions, worldviews, and circumstances that shaped people's practices in a given moment in time. Recognizing difference is by itself not enough, however, if the past is dismissed for being unenlightened or immoral. Students must also be able to reconstruct the plausibility of other people's perspectives and actions within their own frame of reference. Contextualization does not mean identification (we can understand another's viewpoint without accepting it as our own), facile claims to knowing (we can never directly know others' experiences and perceptions), or an emotional response (the goal is understanding, not necessarily admiration or sympathy). Rather, students should be able to make sense of actions, social practices, and institutions in terms of people's reasons for doing or believing what they did.

Construct Acceptable Historical Accounts

Students must be able to construct acceptable historical accounts that interpret the past using sources as evidence for knowledge claims in ways that demonstrate understanding of historical concepts, especially the nature of historical evidence, interpretation, and perspective. More specifically, students should be able to do the following: pose historical questions; select and utilize relevant and reliable primary source evidence to support their historical interpretation; extract information and supportable inferences from a wide range of primary and secondary sources, acknowledging, conceding, or refuting evidence that runs counter to the overall argument; recognize the limitations of evidence; and persevere through uncertainty, renouncing simple certitude (proof and inevitability) and easy relativism (every view is equal) for the disciplinary standard of limited relativism (plausible–implausible, acceptable–unacceptable).

Reflections on the List of Essential Concepts and Competencies

A definitive list of learning outcomes for history is, of course, a chimera. We offer this list of essential concepts and competencies as our best summation of what history students in college should know, do, and value based on our study of a century and more of historians thinking out loud about history education and more recent attempts by historians, philosophers, history educators, and cognitive scientists to define the nature of expertise in history. Before we turn to the problem of how to design assessment tools that are worthy of historical understanding, we pause to consider two important questions raised by our list.

In college, what is the study of history for?

When thinking about learning outcomes for history education, questions about the purpose of a BA in history—or even the value of taking a single history course in college—cannot be avoided.

In today's career-minded environment, students are drawn to preprofessional programs because it is obvious what such majors train students to do. The premedical (premed) major prepares students for graduate education in health-related professions. The education major is for future teachers. The business major is for those who want to work in business fields. History programs suffer by comparison because a bachelor of arts in history is not a ticket to employment as a historian, and the demand for history MAs and PhDs is small. So why study history in college?

The answer, we believe, is that a course of study in history does two important things very well. In good history programs, the study of history effectively marries the analytic and synthesizing strengths associated with the liberal arts and sciences—America's premier educational tradition—with the problem-solving and practical strengths necessary to help companies and organizations succeed and grow. Better perhaps than most other disciplines or at least as well as any, history is positioned to help people become civic and workplace leaders who think critically, communicate clearly, and solve complex problems. The reasons that this is so are apparent in our list of essential concepts and competencies.

In a paper published by the National History Center in 2008, "The Role of the History Major in Liberal Education," Stanley Katz and James Grossman noted the close linkages between historical study and the broad aims of liberal learning. Katz and Grossman warn historians not to regard undergraduates as miniature graduate students, teaching history as the professors themselves were taught on the way to the PhD. Rather, they argue, undergraduate programs should be designed to "nurture [students'] liberal and civic capacities, in part by integrating disciplinary knowledge, methods, and principles into the broad experience of undergraduate education" (Katz and Grossman 2008). We concur wholeheartedly, and we call attention to the significant overlap between our list of essential history concepts and competencies and efforts by the Association of American Colleges and Universities (AAC&U) to invigorate liberal education for the 21st century through the decade-old LEAP initiative (Liberal Education and America's Promise). To prepare students for responsible citizenship and a global economy, LEAP's Essential Learning Outcomes for a liberal education are as follows: (a) knowledge of human cultures and the physical and natural world; (b) intellectual and practical skills (e.g., inquiry and analysis, critical and creative thinking, written and oral communication, and quantitative and information literacy); (c) teamwork and problem solving; (d) personal and social responsibility (e.g., civic knowledge and engagement—local and global, and intercultural competence); and (e) integrative and applied learning (e.g., synthesis across general and specialized studies demonstrated through complex problem solving). When we compare the LEAP outcomes with our list of essential concepts and competencies for history, we find that a course of study in history closely aligns with the AAC&U's outline for liberal learning in the 21st century (AAC&U 2015).

But students may find another purpose for history education even more valuable, at least at first. Surveys of employers' priorities for the kinds of learning students need to succeed in today's competitive and global economy show that history is well positioned to provide what business and nonprofit leaders want. A 2013 AAC&U study conducted by Hart Research Associates found that 93 percent of employers believe "a demonstrated capacity to think critically, communicate clearly, and solve complex problems" is more important than a student's particular major. When employers were asked to endorse educational practices that would be helpful in preparing college students for workplace success, the practices they selected amount to a précis of the essential competencies we describe, including (a) conduct research and use evidence-based analysis; (b) gain in-depth knowledge and analytic, problem solving, and communication skills; and (c) apply learning in real-world settings (Hart Research Associates 2013). On the basis of surveys like this, we believe that history programs can capitalize by design on students' desire to prepare for career opportunities and success.

Why study history? An 1898 AHA pamphlet stated that "the chief purpose [of historical education] is not to fill the boy's head with a mass of material which he may perchance put forth again when a college examiner demands its production" (Sipress and Voelker 2011, 1051). By contrast, our list of concepts and competencies for a history BA foregrounds a very different purpose for undergraduate history education. The history BA prepares future civic and workforce leaders to grapple productively with ill-defined problems by bringing inquiry, analysis, and communication and application of knowledge to bear on specific complex questions. Historical study trains people to be citizens committed to liberal learning and innovative problem solvers in real-world settings.

How do the essential concepts and competencies relate to introductory history courses?

Unlike disciplines that offer one or two clearly delineated courses introducing students to the major, history has many pathways to the major and relatively little sequencing within it. Furthermore, introductory courses are taught in different ways and for different purposes. In some departments, introductory courses are small courses organized around doing history, aiming to introduce students to historical thinking and methodology through a focused topic. In many others—probably most—introductory courses remain broad surveys of historical knowledge and are commonly large lecture courses that also serve general education goals for the university. As our earlier summary of the history of learning outcomes suggests, in many of these courses the goal of cultural literacy and the methods of coverage are still embraced. Although some professors aim to infuse historical thinking into these surveys, many others emphasize broad exposure to content knowledge as the primary aim.

We believe that introductory courses can and should introduce students to the disciplinary concepts and competencies we propose and that this can exist alongside knowledge transmission goals. We believe this on the basis of the learning science that rejects the attic theory of cognition, which considers a stockpile of knowledge accumulated over years of study to be the prerequisite for advanced analytic work. We now know that students learn more when they are engaged early, often, and cumulatively in problem-centered inquiries requiring disciplined ways of thinking. Introductory courses, whether small seminars or large lectures, should aim to introduce and develop some or all of the essential concepts and competencies outlined here. However, we acknowledge that there might be considerable disagreement within the profession on this point, and some, perhaps many, historians view the traditional survey as serving legitimate, valuable, and important ends, including establishing a foundation of knowledge for later study or promoting cultural and civic literacy. Many departments face real constraints that make doing history in small seminars seem unfeasible; reimagining the large introductory course to emphasize historical thinking, including its goals, methods, and assessments, is a project still in development.

Consequently, at this moment, even though we are confident that the learning outcomes we have defined are universally applicable to the BA in history, we do not believe the assessment imagined in this white paper will be considered appropriate by all instructors to measure student learning in introductory courses. Those still wedded to coverage methods as the best way to attain cultural literacy likely will object to our recommended assessment tools. On the other hand, those looking to build introductory courses on the platform of historical thinking for liberal learning and expanded opportunities in the workplace likely will be intrigued.

Student Learning in History: Past, Present, and Future Assessments

Assessment is integral to history teaching and learning. History faculty members routinely assess student learning in individual courses, most often through papers and in-class examinations. Examinations in history often include multiple-choice questions, short answers (e.g., identifications), or essays that ask students to demonstrate knowledge or skills valued by the instructor. Essay assignments may ask students to analyze and synthesize a historical theme or historical narratives, interpret one or more primary sources, or conduct historical research by asking a historical question and answering it with primary and secondary sources. History faculty also employ a range of other assignments to assess student learning in courses: constructing primary source readers; oral presentations; short written assignments to assess particular skills like distinguishing between primary and secondary sources; questions for class discussion; and historical role-playing games like Reacting to the Past.[4] Ideally, these assignments are carefully aligned with the instructor's learning goals, thereby providing valid evidence of students' achievement of those goals. Unfortunately, as Sipress and Voelker found in their analysis of introductory courses, though most historians claim to be teaching historical thinking, common assessments show otherwise. Constraints such as large class sizes and inadequate faculty development lead many instructors to settle for assessments requiring students to merely memorize and reproduce expert knowledge.

Less common are efforts to assess history learning across courses at the level of the history major. Most departments assume that successful completion of requirements, which may include standards for grade point average, breadth or specialization, and methods, demonstrates successful learning. However, an increasing number of history departments are making efforts to assess student learning more directly, using portfolios of student work, senior theses, capstone projects, or senior seminar courses to evaluate whether graduating seniors have "gotten it" and are able to demonstrate historical knowledge and thinking. Many of these efforts attempt to assess everything at once, providing relatively little feedback on which particular historical concepts and competencies majors have achieved. A thesis, for example, asks students to exhibit attainment of a great number of learning objectives simultaneously. Consequently, if the final product is unsatisfactory, in the absence of fine-grained rubrics it can be difficult to pinpoint the specific skills that need further development.

At the level of elementary and especially secondary education, there have been more efforts to develop large-scale assessments that provide information about student learning in history. The SAT Subject Tests offer exams in U.S. history and world history that can be taken by prospective college applicants and submitted

---

[4] See https://reacting.barnard.edu for more information on Reacting to the Past.

for college admission, although institutions rarely require them. The exams are composed entirely of multiple-choice questions that ask students to demonstrate breadth of knowledge above all else. The exams purport to incorporate social science concepts, methods, and generalizations by including short document excerpts including quotations and images as part of questions, but the overriding emphasis is on recall of content. A sample question in a practice guide, for example, asks students to identify the likely source of a quotation. The item requires examinees to read and comprehend the quotation, but ultimately it is assessing whether they can identify the individuals listed to discern the most likely author (College Board 2015).

The National Assessment of Educational Progress (NAEP) offers an assessment in U.S. history every five to eight years and is developing a test for world history. NAEP aims to measure what the nation's students in Grades 4, 8, and 12 know and can do in given subjects, rotating the subjects examined every year. NAEP exams use a matrix-sampling method in which every student is given only a portion of the test; rather than reporting the scores of individuals, NAEP reports the scores of groups of students. This allows them to examine students on a much wider range of materials. The U.S. history subject exam was first administered in 1986 as a multiple-choice exam that tested breadth of knowledge about U.S. history. In subsequent years and in light of the Bradley Commission, National History Standards, and burgeoning scholarship on history teaching and learning, NAEP decreased its multiple-choice portion to 50 percent, incorporated more open-ended responses and performance exercises on the exam, and infused ways of knowing and thinking about U.S. history into the four themes and eight periods that it examines. Today the NAEP U.S. history exam focuses strongly on breadth of historical knowledge, but it also uses multiple-choice questions and constructed responses to measure depth of learning and cognitive skills, including the ability of students to marshal facts and organize and express thoughts.

In some cases, students are given a textual or visual source and asked to respond to multiple-choice questions or write short open-ended responses to questions posed about it. The NAEP exam tests for historical knowledge and perspective and historical analysis and interpretation. The former asks students to identity, define, describe, and place knowledge, whereas the latter asks students to explain cause and effect, interpret different points of view, and define significance.

A third major history assessment in use today is perhaps the most well known to college faculty: the Advanced Placement exams in U.S. history, European history, and world history. Taken most often by high school juniors and seniors, these exams are meant to certify competence in the introductory college survey course to qualify for college credit. The exams are roughly half multiple-choice questions assessing students' knowledge of historical facts, one-quarter short essays measuring deeper knowledge about a topic and historical reasoning, and one-quarter a single document-based question (DBQ) that provides short primary source excerpts and asks students to write an essay interpreting the sources while drawing on background content knowledge. The examinations consequently involve writing and interpretation of sources but are heavily weighted toward assessing content knowledge. Recently the AP U.S. history exam underwent a redesign to address some of the criticisms of college faculty that it placed too much emphasis on recall of discrete facts, reinforcing a coverage model pedagogy and shortchanging important historical thinking skills. The new exam decreases multiple-choice questions to 40 percent of the score, emphasizes thematic learning objectives to help focus preparation for the exam and allow greater depth in teaching, and increases emphasis on historical thinking skills outlined in its curriculum framework.

These three major national assessments in history have several things in common and some important differences. All three examinations place strong emphasis on assessing specific content knowledge about the past, be it U.S., European, or world history. Since the examinations are meant to assess learning in K–12 school subjects and, in the case of the AP exams, to substitute for a particular college course, this emphasis on demonstrating knowledge about major themes, events, and figures is understandable. NAEP and the AP exams have developed increasingly sophisticated frameworks for defining and assessing historical thinking within the context of a particular regional history; students might be asked, for example, to interpret a political cartoon that requires them not only to know something about the people and time being depicted but also to interpret a source. Yet for the reasons already outlined, an assessment of learning in the college history major will not place the same emphasis on evaluating a student's content knowledge. This raises thorny questions about assessment design that will be addressed in the next section: Since content knowledge is necessary for historical thinking, how can a history test be designed for diverse college curricula that require no common historical subject for the BA?

Another similarity between the three exams is that they all use multiple-choice questions to assess student knowledge and, to some extent, historical cognition. For large-scale standardized assessments, reliance on multiple-choice questions is unsurprising: They are easy, fast, and inexpensive to administer and score. In a shorter amount of time and at less cost than other methods of assessment, multiple-choice items can gather more information about student learning. Assessment experts also have great faith in the validity (how well they represent the learning outcome desired) and reliability (how consistent the results are) of multiple-choice items once they have been rigorously field tested and refined.

However, we caution that multiple-choice items might face a hostile reception among college history faculty. Some researchers in history teaching and learning have rejected multiple-choice questions as appropriate assessments for the field because they do not reveal the cognitive processes behind an answer.

Moreover, multiple-choice items privilege a single, right answer when historical interpretation is by nature complex, nuanced, and multiple, allowing for several acceptable answers. Some have raised concerns that multiple-choice items can be skewed by strong test-taking skills; students can puzzle out the correct response even when they cannot come up with it on their own (Ercikan and Seixas 2015). Discussions with our MCL faculty panel indicated that most historians in the room associated multiple-choice items with memorization of facts and lower order thinking skills. Even when given questions from the redesigned AP U.S. history exam that aim to measure deeper cognitive processes, the MCL historians remained skeptical, faulting the validity of the items. When items are subject to multiple interpretations, will the best students choose the wrong answers? Some historians in the group did!

A final observation about existing large-scale assessments is that the most respected tests, NAEP and AP, use constructed responses—open-ended writing—to evaluate knowledge and thinking in deeper ways. Short constructed responses and essay questions ask students to demonstrate knowledge, make and support claims about changes and continuity over time, identify relevant and significant information, and organize and cogently communicate ideas. Consequently these exams allow more opportunity to gather evidence about students' cognitive moves, including their mastery of concepts and competencies. The DBQ in particular has often been regarded as a gold standard in history assessment because it is an authentic assessment, meaning it assesses students' ability to complete a task that replicates the work historians actually do. The faculty panel was relatively impressed by the DBQ, although some noted ways it might be adjusted to measure additional facets of historical thinking. For example, some historians thought the document excerpts were too obviously targeted to the question, a problem that could be fixed with longer excerpts and the inclusion of less useful or relevant sources to evaluate students' abilities to evaluate and select sources. Others noted potential for

a DBQ to include secondary sources or to be designed around evaluating historical interpretations instead of only primary sources.

The DBQ is highly regarded, but a difficulty with this type of
assessment is that it measures many different learning outcomes
simultaneously, meaning the information it gives about student
learning is not as clear and precise as more targeted assessments
that isolate concepts and competencies. This weakness has inspired
the Stanford History Education Group (SHEG), headed by Sam
Wineburg, to develop and make available to teachers through its
free website a range of short constructed-response items called
History Assessments of Thinking (HATs) that can be used in the
classroom to inform instruction. HATs isolate and measure specific
cognitive moves that define historical thinking, such as sourcing,
corroborating, and contextualizing. For example, one HAT gives
students the 1932 painting *The First Thanksgiving 1621* depicting
Native Americans and Pilgrim settlers sharing a meal. The title,
painter, and date are given along with the prompt, "The painting
The First Thanksgiving 1621 helps historians understand the relationship between the Wampanoag Indians and the Pilgrim settlers
in 1621. Do you agree or disagree? (Circle one.) Briefly support
your answer." Students are given several lines to answer, which is
enough space to explain their reasoning but requires them to be
succinct. This particular HAT evaluates students' ability to source
material by evaluating whether they understand the importance of
the painting date—1931—in relation to the event being depicted.
HATs are designed to be relatively fast assessments to administer
and score so that teachers can use them in the classroom as formative, or baseline, assessments. The benefit of this approach is
twofold. First, unlike a complex task like the DBQ, HATs allow
assessors to isolate specific concepts and competencies, thereby
supplying more targeted information about student learning.
Second, unlike multiple-choice exams, HATs do not assume a
single, right answer but instead put the focus on how students
justify their conclusions. In the *First Thanksgiving* example, one

can imagine strong responses that both agree and disagree with the prompt. One might disagree that the painting helps historians understand the relationship between natives and settlers because it was painted over three hundred years later and was based on the artists' imagination, not historical research. However, one might also agree with the statement by stipulating reasons to believe the painter based the depiction on historical documents and aimed for historical accuracy. HATs provide an innovative model for assessing historical thinking that might be expanded to target additional learning outcomes, including specific skills with secondary texts as well as primary sources (SHEG, "Beyond the Bubble").

It is also possible to imagine new forms of assessment that utilize technology to create authentic assessments that mimic the work historians do. In other disciplines, testing companies are experimenting with computer simulations, such as performing a virtual scientific experiment or cooperating on a group problem-solving task. These interactive assessments allow students to perform a task that measures essential concepts and competencies in that discipline. In history, one might imagine a virtual archive, for example, that allows students to find, select, and utilize sources out of many possibilities, assessing their ability to ask a historical question, sift and identify relevant and significant sources, and interpret those sources. One might also imagine a simulation that asks students to role play in some fashion, demonstrating ability to take perspectives, understand context, and reason historically.

An Assessment for the History Major: Form, Uses, and Next Steps

Historians should use multiple forms of assessment to gather as much evidence as possible about student learning in history. Different assessments can focus on evaluating different things and for different purposes: for example, assessment can focus on certifying the learning of individual students or it can be used to evaluate a department's curriculum by focusing on the performance of majors as a whole; it can be used to inform and improve instruction as it is happening or to measure achievement of learning outcomes as seniors finish the major. Multiple forms of assessment allow stronger conclusions about student learning and ensure that no single measure is invested with so much authority that it narrows or distorts teaching and learning. Historians already have some assessments available—like portfolios and senior theses—and we urge that departments think about how to utilize these in more systematic ways to gather evidence about student learning that will inform teaching and curriculum. In addition, however, we believe that rigorously developed, standardized instruments can be a valuable contribution to these efforts and have important uses for history departments.

As a first step, we recommend the development of a voluntary, standardized assessment under the control of departments to evaluate whether students completing their history major have mastered foundational disciplinary concepts and competencies in history. We hope this is the first of many such tools developed for departments and that standardized instruments form only one component of a larger assessment toolkit.

A professionally developed assessment of the major at the level of the department has several potential benefits. In the first place, it will allow departments to collect and analyze evidence about the achievement of graduating seniors. In doing so, it can help departments to identify strengths and weaknesses in student learning that can guide curriculum development and instructional choices. In addition, this evidence can help strengthen the case to students, parents, university administrators, employers, and the larger public about the value of the history major. The AHA Tuning Project has taken an important first step in making this case but a trustworthy, objective assessment of student learning would strengthen it considerably. Relatedly, many departments face pressure from university administrators or external entities likes accreditors, state legislatures, and regulatory bodies to demonstrate their effectiveness. An assessment of student learning in the major provides far more meaningful evidence of departments' work than most other measures available. Perhaps it can also direct conversations about assessment that are already gaining steam in recent years into directions that history faculty find more valuable and legitimate. In states like Texas, for example, a growing conversation about assessment has many faculty fearing, not without reason, that externally imposed assessments will draw from models like the SAT Subject Tests that prioritize low-order thinking skills and memorization of historical facts, thereby narrowing and misdirecting history teaching and learning. In developing an assessment that has legitimacy among college history faculty, perhaps we can help to shape the conversation and the efforts that are bound to continue in the coming years. Finally, a standardized assessment has the potential to offer new knowledge about history teaching and learning. It could provide a large body of evidence about student learning in history that will allow researchers to ask and answer important questions.

In thinking about the forms that an assessment for the major might take, it is essential that the discussion continues among history faculty and that historians take the lead role in defining the goals, forms, and uses of assessment. With that in mind, we urge consideration of a few key issues and offer some preliminary recommendations to serve as a starting point for discussions.

First, careful attention should be given to the issue of the *assessment's primary purpose*. Specifically, should the test measure and report individual student scores, or should it instead measure and report at the aggregate level of the department? The assessment could be designed in a way to report individual students' scores, enabling tracking of specific students' learning over time if the assessment is administered at different points, such as at the time of declaring the major and at the time of graduation. Aggregated, these scores could serve as a measure of the effectiveness of the curriculum overall. But individual reporting could have other uses, too. Students might want to use the test for signaling purposes when applying for jobs. Instructors could use individual scores as formative assessment for guidance purposes; it could help to diagnose areas for improvement and additional emphasis to guide students in their history studies. Alternately, the assessment could eschew reporting individual student scores and instead report about student learning as a group as NAEP and the Collegiate Learning Assessment (CLA) do, effectively making the department as a whole the object of assessment. One benefit of this approach is that it allows for matrix sampling, meaning that students can be given different versions of the assessment and therefore evaluated on a much broader range of items and in less time. If the object is to measure departments rather than individuals, it also gives more flexibility for test items including performance tasks since the standards for validity for measuring group performance versus individuals are different.

Second, it is important that a history assessment have substantial focus on revealing cognitive processes of historical thinking, not simply assessing the ability to arrive at a correct answer. Short constructed-response items like HATs may be the best way to do this. However, it is possible that these cognitive processes can be assessed using carefully constructed multiple-choice questions, an approach that has important benefits from the standpoint of assessment: namely, multiple-choice items are easier and less costly to score and faster to take, allowing the assessment to collect more discrete pieces of information about student learning in a faster amount of time and for less cost. Recently, Bruce VanSledright has put forward suggestions for how multiple-choice tests might be made more responsive to the complexity of historical thinking by providing statements that are weighted according to their defensibility (VanSledright 2013). If multiple-choice approaches are pursued, however, it is essential to first explore their legitimacy among historians, because if our MCL panel is representative, there may be too much skepticism among academic historians to use them.

Third, the assessment should have a strong authentic component, meaning it asks students to demonstrate the concepts and competencies in performance tasks that approximate the real work historians do, namely, analyzing sources and constructing historical explanations and arguments in writing. An assessment of history majors that does not have a significant writing component or ask students to do history in some form will not be accepted as legitimate by many college faculty. Furthermore, although assessing concepts and competencies individually offers important information about student learning, it is also important that students synthesize them because the concepts and competencies are interrelated. Consequently, a DBQ-type performance exercise that asks students to demonstrate the ability to think historically should be an important component of the assessment.

Finally, a significant issue to address in designing a history assessment is the question of which subject matter content will be used in the assessment. For reasons outlined earlier, historical knowledge is not among the essential concepts and competencies that would be assessed. Theoretically, then, the content of the exam should not matter since the assessment will be rigorously field tested and validated to ensure that it measures a given concept or competency regardless of a student's background knowledge. However, we believe the choice of content for the exam will matter greatly to historians, both in terms of what it communicates about how the test defines and privileges particular fields, and because many of us suspect that no matter how rigorously developed, a history assessment cannot and ought not to entirely strip historical content away. Students will bring content knowledge to the exam that will shape their encounter with test items. Content informs and is embedded in most facets of our core disciplinary concepts and competencies: how does one demonstrate proficiency in contextualization without being able to draw on knowledge of a particular time and place to locate a source or event in context? Consequently the question of what content will be on the exam is a thorny, but important, issue to resolve. Existing history assessments do not face this issue since they assess historical knowledge and ground historical thinking skills within a specified body of content knowledge, be it U.S., European, or world history.

Based on our discussions with the MCL faculty panel, assessment experts, and one another, we offer the following description of a potential assessment as a starting point for further discussion among history faculty. We propose that the test contain two distinct parts. The first part would assess historical concepts and competencies in isolation or in small combinations to give targeted information on student learning. We recommend that this part be composed entirely of HAT-type short constructed responses or, if further discussions in the field warrant it, half HAT-type responses and half multiple-choice questions. This part of the exam could draw its questions from all regions and time periods and would have to be rigorously field tested to ensure that it assessed the given historical concept or competency rather than content knowledge. Students might have to evaluate historical accounts from early modern Britain, source primary texts from 19th-century Ghana, and interpret primary sources from 20th-century Mexico. It may be that the assessment could supply necessary background knowledge to isolate the concept or competency. To keep the time needed to take this section reasonable, it may be that a single piece of evidence could be used to ask several distinct questions or that these HATs could be combined with the sources used in the second part of the exam.

The second part of the assessment would be a DBQ or similar lengthy performance task that asks students to do history in a meaningful way, drawing on most concepts and competencies in the process. For part two, students should be given a choice of questions that would allow them to select a DBQ for a geographic area or time period in which they have some familiarity through course work. A computer-based assessment would make this particularly feasible.

The exam should be administered at point of entry to the major and again at completion to allow departments to assess learning within the major over time. We recommend that scores be reported to institutions and under their control (like the CLA is currently done) to avoid sensationalized comparisons and allay some of the concerns of historians about how external authorities might misuse these assessments.

In moving forward there are two major problems to address: (a) the technical problems and cost of developing an assessment; and (b) suspicion and mistrust of college faculty to standardized assessment. The technical challenges and cost can be overcome but will require substantial interest and investment by one or more organizations with expertise in assessment such as the Educational Testing Service, the Stanford History Education Group, or other entities. Proposed items must be rigorously field tested and validated against other kinds of measures to ensure that each task or question measures what it claims to measure and does so without measuring other things that will skew the results and weaken the inferences that can be made about student learning. These problems could only be discovered through repeated trials and adjustment of items and by comparing results with alternative forms of assessment meant to measure the same learning goals. Developing a good assessment is far more difficult, involved, and technical than simply having an expert produce a set of tasks she believes is good. Given the time and expense involved, for historians to undertake development of an assessment tool, we would have to be confident about finding a receptive market.

This leads to the second challenge: although there are encouraging signs that some historians and departments are receptive to framing and assessing learning outcomes, on the whole, there is still considerable suspicion, even outright opposition, among college history faculty to the project of assessment. This opposition is rooted for some in philosophical objections—rejection of the very project of defining behavioral objectives and attempting to measure them—and for many others on the experience of testing at the K–12 level, including the lower order fact retention many of us associate with standardized history assessment and the perverse effects that testing has had on K–12 education in general. We share these concerns.

Yet the inability to measure everything we value about history—such as its ability to stimulate curiosity and generate meaning—does not mean historians can abdicate our responsibility to think carefully about what we *can* assess and use it to improve our teaching. Furthermore, our critiques of K–12 assessment examples should inspire us to engage in and shape the conversation, not run from it. Historians can choose to take a leading role in designing assessments that are worthy of the history we teach, or we can do nothing and hope that calls for accountability in higher education will go away. The latter course of inaction, we fear, will see historians being forced to assess courses and programs with odious tests designed by others.

Opposition within the field is a serious obstacle since a disciplinary assessment meant to measure student learning in history at the level of the department will be effective and meaningful only if faculty accept it as legitimate and use it to inform and improve practice. The experience of QUE suggests such a test will fail in its goals if it is imposed by institutions or external authorities on unwilling departments. Hence, the role of the American Historical Association will be key. As the chief organization of professional historians in the United States, it has an authority and legitimacy among college history faculty that cannot be matched by any other group. AHA has already taken a leadership role in conversations about outcomes. We urge the AHA to stay in the game and continue to lay the groundwork for further conversations about assessment and pedagogies, supported by foundation funding.

One obvious place for AHA to encourage this work would be to expand the scope of the Tuning Project. Tuners might be a particularly receptive audience for conversations about assessment since they already have conducted lengthy discussions about departmental goals. The obvious next question concerns how to know whether these goals are being met. Volunteers could be solicited from departments who have already completed the Tuning process to take the next step and begin planning for assessment of the learning outcomes they have defined. As in Tuning, the process itself will be as important as the product. The search for department-level assessment should model Tuning's emphasis on deliberation and its careful balance of external support and guidance with respect for institutional autonomy and contexts.

Another receptive audience would be historians in states that are already moving to require standardized assessment. These conversations might begin with some of the issues raised in this white paper, including the refinement of essential concepts and competencies, the best models for assessment, the legitimacy of multiple-choice questions, and the question of how to deal with content on the exam. The goal would be to take the temperature of the profession on these issues and work toward areas of consensus and to foster individuals' and departments' engagement with the issues, which we believe is the only way to gain buy-in and support for assessment.

AHA might spearhead conversations about assessment within history in other ways that would be most effective if supported by a foundation or other fiscal support. It might, for example, organize panels at the AHA annual meeting or hold special smaller meetings or workshops devoted to the subject. It might offer seed grants to a small number of departments (perhaps former Tuners) to develop institution-specific plans for assessment or to work on recommendations for a standardized assessment for the field. AHA might create a special section of its website where it collects and shares information on assessment for history departments who are working to develop their own plans. The website could collect useful links, such as to the assessment resources of the Stanford History Education Group, and could provide concrete examples of what institutions are doing to assess student learning among history majors, such as a description of how history faculty at California State University, Long Beach use and evaluate portfolios of student work. Even if a standardized assessment for the discipline is never developed, it is important that departments work to be more deliberate, systematic, and thoughtful about student learning in the major and how to evaluate it. AHA can perform a real service by helping to organize discussions of assessment and share best practices among institutions so that individual departments are not required to reinvent the wheel.

We have argued that a standardized history assessment would be a valuable tool for capturing usable information about student learning. One reason for doing so is to be ready with answers when students, parents, administrators, and public representatives ask about the value of a history degree. Of course, departments can hand out degree specifications and other documents articulating how the study of history instills crucial skills and habits of mind for citizenship, employment, and personal well-being. And history teachers can point to their grade books as evidence of achievement in these areas. But is this really the best we can do, asking the public to take our word for it? In this moment of crisis in higher education, historians need an assessment tool worthy of our discipline, one that will measure the most crucial concepts and competencies gained in the course of undergraduate study in history. We need such a tool not only to justify the value of our degree programs to others but also for ourselves. As historians, we know that corroborated evidence is preferable to no evidence or just a little evidence. The information gained from a standardized history assessment tool could be used to strengthen history curricula at the department level and inform research about history teaching and learning. For this, historians do not need a crisis; already we have our curiosity and responsibility as professionals.

Thus, we urge our fellow historians to carefully consider the potential—and the risks—of new assessment tools for history teaching and learning, especially those that would inform decisions about improving the history major as a whole. It is not enough to make stirring pronouncements about what a history degree aims to teach. We also should attend to evidence for what students are learning.

References

Association of American Colleges and Universities (AAC&U). 2015. *The LEAP Challenge: Education for a World of Unscripted Problems*. Washington, DC: AAC&U.

American Historical Association (AHA). 2013. "AHA History Tuning Project: History Disciplinary Core." http://www.historians. org/teaching-and-learning/current-projects/tuning/history-discipline-core.

American Historical Association (AHA). n.d. "About Tuning." http:// www.historians.org/teaching-and-learning/current-projects/tuning/about-tuning.

Andrews, Thomas, and Flannery Burke. 2007. "What Does It Mean to Think Historically?" *Perspectives on History* 45: 32–35.

Barr, Robert B., and John Tagg. 1995. "From Teaching to Learning: A New Paradigm for Undergraduate Education." *Change* 27, no. 6: 13–26.

Bloch, Marc. 1953. *The Historian's Craft*. New York: Alfred Knopf.

Bradley Commission on History in Schools. 1989. "Building a History Curriculum: Guidelines for Teaching History in Schools." *The History Teacher* 23, no. 1: 7–35.

Calder, Lendol. 2006. "Uncoverage: Toward a Signature Pedagogy for the History Survey." *Journal of American History* 92: 1358–1369.

Calder, Lendol, William W. Cutler III, and T. Mills Kelly. 2002. "History Lessons: Historians and the Scholarship of Teaching and Learning." *Disciplinary Styles in the Scholarship of Teaching and Learning*, edited by Mary Taylor Huber and Sherwyn P. Morreale, 45–68. Washington, DC: American Association for Higher Education and The Carnegie Foundation for the Advancement of Teaching.

Carr, Edward H. 1961. *What Is History?* New York: Cambridge University Press.

College Board. 2015. *Getting Ready for the SAT Subject Tests*. New York: College Board.

Collingwood, R. G. 1939. *An Autobiography*. New York: Oxford University Press.

Collingwood, R. G. 1946. *The Idea of History*. New York: Oxford University Press.

Ercikan, Kadriye, and Peter Seixas, Eds. 2015. *New Directions in Assessing Historical Thinking*. New York: Routledge.

Evans, Richard J. 2000. *In Defense of History*. New York: W.W. Norton.

Flaherty, Colleen. 2015. "Text Anxiety." *Inside Higher Education*, January 28. https://www.insidehighered.com/news/2015/01/28/purdues-president-and-faculty-clash-over-student-learning-assessment.

Florida K-20 Education Code. 2015. "Public K–12 Educational Instruction: Required Instruction." 1003.42.

Furay, Conal, and Michael J. Salevouris. 1988. *The Methods and Skills of History: A Practical Guide*. Wheeling, IL: Harlan Davison.

Gaddis, John Lewis. 2004. *The Landscape of History: How Historians Map the Past*. New York: Oxford University Press.

Hart Research Associates. 2013. *It Takes More than a Major: Employer Priorities for College Learning and Student Success: Overview and Key Findings*. Washington, DC: AAC&U.

Holt, Thomas. 1995. *Thinking Historically: Narrative, Imagination, and Understanding*. New York: College Entrance Examination Board.

Jenkins, Keith. 1991. *Re-Thinking History*. New York: Routledge.

Katz, Stanley N., and James R. Grossman. 2008. *The History Major and Undergraduate Liberal Education: Report of the National History Center Working Group to the Teagle Foundation*. Washington, DC: American Historical Association.

Lerner, Adam. 2015. "History Class Becomes a Debate on America." *Politico*, February 21. http://www.politico.com/story/2015/02/ap-us-history-controversy-becomes-a-debate-on-america-115381.html.

National Commission on Excellence in Education. 1983. *A Nation at Risk: The Imperative for Educational Reform*. Washington, DC: U.S. Department of Education.

Pace, David. 2004. "The Amateur in the Operating Room: History and the Scholarship of Teaching and Learning." *American Historical Review* 109: 1171–1192.

Rothstein, Richard. 2004. "We Are Not Ready to Assess History Performance." *Journal of American History* 90: 1381–1391.

Seixas, Peter. 1994. "Students' Understanding of Historical Significance." *Theory and Research in Social Education* 22, no. 3: 281–304.

Sipress, Joel M., and David Voelker. 2011. "The End of the History Survey Course: The Rise and Fall of the Coverage Model." *Journal of American History* 97: 1050–1066.

Stanford History Education Group (SHEG). n.d. "Beyond the Bubble: A New Generation of History Assessments." https://beyondthebubble.stanford.edu/assessments.

Taylor, Paul, Kim Parker, Richard Fry, D'Vera Cohn, Wendy Wang, Gabriel Velasco, and Daniel Dockterman. 2011. *Is College Worth It? College Presidents, Public Assess, Value, Quality, and Mission of Higher Education*. Report of the Pew Research Center. Washington, DC: Pew Social & Demographic Trends.

VanSledright, Bruce A. 2013. *Assessing Historical Thinking and Understanding: Innovative Designs for New Standards*. New York: Routledge.

Voss, James F., and Jennifer Wiley. 2006. "Expertise in History." In *The Cambridge History of Expertise and Expert Performance*, edited by K. Anders Ericsson, Neil Charness, Robert R. Hoffman, and Paul J. Feltovich, 569–586. New York: Cambridge University Press.

Wineburg, Sam. 2001. *Thinking Historically and Other Unnatural Acts: Charting the Future of Teaching the Past*. Philadelphia: Temple University Press.

3

Measuring College Learning in Economics

Sam Allgood
University of Nebraska— Lincoln

Amanda Bayer
Swarthmore College

This contribution presents a framework of essential learning outcomes and a vision for the future of assessment for undergraduate-level education in economics. The framework includes a set of essential concepts (individual decision making, markets and other interactions, the aggregate economy, and the role of government and other institutions) and essential competencies (apply the scientific process to economic phenomena, analyze and evaluate behavior and outcomes using economic concepts and models, use quantitative approaches in economics, think critically about economic methods and their application, and communicate economic ideas in diverse collaborations). With regard to assessment, the authors argue that future assessments should go beyond measuring content mastery and should include open-ended tasks that allow students to demonstrate higher order skills, such as formulating questions, interpreting data, and constructing and deconstructing arguments.

Introduction

Economics is one of the social sciences, along with sociology, history, political science, and other disciplines. The field is often divided between macroeconomics (i.e., the study of the economy as a whole) and microeconomics (i.e., the study of individual choice or within single markets of the economy). Micro- and macroeconomics provide the foundation for almost all other areas of inquiry in economics, which involve topics as diverse as recessions, currency exchange rates, famines, terrorism, environmental protection, and the allocation of household chores. Economics makes heavy use of formal mathematical models and statistical analysis to understand the economy and human behavior. Economists are known to work with other social scientists and psychologists because of the overlap in these fields.[1]

Economic inquiry is based on the scientific method. Economists build formal models to explain observed phenomena. These models provide testable hypotheses and data are collected to test these hypotheses. This process is as essential to economics as the specific content that economics covers. A student with a thorough education in economics will have the ability to apply this process in developing insights and formulating solutions in their professional and personal lives.

A person with a strong education in economics will have the skills to explain the world around them as it is, and the ability to form predictions about what the future holds. At a basic level, this enables her not only to understand why the Federal Reserve

---

[1] Economics is also unusual on college campuses because some departments are housed in colleges of arts and sciences and some are housed in business colleges. A third of all economics departments are housed in business schools only or in both arts and science and business.

Bank would raise interest rates as the economy exits a recession but also to form an expectation about what the Fed will do with interest rates in the future. This same person will not only know what adverse selection is but will also be able to explain why the Affordable Care Act mandates participation. Thus, economics plays an important role in providing an informed electorate. Moreover, economic education can improve the decisions an individual makes that directly affect her own life circumstances, for example, paying off credit cards monthly (Allgood, Bosshardt, van der Klaauw, and Watts 2011).

Almost 30,000 students per year receive a bachelor's degree in economics (Allgood, Siegfried, and Walstad 2015). This is fewer than in some of the other social sciences but more than in other quantitative disciplines such as math and physics. The number of economics majors is only about a tenth of the number of business majors, but it is incorrect to think about the impact of economics on the postsecondary curriculum by counting majors. The study of economics typically begins with two introductory courses, with over a million students per year enrolled. In addition, business students are often required or elect to take several additional economics courses. Thus, even students whose major is not economics take up to five or more courses before they graduate. The selection of students, however, is not representative of the broader student population. The economics profession, at the undergraduate level and continuing up through faculty ranks, includes disproportionately few women and members of historically underrepresented racial and ethnic minority groups, relative both to the overall population and to other academic disciplines including most STEM— science, technology, engineering, and math—fields (Bayer and Rouse, forthcoming).

A small but committed group of economists have taken economic education seriously for decades. Almost thirty years ago, W. Lee Hansen (1986) wrote of the need to think of education outcomes that go beyond simple knowledge of content, and he articulated a set of proficiencies for the economics major. Although the stated objectives of the largest association of economists, the American Economic Association (AEA), focus on support of research and do not include mention of education, the AEA does have a standing Committee on Economic Education. For the last five years, with a substantial subsidy from the AEA, the committee has organized a conference devoted solely to economic education. The field of economic education has had the peer-reviewed *Journal of Economic Education* since 1969, and three lengthy review articles have been written on scholarly work in economic education (Allgood, Siegfried, and Walstad 2015; Becker 1997; Siegfried and Fels 1979).

That said, there is room for improvement in how economists approach teaching and assessment. The voluminous literature that exists on economic education belies the fact that many economists have no training in teaching, learning, and assessment and many have no experience when taking their first jobs. Additionally, once in those jobs, economists are reluctant to allocate their scarce time to improving their teaching. Economics as taught in most classrooms is increasingly unrelated both to best practices as documented by education research and to economics itself as actually practiced by economists (Colander 2005; Watts and Schaur 2011). Increased attention to teaching and learning in economics would improve outcomes for all students, and particularly for women, students of color, and members of other groups underrepresented in economics (Bayer 2011).

Our hope is to provide a document that will motivate a broad range of economists to think about the outcomes they desire from the classes they teach and how they assess student learning in those classes. Building on prior work in the discipline as well as over two years of discussion with a panel of leading experts in economics education that was convened as part of the Measuring College Learning (MCL) project, we offer a framework for designing productive and inclusive curricula and for developing assessment tools that can be used to assess learning in individual courses and in the economics major.[2]

Specifically, in this paper, we outline a method that instructors and departments can use to develop learning outcomes in economics, and we use this method to articulate a set of representative learning outcomes for undergraduate students of economics. We start by defining four essential concepts, broadly defined, in economics: individual decision making; markets and other interactions; the aggregate economy; and the role of government and institutions. We then identify five essential competencies: ability to apply the scientific process to economic phenomena; ability to analyze and evaluate behavior and outcomes using economic concepts and models; ability to use quantitative approaches in economics; ability to think critically about economic methods and their application; and ability to communicate economic ideas in diverse collaborations. The scope and refinement of the concepts may vary from course to course, but the competencies identified here are essential to an effective undergraduate economics curriculum.

Ultimately, we construct a set of representative learning outcomes in economics by intersecting concepts with competencies; the set is not exhaustive but offers an array of specific learning outcomes we could expect students of economics to achieve. These outcomes are a natural by-product obtained when placing the competencies in the context of the specific content of economics curricula. For example, if the ability to apply the scientific process is a core competency and individual decision making is a content area, then developing a hypothesis to explain an observed behavior would be a representative learning outcome.

---

[2] Although it would be ideal to craft learning outcomes, pedagogy, and assessment together, the issue of pedagogy is beyond the scope of this paper.

Our approach is easily adapted across courses and departments, thus providing a framework by which any instructor, department, or assessment creator can create a set of learning outcomes. The concepts admit study of a broad range of subject matter and methods, whereas the competencies require the educator or assessor to express learning outcomes in terms of what the student can do, not simply what she knows.

By constructing this framework for learning outcomes, we hope to encourage economic educators to be more intentional about their teaching. A reexamination of our role as teachers can help all students and especially those who have less prior exposure to, and social identification with, our field. We need to change our habit of trying to download a set of knowledge to students with the aim of getting them to know or understand but instead to equip students to do—to explain, analyze, predict, ask, and create. The reframing is sometimes subtle; for example, instead of saying that a student should know what free-riding behavior is, a better learning objective would ask the student to use a model of strategic behavior to explain free-riding behavior. The effect is to put focus on higher order cognitive skills beyond memorization and simple acquisition of content knowledge. Creating learning outcomes in this fashion will not only guide the economic educator about what to teach but will also inform decisions of how to teach and how to assess.

Overview of Prior Efforts to Articulate and Assess Learning Outcomes in Economics

Numerous groups have articulated learning outcomes in economics. Many, but not all, of these efforts were for the purpose of developing assessment instruments. In this section, we discuss these prior efforts, contrasting those that focus on content with those that focus on competencies or skills. The dichotomy is not perfect, since some groups consider both content and competencies, but the breakdown provides a useful way of organizing these projects. Furthermore, our construction of learning outcomes makes use of this dichotomy, so it is helpful to view past efforts through this lens. Most of the assessment tools and standards described here are well known to the relatively small number of economists who work in the area of economic education or who are responsible for assessment at their institutions. However, the typical economist is probably not aware of them. Indeed most professors likely teach their courses without thinking explicitly about learning objectives. Thus, one of the tasks of the MCL project is to educate the profession on both past assessment efforts and the current project.

Most of the earlier efforts to define learning outcomes are content centered, producing lists of concepts that should be covered in an economics curriculum. The Voluntary National Content Standards, first published by the Council for Economic Education in 1997 and updated most recently in 2010, lists twenty content standards for microeconomics and macroeconomics that should be taught to students in kindergarten through high school (Siegfried et al. 2010). The writing committee for the Standards includes eight academic economists as content specialists. The list of concepts includes core ideas, such as scarcity, as well as those that may receive less attention, such as entrepreneurship. According to the accompanying documents, the Standards hope to be more than a catalog of content: "As students observe the reasoning process used by economists and practice it themselves, they will acquire analytical skills they can apply to emerging economic issues unforeseen at the time these standards were written" (v). Despite this aim, the Standards present "fundamental economic ideas and concepts" without explicit identification of or reference to competencies such as analytical or communication skills. The Standards have become a widely used tool for curriculum development and assessment at the precollege level.[3]

The College Board's Advanced Placement (AP) program is designed to provide high school students with college-level curricula and assessments.[4] Introduced in 1989, the AP exams in economics can certify that a student has mastered college-level material through rigorous coursework in high school, and many colleges and universities grant course credit and placement to students with high scores. As such, the content of the typical introductory college-level economics course determines the content of the AP Microeconomics and Macroeconomics courses and exams, and thus the current course descriptions include lengthy lists of topics. However, AP economics courses and assessments are in the midst of a major redesign and are making the shift from a content orientation to a competency-based design. After careful surveying of and consultation with economics faculty in higher education, the College Board is refocusing its courses and assessments to reflect current best practices in college-level learning and putting more emphasis on critical thinking, inquiry, reasoning, and communication skills. Currently, each AP exam is two-thirds multiple choice and one-third free response. The exam is required for those wishing to obtain AP course credit; unlike most college-level assessments, the teacher cannot select or create his or her own exam.

---

[3] Another program that attempts to assess precollege learning, the National Assessment of Education Progress, evaluates the economic knowledge of high school seniors and identifies three cognitive skills: knowing, applying, and reasoning (https://nces.ed.gov/nationsreportcard/economics/whatmeasure.aspx). Due to our focus on college learning, we do not discuss this important work here.

[4] For more details, consult the AP Microeconomics and Macroeconomics course home pages (http://apcentral.collegeboard.com/apc/public/courses/teachers_corner/2121.html; http://apcentral.collegeboard.com/apc/public/courses/teachers_corner/2120.html).

The Test of Understanding of College Economics (TUCE) is designed for the assessment of college students at the introductory undergraduate level, but it is not intended for accreditation or certification.[5] Items on the multiple-choice exam are placed into cognitive areas (recognition and understanding, explicit application, implicit application), but the main focus is on content areas in introductory microeconomics (the basic economic problem, markets and price determination, theories of the firm, factor markets, role of government in a market economy, international economics) and introductory macroeconomics (measuring aggregate economic performance, aggregate supply and aggregate demand, money and financial markets, monetary and fiscal policies, policy debates, international economics). Each content area comes with examples of the material covered. For instance, markets and price determination includes determinants of supply and demand, utility, elasticity, and price ceilings and floors. The TUCE has a multiple-choice format, with thirty items in macroeconomics and thirty in microeconomics. It was first developed about forty-five years ago and has since gone through multiple revisions, most recently in 2005.[6] The TUCE provides a nationally normed data set against which students may be compared. Since its development, the exam has become a key tool in empirical research on economic education, used as a pre- and posttest in measuring differences in learning across different treatments.

The stated purpose of the Major Field Test in Economics (MFT), as first developed by the Educational Testing Service in 1989, is to assess "mastery of concepts, principles and knowledge by senior-level undergraduates" (Educational Testing Service 2014). It aims to test economic knowledge more comprehensively,

---

[5] For more information, see Walstad, Watts, and Rebeck (2007).

[6] This project was funded by the Council for Economic Education. For more information, see Walstad et al. (2007) or Walstad and Rebeck (2008).

beyond the micro–macro dichotomy, than is true of the AP exam or the TUCE, because it is intended for assessing students at the end their undergraduate education. The MFT places items into five content areas—introductory concepts, microeconomics, macroeconomics, statistics and econometrics, and quantitative analysis—identifying a set of introductory concepts such as scarcity and opportunity cost common to all economics and including statistics and data analysis as a distinct content area. Quantitative analysis is not assessed through a separate category of items but is involved in at least a quarter of the items across the other content areas. As ETS's description of the MFT asserts, "In addition to factual knowledge, the test evaluates students' abilities to analyze and solve problems, understand relationships and interpret material" (Educational Testing Service 2014, 1). The exam has ninety multiple-choice questions, and, like the TUCE, the MFT provides normalized data against which student scores can be compared. Some departments use the MFT when required to provide assessment data for accreditation.

Some other initiatives that define learning outcomes in economics explicitly emphasize skills or competencies over content. W. Lee Hansen's "Expected Proficiencies for Undergraduate Economics Majors," first published in 1986 and updated in 2001, is one of the earliest efforts to go beyond content knowledge in identifying learning outcomes in economics. As he states, "The proficiencies approach focuses on what graduating majors can do with the knowledge and skills they acquire in the major" (Hansen 2001, 231). Hansen identifies six expected proficiencies: access existing knowledge; display command of existing knowledge; interpret existing knowledge; interpret and manipulate economic data; apply existing knowledge; and create new knowledge. Subject or content knowledge is not ignored but is not seen as the only desired learning outcome, understanding that a good education should provide proficiencies or abilities that go beyond the specific content learned in school. Hansen's proficiencies are sometimes used to inform the development of curriculum and assessment tools.

It is worth noting that the majority of economists support the idea of proficiency-based education. In a survey of more than 202 economics departments, Myers, Nelson, and Stratton (2011) found that over half of the programs agreed with the first five Hansen proficiencies. Respondents put critical thinking as the most important competency, and oral communication was third.

The OECD's Assessment of Higher Education Learning Outcomes (AHELO) directly acknowledges the distinction between subject knowledge and the general human capital developed from a quality education and seeks to assess generic skills, such as critical thinking, and discipline-specific skills in economics and engineering. AHELO assesses the learning outcomes of bachelor's degree recipients and is "intended as a tool for institutional improvement" (OECD 2009, 11). The writing committee for the economics assessment included faculty from over a dozen countries. To guide the design of an internationally relevant economics assessment, the committee produced a list of "agreed learning outcomes," which are somewhat similar, as they note, to Hansen's proficiencies: subject knowledge and understanding, subject knowledge and its applications, effective use of relevant data and quantitative methods, effective communication, and acquisition of independent learning skills. Subject knowledge and understanding is explained not as a list of topics but as a more general set of criteria such as a "consistent and coherent command of the principles of both micro and macroeconomics" and the "ability to articulate critical features and shortcomings in a model or method of analysis" (OECD 2009, 25). The experts on the AHELO project identify four additional skills that should be assessed for economics: abstraction; analysis, deduction, and induction; quantification and design; and framing. The AHELO exam uses multiple-choice items (67 percent) and short and long constructed response items (33 percent). AHELO is unique in that it is designed for international use (OECD 2012a).

To date, the exam has been used once in a feasibility study involving seventeen countries and almost 250 institutions (OECD 2012b).

The economists developing the AHELO learning outcomes relied heavily on benchmarks created in the United Kingdom by the Quality Assurance Agency (QAA), an independent body established to monitor and advise institutions of higher education on standards and quality.[7] QAA subject benchmark statements "describe what gives a discipline its coherence and identity, and define what can be expected of a graduate in terms of the abilities and skills needed to develop understanding or competence in the subject . . . . They are intended to assist those involved in programme design, delivery and review and may also be of interest to prospective students and employers" (QAA n.d.). The QAA benchmark statement for economics, first created in 2000 by economists from a number of schools in the United Kingdom, presents a lengthy, three-part definition of the nature and context of economics: it identifies economic content, places the discipline in context relative to other social science and related fields, and lists the competencies (such as abstraction) that are seen as integral to economics (QAA 2007). The authors then identify nine aims for those obtaining a degree in economics, which go beyond content knowledge and reflect general competencies such as "to develop in students, through the study of economics, a range of generic skills that will be of value in employment and self-employment" (QAA 2007, 2). The QAA benchmark identifies three elements that allow those with an education in economics to apply their decision-making skills

---

[7] The Australian Government has also commissioned the development of economics learning standards for Australian higher education in response to the Tertiary Education Quality and Standards Agency Act of 2011. These standards build off and look similar to QAA and AHELO.

beyond their education: numeracy, subject-specific skills (similar to those listed for the AHELO project), and a framework for decision making. The latter identifies eight key concepts in economics: opportunity cost; incentives; equilibrium, disequilibrium and stability; strategic thinking; expectations and surprises; the relevance of marginal considerations; the possible gains from voluntary exchange; and systems and dynamics.

Overall, the four widely available assessment tools (AP, TUCE, MFT, and AHELO) differ from each other, but each has some elements that align with the goals of the MCL project. The TUCE and MFT are multiple-choice–only tests, a format that has advantages but that is more commonly used to assess content mastery and less suited for assessing competencies. Both exams provide outlines of content knowledge reflecting what has been taught in economics for much of the last forty years; however, neither exam reflects the growing emphasis given to statistics, game theory, and behavioral economics. The redesign of the AP exam and the recently designed AHELO are based more on competencies, and this reflects the direction in which the MCL project would like to move assessment. Understanding the process by which both exams were developed and understanding why the exams are written as they are can provide important insights when it is time to develop an assessment tool based on the essential concepts and competencies developed in this paper. Unfortunately, the AP exam is designed for assessing achievement at the introductory college level, which is not sufficient for the purposes outlined here. AHELO is designed to measure outcomes at the degree level, but the fact that it is designed for international use limits the ability for using it to measure gains in U.S. colleges and universities.

After reviewing the existing tools, we believe there is still a need for assessment instruments that allow professors, departments, and institutions to assess more effectively the level of, or the gain in, learning by college students in economics. Our emphasis on essential competencies is not meant to imply that content is unimportant. It is still important for students to know what does and does not go into the measurement of gross domestic product (GDP), unemployment, and inflation. By defining outcomes as the product of concepts and competencies, as we do later in this paper, we hope to emphasize the importance of what students can do with the knowledge they obtain in school.

Last, we must note the role of textbooks in determining what is taught in economics, especially at the introductory level. Instructors are always able to develop their own material for students, but busy professors are inclined to teach the content found in their text. Some of the more popular textbooks are decades old, and their basic content has not changed much over time. In fact, the textbooks are remarkably similar, both to each other and to Samuelson's classic economics textbook, first published in 1948. Although an analysis is beyond the scope of this paper, any discussion about what students should know or be able to do will have to consider how to move beyond the material in existing textbooks.

Methods

The goal of the economics strand of the Measuring College Learning project has been to create a rigorous but flexible framework that many different economics professors in many different settings can use to define student learning outcomes. This section briefly summarizes the methods we used to compile such a framework.

To inform this effort, the MCL project assembled a group of twelve economists actively involved in the area of economic education, either in curriculum development or in research on the efficacy of different teaching methods. The economists represented a variety of colleges and universities, and many were involved in the initial development or revisions of the efforts described in the preceding section. Four participated in the last revision of the TUCE, three were on the writing committee of the Voluntary National

Content Standards, one participated on the AHELO committee, and one is involved in the redesign of the AP economics curriculum and exam. This group provided invaluable insights into the discussions and the issues faced by previous groups.[8]

After examining these prior efforts, the MCL Economics faculty panel decided to build an original approach from the ground up. To capture the spirit of inquiry and practical problem solving that motivates the practice of economics, we constructed a set of competencies that we believe all students trained in economics should be able to employ. We then checked our set against the lists provided by Hansen's proficiencies, AHELO, and the updated AP curriculum. The Standards and the TUCE offered a good starting point for a listing of content, but for the purposes of the MCL we wanted to distill economics to a small number of essential concepts and to make space for newer and more sophisticated concepts and methods. We wanted students to display an array of competencies rather than knowledge in many content areas that might simply reflect a student's ability to remember facts.

We also consulted sources outside our discipline to construct our list of competencies. In particular, we found it productive to consider learning outcomes developed in other disciplines. Biologists have done a great job developing insights and evidence on the goals, outcomes, and practice of biology education. It was helpful to review the concepts and competencies presented in

---

[8] The members of the MCL Economics faculty panel were Sam Allgood (University of Nebraska, Lincoln), Amanda Bayer (Swarthmore College), Stephen Buckles (Vanderbilt University), Charles Clotfelter (Duke University), Melissa Famulari (University of California, San Diego), Rae Jean Goodman (United States Naval Academy), Mark Maier (Glendale Community College), KimMarie McGoldrick (University of Richmond), John Siegfried (Vanderbilt University), William Walstad (University of Nebraska, Lincoln), and Michael Watts (Purdue University).

Vision and Change in Undergraduate Biology Education: A Call to Action (AAAS 2011) as we developed our own distillation of economics.

But our list, of course, also derived from considerable reflection on our own discipline and on how economists do their work outside the classroom. We decided we can best educate our students by sharing how we as economists learn about the world. Thus, we considered how economists operate, not just what we know but how we come to know what we know. We aimed to be intentional about teaching our methods, and our methods for improving our methods, to our students.

Economics is a dynamic and contested discipline in which there are multiple logical viewpoints that evolve as new evidence is uncovered. Most introductory economics classes use similar textbooks, for better or for worse, but there is growing heterogeneity as game theory, behavioral economics, and other topics are increasingly emphasized. Some faculty and departments also use and teach heterodox approaches such as institutional, feminist, ecological, and Marxian economics. To construct a learning outcomes framework that allows teachers and students to use and integrate multiple approaches in economics, we considered the work of William Perry, who described cognitive development as a process starting from a simplistic view of knowledge as right answers known to authorities and proceeding to increasingly more sophisticated attitudes toward knowledge (Perry 1981). We believe the essential concepts and competencies of economics, as we have defined them, can be studied and developed in many different ways in many different classrooms.

Building on these resources and more, we develop our recommended learning outcomes for students in introductory economics and for economics majors. We merge the content and the competencies considered by others with our own observations and insights to construct a rigorous but flexible framework for a well-designed education in economics. We choose a competency-centered approach but do not neglect the content that distinguishes economics from other disciplines. The end product is an original set of representative learning outcomes in economics, illustrating an array of specific learning outcomes we expect students of economics to achieve.

Essential Concepts and Competencies for the Economics Major

Undergraduate economics education helps students develop potent discipline-specific competencies while working with discipline-specific concepts in core and elective courses. This section presents our vision of a quality education in economics. In an original approach, it defines both concepts and competencies that are essential to an undergraduate economics curriculum and intersects those to provide representative learning outcomes. We start by presenting four essential economic concepts, representing four broad categories of economic content. Next, we state five core competencies we expect economics students to develop. Ultimately, we intersect the competencies with the content areas to illustrate learning outcomes, which is how students majoring in economics can demonstrate their achievement in our discipline.

Essential Concepts

To define our four essential concepts in economics, we divide economic content into four very broad categories: individual decision making; markets and other interactions; the aggregate economy; and the role of government and institutions. Some of the concepts cut across both macroeconomics and microeconomics, such as the role of government and institutions, whereas others are more specific to one branch or the other.

Concept 1: Individual Decision Making

> Individuals, households, firms, communities, countries, and other agents make decisions about how to use the resources they control, which affects their well-being and the welfare of others.

Decision making is the cornerstone of economic analysis. Introductory-level students (commonly known in the discipline as principles students) may be introduced to rational agents making decisions at the margin, strategic thinking, and aspects of behavioral economics. As students advance they learn how to model time, uncertainty, and other aspects of behavior not accounted for in the simple abstracts used at the principles level. This understanding extends to macroeconomics where explanations of price rigidities are based on explanations of how individuals respond to price changes.

Concept 2: Markets and Other Interactions

> Agents interact through markets and other mechanisms, which help to determine the production, consumption, and distribution of goods and services.

Both macro- and microeconomics are less the study of individuals in isolation and more the study of agents interacting with each other. Economists study this interaction at the market (e.g., monopoly) and economy levels (e.g., aggregate demand–aggregate supply) but also have tools like models of comparative advantage and game theory to examine a wide range of interactions, such as those that occur within households or between countries. As one would expect, the tools become more numerous and more sophisticated as students progress through their classes.

Concept 3: The Aggregate Economy

> Individual decisions and interactions combine to form aggregate outcomes for an economy, which are described, predicted, and assessed in macroeconomic analyses.

Measuring the macroeconomy, explaining the causes of changes in these aggregate measures, and predicting future aggregate outcomes is the purview of macroeconomics. Course work in macroeconomics helps students understand the determinants of national income and well-being through systematic examination of business cycles and long-run economic growth. It also provides insight into the distribution of incomes and welfare within and across nations. Macroeconomic classes often include international economics as part of open-economy models.

Concept 4: Role of Government and Other Institutions

> Governments and other organizations and institutions can regulate or influence economic activity in ways that affect the distribution of resources, individual well-being, and social welfare.

Resource and output allocation in most modern economies occurs through markets and government and the interaction of these two. In introductory and advanced courses, students learn how to use the tools of economics to evaluate allocations and to suggest policies that can improve economic outcomes, understanding how individuals and markets respond to government and monetary policy. Furthermore, numerous institutions beyond markets and governments also determine these allocations; students should gain the capacity to understand the roles that institutions such as households, schools, unions, and social norms play in determining economic outcomes.

Essential Competencies

The mainstays of our framework are the competencies we wish to develop in our students. Technological change demands a renewed and explicit focus on developing competencies through higher education. We must teach students how to organize, evaluate, and build from the information at their fingertips. Our job is no longer, if it ever was, to present content for students to memorize. Just as the authors of the Voluntary National Content Standards want students to acquire "skills they can apply to emerging economic issues unforeseen at the time these standards were written" (Siegfried et al. 2010, v), we, too, want to embed such a capacity in students. We believe the best way to achieve this objective is to center learning outcomes on explicit statements of the competencies we expect them to acquire.

Two features of these competencies are worth noting in advance. First, the competencies may not appear to be unique to economics, but we stipulate discipline-specific manifestations. Many fields apply the scientific process, for example, but economists often employ distinctive methods of observation, data collection, and analysis. Second, the competencies may not appear to be mutually exclusive, but we explain how they are distinct.

Competency 1: Apply the Scientific Process to Economic Phenomena

> Students should know how to ask an economic question, gather information and resources, form an explanatory hypothesis, collect data that can be used to test the hypothesis, analyze the data, draw conclusions, and suggest future research.

Most fundamentally, we want our students to acquire habits and capabilities that allow them to nurture and develop their understanding of the world long after they leave our care. Economics students should be curious, observing the world and asking productive questions, and then organizing their observations into hypotheses and testing those hypotheses against careful examination of the evidence. Demonstration of this competency requires a student to possess the spirit and methods of economic inquiry, desiring to learn about the world and integrating skills acquired through the other core competencies to achieve that goal.

Competency 2: Analyze and Evaluate Behavior and Outcomes Using Economic Concepts and Models

> Students should be able to use economic concepts and models to predict or explain behavior and outcomes in novel settings; evaluate choices made by firms, individuals, or groups, and suggest allocations that may help them better achieve their objectives; and evaluate economy-wide allocations using the concepts of efficiency and equity and suggest government policies to improve social welfare.

Economics uses deliberate simplifications to think through complex situations. By exposing students to economic theory, we give them specific analytical tools while also expanding their capacities for abstraction and problem solving. We require students to be able to use economic concepts and models in both positive and normative analyses, thereby explaining, predicting, evaluating, and proposing choices, allocations, and policies. This competency, often practiced and demonstrated in idealized situations, is necessary but not sufficient to describe economists' work or our expectations for students. As social scientists, economists use model-based reasoning in combination with the other competencies identified here to study actual human relations and to improve living conditions locally and globally.

Competency 3: Use Quantitative Approaches in Economics

> Students should be able to work with mathematical formalizations of economic models (e.g., graphs, equations) and perform mathematical operations (e.g., basic

calculus); confront any observed correlation knowing it is not evidence of causation and explain why; explain the design and results of laboratory and field experiments (i.e., randomized controlled trials); and explain the conduct, results, and limitations of basic econometrics (e.g., hypothesis testing, interpreting ordinary least squares estimates, omitted variable, included variable, selection biases).

Economics uses quantitative analysis and mathematical reasoning. We want students to be able to access, interpret, and manipulate economic data and to have knowledge of the primary methods of gathering and assessing evidence in economic investigations. (We will assume our students come to us with fundamental quantitative skills, such as the ability to perform basic calculations without a calculator and understanding concepts such as mean, median, and variance.) In addition to developing comfort in working with numerical data and statistics, we expect students to be competent in representing and analyzing economic behaviors and systems with graphs and mathematical equations.

Competency 4: Think Critically about Economic Methods and Their Application

Students should be able to explain economic models as deliberate simplifications of reality that economists create to think through complex, nondeterministic behaviors; identify the assumptions and limitations of each model and their potential impacts; select and connect economic models to real economic conditions; explain economic data as useful but imperfect recordings of empirical realities; explain the strengths and limitations of economic data and statistical analyses; and think creatively and combine or synthesize existing economic ideas in original ways.

Economics provides a powerful set of tools to analyze human behavior and outcomes. Students need to develop the ability to select appropriate models to conduct analysis of a given situation. They must evaluate how well models and collected data capture relevant features of the setting being analyzed and identify ways an analysis might be improved. Given that economic research is varied, imperfect, and developed and applied in social contexts, students need to explore how theories, assumptions, and research topics can reflect the experiences and values of practitioners, including themselves, and to learn to think about issues from various perspectives. Overall, this core competency requires students to evaluate, think critically, and make connections between the economics they learn and the real world.

Competency 5: Communicate Economic Ideas in Diverse Collaborations

> Students should be able to demonstrate fluency in economic terminology and graphical tools; demonstrate knowledge of major economic institutions and familiarity with magnitudes of common economic statistics; explain economic reasoning and methods to economists and to noneconomists; integrate economic insights with those from other disciplines in multidisciplinary examinations of individuals and societies; and use training to discuss economic issues and policies in ways that promote mutual understanding and inquiry.

Economists must be able to communicate with each other, with policymakers, and with the general public. We expect our students to be able to explain economic concepts and analyses using the terminology and tools of our discipline, including writing clear and concise text, drawing graphs to present an analysis, and using data and statistics to communicate and support a thesis. Communication also requires an ability to listen to others, and we expect our students to glean information and insights from others' explanations whether or not they use the language of economists.

***

Even though they are intrinsically intertwined, these five competencies identify five distinct sets of abilities. For example, a student could hypothesize the impact on unemployment of a higher minimum wage without reference to an economic model and then use simple statistics, such as means, to analyze data to test the prediction, thus employing the scientific method (Competency 1) without using economic models or quantitative methods (Competencies 2 and 3). Alternatively, a student could use a model of supply and demand (Competency 2) to explain how a higher minimum wage may increase quantity supplied and decrease quantity demanded without empirical observation or statistical analysis (Competencies 1 and 3). As a final example, a student could display all three of the first competencies without being aware of the strong assumptions that go into creating the competitive environment and how this impacts the conclusions of the model (Competency 4). Thus, each of these competencies addresses a unique aspect of what an economist does.

Students majoring in economics acquire a quality education by developing these five essential competencies while studying the four essential concepts. To illustrate the kinds of assessable learning outcomes we would expect to see as a result, we can generate representative learning outcomes by intersecting discipline-specific competencies with discipline-specific concepts. Table 3.1 (which begins on page 112) summarizes these concepts and competencies, with concepts in the rows, competencies in the columns, and representative learning outcomes in the cells that intersect competencies with concepts. Students majoring in economics should be able to demonstrate these, or similar, learning outcomes. Although economics is too broad and contested to provide a comprehensive set of learning outcomes, we present those we consider representative of a successful education in economics. The outcomes on our list are neither necessary nor sufficient, but they do require students to display an array of key competencies and understand core concepts of the discipline. They are examples of the sorts of things successful students can do with their economic knowledge and skills.

Table 3.1 Matrix of Essential Concepts and Competencies in Economics (Part 1 of 5)

	Essential Competency 1. Apply the Scientific Process to Economic Phenomena	Essential Competency 2. Analyze and Evaluate Behavior and Outcomes Using Economic Concepts and Models	Essential Competency 3. Use Quantitative Approaches in Economics	Essential Competency 4. Think Critically about Economic Methods and Their Application	Essential Competency 5. Communicate Economic Ideas in Diverse Collaborations
General Description of the Competency	Students should know how to: • Ask an economic question • Gather information and resources • Form an explanatory hypothesis • Collect data that can be used to test the hypothesis • Analyze the data • Draw conclusions and suggest future research	Students should be able to use economic concepts and models to: • Predict or explain behavior and outcomes in novel settings • Evaluate choices made by firms, individuals, or groups, and suggest allocations that may help them better achieve their objectives • Evaluate economy-wide allocations using the concepts of efficiency and equity, and suggest government policies to improve social welfare	Students should be able to: • Work with mathematical formalizations of economic models (e.g., graphs, equations) and perform mathematical operations (e.g., basic calculus) • Confront any observed correlation knowing it is not evidence of causation and explain why • Explain the design and results of laboratory and field experiments (i.e., randomized controlled trials)	Students should be able to: • Explain economic models as deliberate simplifications of reality that economists create to think through complex, nondeterministic behaviors • Identify the assumptions and limitations of each model and their potential impacts • Select and connect economic models to real economic conditions	*Students should be able to:* • Demonstrate fluency in economic terminology and graphical tools • Demonstrate knowledge of major economic institutions and familiarity with magnitudes of common economic statistics • Explain economic reasoning and methods to economists and to non-economists • Integrate economic insights with those

• Explain the conduct, results, and limitations of basic econometrics (e.g., hypothesis testing, interpreting ordinary least squares estimates, omitted variable, included variable, and selection biases)	• Explain economic data as useful but imperfect recordings of empirical realities • Explain the strengths and limitations of economic data and statistical analyses • Think creatively and combine or synthesize existing economic ideas in original ways	from other disciplines in multidisciplinary examinations of individuals and societies • Use training to discuss economic issues and policies in ways that promote mutual understanding and inquiry

Table 3.1 Matrix of Essential Concepts and Competencies in Economics (Part 2 of 5)

	Essential Competency 1. Apply the Scientific Process to Economic Phenomena	Essential Competency 2. Analyze and Evaluate Behavior and Outcomes Using Economic Concepts and Models	Essential Competency 3. Use Quantitative Approaches in Economics	Essential Competency 4. Think Critically about Economic Methods and Their Application	Essential Competency 5. Communicate Economic Ideas in Diverse Collaborations
Essential Concept 1. Individual Decision Making	Learning outcomes include: • Explain how economists have used the scientific process to expand understanding of individual decision making, and identify the main methods and findings in the field of behavioral economics (e.g., experiments on status quo bias and fairness preferences) • Develop a hypothesis to explain observed behavior, identifying what model or models are appropriate for analyzing the behavior, and design an appropriate experiment to test the hypothesis	Learning outcomes include: • Use the concepts of opportunity cost and sunk cost to analyze and make decisions • Use marginal analysis to make and defend allocation decisions • Use marginal analysis to analyze and predict the choices of individuals, firms, and other decision makers • Explain the strengths, and limits of, cost-benefit analysis	Learning outcomes include: • Explain that accounting profit is not economic profit and other applications of opportunity cost • Explain the relationships between total, average, marginal, and fixed costs (and revenue and product) with tables, graphs, and words • Compute and use elasticities, present discounted value, expected value, and conditional probabilities (Bayesian updating)	Learning outcomes include: • Explain how consumer choices are constrained and influenced by forces other than budgets and inborn preferences (e.g., health, social norms, networks, discrimination, and credit constraints) • Use, and explain the limitations of, labor–leisure models to explain observed time allocation decisions; compare to analyses using models of market goods versus nonmarket time	*Learning outcomes include:* • Read and explain popular press writings on how individuals respond to changes in incentives (e.g., going to college and the returns to education) • Read and explain (the less technical sections of) papers from economics journals that investigate consumer choice

• Analyze consumer and producer choice using indifference curves and isoquants • Identify behaviors that are not explained well by rational models (e.g., risk aversion versus loss aversion), and incorporate deviations from rational decision making into choice models • Use calculus to find the profit-maximizing quantity for a monopolist and for a Cournot duopolist	• Compute and use information about distributions of continuous random variables (e.g., mean, s.d., probability density and cumulative distribution functions, and uniform and normal distributions)	• Analyze how choices (e.g., occupation) help explain differences in income and what factors might explain those choices • Explain how the rational choice model provides the foundation to the conclusion that voluntary exchange is mutually beneficial • Identify potential unintended consequences of individual decision making under various policies or conditions

Table 3.1 Matrix of Essential Concepts and Competencies in Economics (Part 3 of 5)

Essential Concept	Essential Competency 1. Apply the Scientific Process to Economic Phenomena	Essential Competency 2. Analyze and Evaluate Behavior and Outcomes Using Economic Concepts and Models	Essential Competency 3. Use Quantitative Approaches in Economics	Essential Competency 4. Think Critically about Economic Methods and Their Application	Essential Competency 5. Communicate Economic Ideas in Diverse Collaborations
Essential Concept 2. Markets and Other Interactions	Learning outcomes include: • Explain how economists use the scientific process to explore the effects of changes in factors affecting demand and supply • Identify how economists use assumptions to reflect and focus on different market structures (e.g., price taker versus price setter) • Explain why it is difficult empirically to isolate the effects of a particular factor or structure to provide evidence of its effects	Learning outcomes include: • Apply the theory of comparative advantage to situations faced by individuals and countries • Analyze perfectly competitive markets using the model of supply and demand • Analyze markets involving monopoly, negative and positive externalities, public goods, or asymmetric information • Evaluate allocations using specific concepts of efficiency (Pareto and Kaldor-Hicks) and equity (Utilitarian, Rawlsian, Entitlement Theory, and the Capability Approach)	Learning outcomes include: • Identify comparative advantage and relate to slopes of production possibilities frontiers • Explain the determinants of exchange rates and use exchange rates to calculate nominal currency values • Identify deviations from purchasing power parity • Solve a simple set of equations to identify an equilibrium	Learning outcomes include: • Explain the possible disadvantages of specialization • Using a model of supply and demand, explain and predict prices and quantities in various markets, and identify differences between conditions assumed in the theoretical model and those in the real market • Select and apply models of monopoly, duopoly, externalities, public goods, and asymmetric information to real markets and situations (e.g., environmental pollution)	Learning outcomes include: • Explain concepts in economic terms (e.g., theory of liquidity preference) so that economists understand • Demonstrate deep understanding by explaining technical economic concepts so that a person not trained in economics understands • Integrate economic ideas with information from the medical sciences to evaluate tobacco taxes and regulation

• Explain how differences in economists' methods, evidence, or theories can generate differences in conclusions	• Find the general equilibrium of an economy and distinguish from partial equilibrium analyses • Identify and explain Nash equilibria in simultaneous games and subgame perfect equilibria in sequential games • Describe various types of auctions and the conditions under which they may be used, and explain possible outcomes	• Use graphical analysis to conduct comparative statics of basic economic models	• Identify and use an appropriate market model to analyze a current event or environment (e.g., given data on industry concentration or pricing behavior) • Use models of factor markets to explain differences in earnings and changes in wage inequality • Use economic models of asymmetric information to analyze insurance and healthcare markets	• Discuss, with other students or administrators, the efficiency and equity of the allocation of campus housing

Table 3.1 Matrix of Essential Concepts and Competencies in Economics (Part 4 of 5)

	Essential Competency 1. Apply the Scientific Process to Economic Phenomena	Essential Competency 2. Analyze and Evaluate Behavior and Outcomes Using Economic Concepts and Models	Essential Competency 3. Use Quantitative Approaches in Economics	Essential Competency 4. Think Critically about Economic Methods and Their Application	Essential Competency 5. Communicate Economic Ideas in Diverse Collaborations
Essential Concept 3. The Aggregate Economy	Learning outcomes include: • Know how to access credible sources of economic statistics • Collect and present data (from sources such as St. Louis FRED and the IMF) • Develop a hypothesis (e.g., approaching recession or growth) based on interpretation of data	Learning outcomes include: • Use a country's position on a concave production function to interpret if they are a candidate for a large or small growth rate (Solow) • Analyze simplified economies using the aggregate demand–aggregate supply model • Analyze business cycles using the IS-LM model • Analyze long-run growth using the Solow model	Learning outcomes include: • Interpret and critique key economic statistics (GDP and alternatives, unemployment, inflation, interest rates, poverty rates) • Analyze and interpret data using appropriate statistical methods • Compute and use real and nominal values • Compute inflation from a price index	Learning outcomes include: • Analyze the effects of past, present, or possible future events on the macroeconomy • Describe the distribution of income and wealth in the United States in general terms, and use Gini coefficients to compare distributions across time periods and countries • Explain the relationship of financial markets to growth and stability of the aggregate economy, and design government policy to prevent bubbles and crashes	Learning outcomes include: • Read or hear opinions about the macroeconomy and recognize when the opinions are not based on economic theory or evidence • Read views of economists and explain subtle differences and what evidence, methods, or theories generate these differences

• Analyze the impact of changes in exchange rates in an open-economy macroeconomic model	• Explain causes and consequences of secular trends in the extent of nonmarket production	• Explain what information an economist would like to have to provide a more complete economic analysis of a current issue, such as unemployment or income inequality

Table 3.1 Matrix of Essential Concepts and Competencies in Economics (Part 5 of 5)

	Essential Competency 1. Apply the Scientific Process to Economic Phenomena	Essential Competency 2. Analyze and Evaluate Behavior and Outcomes Using Economic Concepts and Models	Essential Competency 3. Use Quantitative Approaches in Economics	Essential Competency 4. Think Critically about Economic Methods and Their Application	Essential Competency 5. Communicate Economic Ideas in Diverse Collaborations
Essential Concept 4. Role of Government	Learning outcomes include: • Explain how economists use the scientific process to explore the effects of policies (e.g., minimum wage policies) • Explain why it is difficult to isolate the effects of a policy empirically to provide evidence of its effects • Analyze how differences in economists' methods, evidence, or theories can generate differences in conclusions	Learning outcomes include: • Propose government policies to improve allocations in the presence of monopolies, externalities, public goods, and asymmetric information • Explain the effects of price controls, taxes, and subsidies in perfect markets and in markets with imperfections • Analyze the effects of fiscal and monetary policies on macro aggregates using the aggregate demand—aggregate supply model • Hypothesize how government policies (e.g., SNAP) impact individual choice	Learning outcomes include: • Compute simple fiscal and monetary policy multipliers • Explain the difference between government deficit and debt and, more generally, between flow and stock variables • Compute, interpret, and explain the difference between marginal and average tax rates, marginal and average benefit, and marginal and average cost	Learning outcomes include: • Analyze the effects of existing government policies to address monopolies, externalities, public goods, and asymmetric information • Explain how government trade policies impact domestic and foreign economies • Connect concepts of adverse selection and moral hazard to recent events in financial markets • Suggest and explain fiscal and monetary policies in light of current economic conditions	Learning outcomes include: • Read and correctly explain portions of the Economic Report of the President • Explain the primary role of the Federal Reserve System • Contribute economic insights on the causes and effects of the evolving role of labor unions in the economy

• Explain free-riding behavior using models of strategic behavior • Analyze financial markets using economic models of asymmetric information	• Compute and explain the rate of return on an investment	• Explain how financial intermediaries, instruments, and markets have evolved in recent decades, and suggest government policies to adapt to changes in financial markets • Use both rational and behavioral models to propose and analyze government policies (e.g., different policies to encourage saving)

Essential Concepts and Competencies for the Introductory Course

Faculty goals for the introductory course are both similar to and different than faculty goals for the major. This section provides guidance on how to refine the essential concepts and competencies for majors in economics, as presented in the previous section and in Table 3.1, to guide student learning in an introductory course. Using the concepts and competencies framework, the learning outcomes can easily be adjusted to the level of the students for which they are intended.

First, it is both feasible and desirable for students in introductory economics courses to develop the same five essential competencies, though with more moderate benchmarks. As is standard, we expect introductory economics courses to expose students to both microeconomic and macroeconomic principles while recognizing that they cover different content at a different level of difficulty than more advanced courses do. For instance, introductory courses might use AS–AD (Aggregate Supply – Aggregate Demand) to model the macroeconomy, whereas intermediate courses might use IS–LM (Investment-Saving/Liquidity Preference-Money Supply) to analyze the same situations.

Second, the introductory course should involve a different kind of exposure to quantitative methods in economics. Effort should be focused on building and reinforcing basic quantitative and numerical literacy, helping students connect basic mathematical tools such as solving equations or drawing graphs to the real world situations economists study. The development of quantitative reasoning should be an explicit goal, but, rather than requiring advanced techniques such as calculus or econometrics, instructors should focus on building appreciation, fluency, and confidence in mathematics as used in economics.

Most departments choose to teach statistics and econometrics in one or two separate courses for the major, but introductory courses should nevertheless expose students to the need for and results of

more sophisticated empirical investigation. Most certainly, introductory curricula should include discussion of causation versus correlation and provide a sense of the methods economists use to tell
the difference. If students are taught how randomized controlled
experiments are designed and how their results are interpreted,
they will better understand why other forms of analysis are less
able to identify cause–effect relationships.

Third, as we bring what we teach closer to what we do as economists, we must help students be comfortable with uncertainty,
helping them progress beyond seeing their task as learning the
"right" answers to questions to appreciating economics as a collection of effective but imperfect methods with which to construct
an understanding of the world. Economics is an exciting, dynamic,
and multifarious field of inquiry, aiming to understand complicated,
non-deterministic behaviors and outcomes. To promote the intellectual development of our students, we must introduce them "not
only to the orderly certainties of our subject matter but to its unresolved dilemmas" (Perry 1981, 109). We help students develop the
competencies they need to navigate a complex world by exposing
them to the messiness of doing real economics. It is important to
complement study of idealized situations that have clean conclusions with critical analysis of models and evidence, alternative
models, and study of current economic experiences and issues.

Two insights about introductory economics courses come from
our concepts and competencies approach to constructing learning
outcomes. First, students would benefit from an explicit statement
of the competencies we wish them to develop through the course;
with this explicit focus, instructors could improve the way they
design their curriculum and pedagogy, and students would have a
better sense of what goals they should be working toward. Second,
the breadth of economics makes it impossible to develop a complete list of all possible outcomes, but it also allows for a variety
of approaches and subject matter that can appeal to all students,
regardless of their background or interests. Once instructors understand education as developing competencies, instead of covering

content, they can choose materials and topics that show students the scope and power of economics. The matrix of competencies and concepts presented in this paper gives structure to the curriculum without limiting an instructor's ability to teach a wide range of models and topics.

Recommendations for Future Assessments

Given that economists and other stakeholders have already devoted a substantial amount of time to developing assessment instruments in economics, any new efforts must be motivated by a desire to do something that is truly different. With this in mind, we make some recommendations that build on yet deviate from what has been done in the past. In this section, we make recommendations regarding the development of a large-scale assessment tool and for the development of a smaller-scale assessment tool that could be used in individual courses or departments. Although we make these recommendations with the understanding that cost is often a binding constraint in the choice of assessment, we are purposefully ambitious with an eye toward future changes in technology and incentives to conduct assessment. In other words, we attempt to describe the contours of the objective function so we know what direction to move in if and when the constraint is relaxed.

In any discussion or instance of assessment, it is important to be mindful of its dual purposes. Assessment on any scale is so much more than declaring a student, or course, or program a success or failure. Assessment can and should be used formatively, not just summatively. Faculty and departments can learn and make improvements in curricula and pedagogy while writing and reviewing the results of assessments. Likewise, students learn about themselves, the material, and their progress through preparing for, taking, and reviewing the results of assessments. For this reason, self-assessment is a viable and productive option for both large and small classes or departments.

Large-Scale Assessment

Past national and international efforts to assess economics learning at the introductory level or at the level of the major have relied heavily on multiple-choice exams. The four instruments we have discussed (AP, TUCE, MFT, AHELO) are two-thirds multiple choice or all multiple choice. This format is also ubiquitous in the classroom—often a necessity for faculty teaching very large sections of courses. Multiple-choice and true–false items are also useful when an exam covers a large amount of material, as could be the case when assessing learning at the introductory level or for the major itself.

Although multiple-choice exams do provide the greatest ease of assessment, many educators believe that fixed-response items are incapable of testing critical thinking or other deeper learning. In *Vision and Change in Undergraduate Biology Education: A Call to Action*, biologists identify an assessment gradient that looks at the ease of grading versus the "potential for assessment of learning." Five types of assessments are identified in order of ease of assessment and reverse order of potential for assessing learning: (a) multiple choice and true–false; (b) models, concept maps, quantitative response; (c) short answers; (d) essays, research papers, reports; and (e) and oral interviews (AAAS 2011, Figure 3.2). We will not debate whether this is the correct ordering of these items, but we argue that a large-scale assessment tool based on the principles set out in this document ideally requires some elements of (d).

We use two commonplace expressions to communicate why assessment in economics should rise to the level of essays and reports, requiring economics students to demonstrate competency in all phases of the scientific process including hypothesis formation, model selection, and data analysis. First, "economics is what economists do."[9] This definition of economics fits well with the concepts and competencies framework outlined in this document.

---

[9] This phrase is often attributed to Jacob Viner, but the authors are unaware if there is historical documentation.

This is not to say that we expect all our students to become economists, but the concepts and competencies that economics students gain are certainly useful in a wide range of careers and pursuits. To assess what students have learned, they must demonstrate that they can do economics. Economists do not answer multiple-choice questions. They formulate productive questions, and they convey their analyses in short and long form. They interpret data and construct and deconstruct arguments that explain observed phenomena. Communication is part of this process. An oral communication device is not realistic for large-scale assessment, but written communication is. A person well trained in economics must be able to take information, whether statistical data or written material, and apply the appropriate economic methods to explain the context by which the information is created or the potential implications of this information. This will be difficult to do with any short form of response.

Second, the expression "economics is a way of thinking" is uttered by many professors at the start of their courses. If we accept this claim, then it becomes difficult to assess learning using fixed-response and short-form answers because these formats tell us only what answer the student gets, not *how* they got the answer. For example, a multiple-choice item can cover a very complex problem but a correct response does not tell whether the student used the appropriate economic method to reach the answer. Assessing the student's thinking process requires that the student demonstrate and explain how they obtain the answer. To conduct this sort of assessment, we must allow the student more space and time to express her response.

Whether or not assessment includes some form of fixed response is still open to debate. Recent research suggests that well-written multiple-choice questions can eliminate the effects of guessing (Kubinger and Gottschall 2007) but does not address the concern that multiple-choice questions cannot measure all elements of in-depth understanding of economics (Buckles and Siegfried 2006).

If one wants to assess how students are forming their answers, free response provides the best approach. Whether the response is short or long, free-response items mean the student begins the answer with a clean piece of paper. Free response requires the student to choose the path they take to answer a question, providing the most insight about her competencies.[10]

Any disciplinary standard or assessment, even within our framework, requires decisions about which topics to include and which to exclude. Does one simply base an exam on content found in the department's core (two introductory courses, statistics, and two intermediate courses), or is it necessary that a student demonstrate an understanding of Heckscher-Ohlin or some other field-specific model? Although such decisions must be made while writing test items, ultimately if a student demonstrates a general ability to use economic models appropriately, the competency implies she would be able to use the Heckscher-Ohlin model if adequately introduced to it. If some instructors still wish to assess a learning outcome relating to this model specifically, the large-scale exam would likely have to be modular, allowing instructors to select items addressing specific fields or topics within economics.

More generally, defining a set of relevant content can be difficult in a discipline such as economics, where even the fundamentals can vary over time and across faculty members. For example, existing assessment efforts make little or no reference to behavioral economics, a burgeoning field that incorporates insights and methods from psychology and neuroscience into the study of economic decisions. The field began to develop slowly in the 1970s, gained traction in the 1980s, and has grown greatly in prominence over the past twenty years. Most introductory economics textbooks currently deal with behavioral economics in passing or devote a chapter to it; however, some economists believe that the behav-

---

[10] See Colander and McGoldrick (2009) for more on the educational value of open-ended, "big think" questions.

ioral approach will eventually supplant the neoclassical model as the dominant paradigm. Similarly, major economic events, such as the financial crisis and recent increases in economic inequality, are leading to changes in both the body of economic knowledge and what is typically taught in undergraduate courses (see, e.g., Caballero 2010). Any newly developed assessment tool will have to decide how to navigate the current and anticipated variety of approaches within the discipline. In our view, our concepts and competencies approach to defining learning outcomes, in tandem with a modular structure for the assessment, is the optimal way to proceed.

Small-Scale Assessment

Within the context of a particular course or department, if one is assessing economic learning by a student's ability to do economics, then this opens the door for better-targeted and additional forms of assessment. Recognizing the formative role of assessment, repeated low-stakes testing can help students develop desired competencies. It may be wise to supplement traditional assessment embedded in the curriculum (exams, homework) with small quizzes, student self-assessment, and daily conversations. Another option is to require students to produce and present original research in a senior paper, for example, with the aim of developing and demonstrating all five essential competencies.

Assessment may also be external to the curriculum (Myers, Nelson, and Stratton 2008). External assessment would be, for example, the use of co-curricular experiences as assessment. Internships and service learning projects provide opportunities for students to develop economic competencies. Advanced students can be hired as peer tutors. Teaching economics is a fundamental way of developing and demonstrating competencies. There are limits of course, but there are also numerous options for faculty who want to go beyond standard methods of assessment.

Some of these nontraditional forms of assessment may be too costly to employ in departments with a large number of majors relative to the number of faculty. In these cases, faculty should be educated in the various ways that students can be assessed beyond standard homework and exams—many of these methods, including those employing clickers, can be used in large class settings. More importantly, if instructors accept that the relevant assessment involves what the student does, then the process by which the student obtains their answer is of primary importance and the answer itself is secondary (Myers et al. 2008).

Conclusion

We economists have paid far too little attention to our teaching. It is time to change that, and this white paper provides a framework to help. Neither the paper nor the learning outcomes we develop here are designed to provide a specific how-to list for professors and departments. Appropriate learning outcomes will vary across institutions, given differences in student bodies and institutional characteristics. We have tried to provide a framework that is general enough, however, to be used by all.

It is our hope that faculty members and departments will use this framework to construct and redesign courses. We are not implying that departments have not put time and thought into their curriculum. Instead, the approach suggested here may lead many departments to redesign their curriculum in a way that ensures students are receiving the education envisioned for them. Specifically, curriculum development should begin with the identification of competencies, which puts the focus on action words that describe skills or what students can do. Once competencies are identified, courses, course content, teaching methods, and assessments can be developed that enable students to obtain the competencies. This can be thought of as a backward design approach to economics curricula (Wiggins et al. 1998). Relying on lists of content is inefficient and counterproductive, as it encourages memorization. Since we all agree we want students to develop skills, we should specify competencies explicitly and construct our curriculum and pedagogy around them.

The efficacy of this approach will be enhanced if faculty and departments share competency statements and desired learning outcomes with students. When economists engage in research, they do not typically know the answer to their research question, but they do understand what actions and steps they must take to obtain an answer—they know what to do. In many cases, the answer to the research is less important than the process by which it is created because the research adds to our knowledge if the process is done correctly. The same can be true for student learning and assessment. Just as we are skeptical of research conclusions if we are skeptical of the research methods, we should not have faith that a student has learned if we are unaware of the process by which he or she forms an answer. Sharing competency statements with students from the beginning illuminates the process and enhances their ability to achieve the learning outcomes.

The approach we are recommending will not necessarily be easy at first since faculty and departments will have to rethink how they approach curriculum and pedagogy. As economists, we suspect that this is unlikely to occur at the many institutions where teaching is valued secondarily to research, and especially at large universities where the vast majority of undergraduate students study and learn economics. Administrators and professional associations should change incentives to value and reward attention to teaching. This may have implications for graduate education as well. Even though teaching will be the primary job for most economics faculty, few graduate students in economics currently receive training on developing pedagogy or assessing students.

Our work can help meet demands for assessment. The framework can be used to develop assessments for individual classes and to evaluate learning in the major. Establishing competencies concerning what students can do, versus what they know, provides a direct link to what an assessment item should require of a student.

Although the approach we outline here does not provide a method for evaluating the quality of instruction in the classroom, faculty and programs can credibly demonstrate the quality of the education they offer by developing and publishing careful and coherent course design. The framework presented here encourages faculty to be purposeful in identifying learning outcomes without imposing on them a specific pedagogy or requiring the teaching of specific content, thus preserving academic freedom.

This work adds value to the existing set of efforts to articulate and measure learning outcomes in economics in several ways. First, our framework enhances economists' awareness of the underlying competencies being developed, such as quantitative reasoning, as they teach a particular skill, such as computing real values of variables. Second, it creates a competency-based set of learning outcomes for students in economics, in contrast to the more common content-based orientation and with a set of competencies that are distinct from prior efforts. Third, our approach allows us to define learning outcomes in newly important areas within the discipline, such as behavioral economics, financial markets, and experimental methods, which existing assessments omit. Fourth, the general framework we develop, in which competencies are intersected with specific content areas, accommodates change within the discipline across time or instructors: Using the examples presented here, readers can construct learning outcomes for specific courses they must teach or assess. The focus remains on the core competencies we seek to develop through an education in economics.

References

Allgood, Sam, William Bosshardt, Wilbert van der Klaauw, and Michael Watts. 2011. "Economics Coursework and Long-Term Behavior and Experiences of College Graduates in Labor Markets and Personal Finance." *Economic Inquiry* 49, no. 3: 771–794.

Allgood, Sam, John J. Siegfried, and William B. Walstad. 2015. "Research on Teaching Economics to Undergraduates." *Journal of Economic Literature* 53, no. 2: 285–325.

American Association for the Advancement of Science (AAAS). 2011. *Vision and Change in Undergraduate Biology Education: A Call to Action*. Washington, DC: AAAS Press.

Bayer, Amanda, 2011. *Diversifying Economic Quality: A Wiki for Instructors and Departments*. The American Economic Association Committee on the Status of Minority Groups in the Economics Profession. http://www.diversifyingecon.org.

Bayer, Amanda, and Cecilia E. Rouse. Forthcoming. "A New Look at Diversity in the Economics Profession." *Journal of Economic Perspectives*.

Becker, William E. 1997. "Teaching Undergraduate Economics." *Journal of Economic Literature* 35, no. 3: 1347–1373.

Buckles, Stephen, and John Siegfried. 2006. "Using Multiple-Choice Questions to Evaluate In-Depth Learning of Economics." *Journal of Economic Education* 37, no. 1: 48–57.

Caballero, Ricardo J. 2010. "Macroeconomics After the Crisis: Time to Deal with the Pretense-of-Knowledge Syndrome." *Journal of Economic Perspectives* 24, no. 4: 85–102.

Colander, David. 2005. "What Economists Teach and What Economists Do." *Journal of Economic Education* 36, no. 3: 249–260.

Colander, David, and KimMarie McGoldrick. 2009. "The Teagle Foundation Report: The Economics Major as Part of a Liberal Education." In *Educating Economists*, edited by David Colander and KimMarie McGoldrick, 3–39. Cheltenham, UK: Edward Elgar.

Educational Testing Service (ETS). 2014. "The Major Field Test in Economics." https://www.ets.org/s/mft/pdf/mft_testdesc_economics_4emf.pdf.

Hansen, W. Lee. 1986. "What Knowledge Is Most Worth Knowing—for Economics Majors?" *American Economic Review* 76, no. 2: 149–152.

Hansen, W. Lee. 2001. "Expected Proficiencies for Undergraduate Economics Majors." *Journal of Economics Education* 32, no. 3: 231–242.

Kubinger, Klauss D., and Christian H. Gottschall. 2007. "Item Difficulty of Multiple Choice Tests Dependent on Different Item Response

Formats—an Experiment in Fundamental Research on Psychological Assessment." *Psychology Science* 49, no. 4: 361–374.

Myers, Steven C., Michael A. Nelson, and Richard W. Stratton. 2008. "Assessing a Proficiency Based Economics Program: Weathering the Perfect Storm while Thriving in a New Environment." Paper presented at the annual meeting of the American Economic Association, January 4–6. https://www.aeaweb.org/annual_mtg_papers/2008/2008_619.pdf.

Myers, Steven C., Michael A. Nelson, and Richard W. Stratton. 2011. "Assessment of the Undergraduate Economics Major: A National Survey." *Journal of Economic Education* 42, no. 2: 195–199.

Organisation for Economic Co-operation and Development (OECD). 2009. *Tuning-AHELO Conceptual Framework of Expected and Desired Learning Outcomes in Economics*. Paris: OECD Publishing. http://www.oecd.org/education/skills-beyond-school/43160495.pdf.

Organisation for Economic Co-operation and Development (OECD). 2012a. *Economics Assessment Framework: AHELO Feasibility Study*. Paris: OECD Publishing. http://www.oecd.org/officialdocuments/publicdisplaydocumentpdf/?cote=edu/imhe/ahelo/gne(2011)19/ANN3/FINAL&doclanguage=en.

Organisation for Economic Co-operation and Development (OECD). 2012b. *Testing Student and University Performance Globally: OECD's AHELO*. Paris: OECD Publishing. http://www.oecd.org/edu/skills-beyond-school/testingstudentanduniversityperformancegloballyoecdsahelo.htm.

Organisation for Economic Co-operation and Development (OECD). 2013. *Assessment of Higher Education Learning Outcomes Feasibility Study Report: Executive Summary*. Paris: OECD Publishing. http://www.oecd.org/edu/skills-beyond-school/AHELO percent20FS percent20Report percent20Volume percent201 percent20Executive percent20Summary.pdf.

Perry, William G., Jr. 1981. "Cognitive and Ethical Growth: The Making of Meaning." In *The Modern American College*, edited by Arthur W. Chickering, 76-116. San Francisco: Jossey-Bass.

Quality Assurance Agency for Higher Education (QAA). n.d. "The UK Quality Code for Higher Education: Subject Benchmark

Statements." http://www.qaa.ac.uk/assuring-standards-and-quality/
the-quality-code/subject-benchmark-statements.

Quality Assurance Agency for Higher Education (QAA). 2007. *Subject Benchmark Statement for Economics*. Gloucester, UK: QAA. http://www.qaa.ac.uk/Publications/InformationAndGuidance/Documents/economics.pdf.

Samuelson, Paul A. 1948. *Economics*. New York: McGraw-Hill.

Siegfried, John J., and Rendigs Fels. 1979. "Research on Teaching College Economics: A Survey." *Journal of Economic Literature* 17, no. 3: 923–969.

Siegfried, John, Alan Krueger, Susan Collins, Robert Frank, Richard MacDonald, KimMarie McGoldrick, John Taylor, and George Vredeveld. 2010. *Voluntary National Content Standards in Economics 2nd edition*. New York: Council for Economic Education. http://www.councilforeconed.org/wp/wp-content/uploads/2012/03/voluntary-national-content-standards-2010.pdf.

Walstad, William B., Michael Watts, and Ken Rebeck. 2007. *The Test of Understanding of College Economics: Examiner's Manual*. New York: Council for Economic Education.

Walstad, William B., and Ken Rebeck. 2008. "The Test of Understanding of College Economics." *American Economic Review* 98, no. 2: 547–551.

Watts, Michael, and Georg Schaur. 2011. "Teaching and Assessment Methods in Undergraduate Economics: A Fourth National Quinquennial Survey." *Journal of Economic Education* 42, no. 3: 294–309.

Wiggins, Grant P., Jay McTighe, Leslie J. Kiernan, and Frank Frost. 1998. *Understanding by Design*. Alexandria, VA: Association for Supervision and Curriculum Development.

4

Measuring College Learning in Sociology

Susan J. Ferguson
Grinnell College

William Carbonaro
University of Notre Dame

This contribution offers a review and synthesis of the current state of learning outcomes and assessment within the discipline of sociology. Based on their review of the literature and discussions with faculty experts, the authors construct a Sociological Literacy Framework, consisting of a set of essential concepts (the sociological eye, social structure, socialization, stratification, and social change and social reproduction) and essential competencies (apply sociological theory to understand the social world, critically evaluate explanations of human behavior and social phenomena, apply scientific principles to understand the social world, evaluate the quality of social scientific data, rigorously analyze social scientific data, and use sociological knowledge to inform policy debates and to promote public understanding). Following their presentation of the Sociological Literacy Framework, the authors describe and critically evaluate current assessments in sociology and conclude with several recommendations for how a new assessment of student learning in sociology should be constructed.

Introduction

Sociology is a scientific discipline that is concerned with understanding the social forces that shape and direct human behavior. Sociologists think that human life and human interactions are distinctively patterned, and that these patterns are observable, predictable, and reflect status differences in society. Sociologists also have a nuanced understanding of social structure, and they study the social relationships between individuals, groups, social institutions, and nations. In addition, sociology is both a theoretical and evidence-based discipline that resembles other social science disciplines. Sociology, however, offers a view that is distinctive from the other social sciences in that it attempts to identify how social context influences individuals and groups. No particular theoretical framework dominates; instead, sociology is informed by various theoretical traditions and research methodologies. The discipline formally developed in Europe during the early 19th century in response to social upheaval and a positivist ambition to scientifically measure social forces. Sociology came to the United States after the Civil War with many early American sociologists influenced by Herbert Spencer's evolutionary theories of social Darwinism. Other American sociological traditions, such as the Chicago School, challenged laissez-faire understandings of industrialization and advocated for social reform (Calhoun 2007). Since the late 19th century, both the European and American traditions in sociology have flourished with increasing theoretical and methodological diversity. As a UK curricular document explains:

> An understanding of the distinctive social features of human life is largely a product of the nineteenth and twentieth centuries, but sociology is not restricted to the study of contemporary societies. A sociological perspective is fruitfully employed in historical, cross-cultural and transnational comparative studies of

changing forms of human life. Sociology seeks to understand how and why societies, institutions and practices
of all kinds came into being, change over time and how
they are currently organized, and the likely impact of
this on human life and the human environment in the
future. (QAA 2007, 2)

Sociology is valuable because it provides scholars, students, and
society with useful concepts, theories, and methods to evaluate
social institutions and social behavior. Sociology also is exciting
to scholars and students because the discipline's concepts and
theories can help to clarify aspects of social life that may have
hitherto been opaque. Additionally, as the scientific study of society, scientific methods applied in both quantitative and qualita-
tive research and in mixed method approaches are a large part of
sociology. As a result, sociology provides practitioners with critical
analytical skills and the ability to use scientific methodology to
understand social problems. Another measure of the magnitude of
the discipline is reflected in the dramatic growth of undergraduate
sociology majors. The American Sociological Association reports
that in 1987 there were 13,584 bachelor's degrees awarded, but in
2013 there were 42,155 bachelor's degrees awarded in sociology
programs across the United States (Curtis 2015).

As our review of the scholarly literature illustrates, sociologists
have been debating the parameters of a core curriculum in sociology for over a century. Although much of this prior scholarship has
concentrated on all the places the sociology curriculum does not
overlap, we believe that the deliberation should now emphasize
the common ground in the literature. Some factors that compli-
cate this task are found within the discipline of sociology. These
aspects include the breadth and diversity of subfields within sociology, the variability in reasons that college students are attracted
to sociology, and the lack of clarity regarding how the sociology
major is connected to the labor market. Nevertheless, our review

of the literature and our discussions with sociology faculty show more consensus about essential sociological concepts and competencies than first appears. Thus, instead of focusing on disagreement, our aim in this white paper is to highlight agreement by sociologists on learning outcomes in the introductory course and for the sociology major.

For this review, we consulted both the published literature and a panel of sociology faculty. The Measuring College Learning Sociology faculty panel was composed of sociologists who have demonstrated a strong commitment to improving the overall quality of undergraduate teaching and learning in their field. They represented a variety of institutions, including liberal arts colleges, larger universities, and our disciplinary association.[1] The faculty panel met twice in 2014, and again in 2015, to discuss the sociology curriculum and learning outcomes for introductory sociology and for the sociology major. There were three main goals for the meetings: (a) to discuss and evaluate previous and ongoing efforts to define a set of common learning outcomes for sociology undergraduates; (b) to identify essential representative learning outcomes for both the introductory sociology course and the sociology major; and (c) to evaluate current assessments of student learning in sociology and to envision possible and preferable alternatives.

---

[1] The MCL Sociology faculty panel included twelve faculty members and two officers from the American Sociological Association. Participants were Richard Arum, New York University; Jeanne Ballantine, Wright State University; William Carbonaro, University of Notre Dame; Paula England, New York University; Susan Ferguson, Grinnell College; Sally Hillsman, American Sociological Association; Katherine McClelland, Franklin and Marshall College; Matt McKeever, Mount Holyoke College; Aaron Pallas, Teachers College, Columbia University; Richard Pitt, Vanderbilt University; Josipa Roksa, University of Virginia; Margaret Weigers Vitullo, American Sociological Association; Theodore Wagenaar, Miami University; and Sarah Willie-LeBreton, Swarthmore College.

The MCL Sociology faculty panel generally agreed that sociology has distinct disciplinary knowledge and that building consensus around a set of shared learning outcomes for sociology students is crucial and valuable for the purposes of improving undergraduate education. Moreover, several panelists argued that defining this core in sociology is critical because other entities (e.g., school boards, the makers of the MCAT exam, and numerous assessment companies) are forging ahead with their own initiatives to measure college learning in sociology. The faculty panel also discussed at length the current criticisms of higher education, including concerns about rising costs, high student debt, and whether students are being sufficiently trained for the nation's workforce or for the global economy. In 2011, for example, the Pew Research Center conducted a survey of the general public on the value, quality, and mission of higher education. A majority of Americans (57 percent) said the U.S. higher education system fails to provide students with good value for the money that they and their families spend (Taylor et al. 2011, 1). In addition, much recent attention has focused on the White House's College Scorecard, and former Education Secretary Arne Duncan advocated for greater accountability in higher education by having the federal government collect more complete and accurate data on learning outcomes from colleges and universities (Duncan 2015). Given these and other concerns about higher education, the sociology panel believes the sociological community should be active participants in endeavors to improve college learning. Since faculty have always assessed student learning, the panelists see this project as a significant faculty-driven endeavor. The faculty panel is most interested in determining learning outcomes for the introductory course and in measuring the knowledge and skill development over the college career of students, and they are eager to participate in institutional improvement.

One lesson from our research is that the use of the term *core* is problematic because of a long-standing debate in the discipline about whether there is a core or not in sociology. Instead, we concentrate on several different areas of learning, including content, skills, and abilities. With our faculty consultants, we initially brainstormed a number of other terms to replace this idea of a core in sociology, including *key sociological ideas, foundations of sociology*, and *sociological contributions to understanding the social world*. What we eventually developed using the American Association for the Advancement of Science's (2011) *Vision and Change* report were two broad categories that organize learning outcomes for sociology. The first category, labeled the *Sociological Perspective*, contains five organizing concepts or themes we think are central to the discipline of sociology. These five organizing themes or sociology principles are essential concepts or themes and should be introduced in the introductory sociology course and then explored in-depth as the student proceeds through the major. We believe that in addition to having an understanding of these essential sociological themes or principles, students also need to develop and apply disciplinary skills. Thus, the second category is labeled the *Sociological Toolbox*, and it contains six essential competencies or disciplinary skills that sociology majors should obtain. We refer to these skills as essential competencies. These two broad categories will be more fully defined later in this white paper as part of our Sociological Literacy Framework. Briefly, defining essential concepts and competencies helps to advance the quality of undergraduate education in sociology by giving us more effective approaches and goals that increase our understanding of teaching and learning. These essential concepts and competencies are what sociology faculty see as fundamental to the discipline and are learning outcomes worth emphasizing given limited time and resources.

This white paper is a review and synthesis of the current state of learning outcomes and assessment within the discipline of sociology. It reflects a comprehensive summary of prior literature and faculty engagement in discussions about priorities for sociology-specific student learning. It outlines sociology's curricular priorities and demonstrates sociology's value for college students, faculty, and other key stakeholders. Since we believe that the best interests of students need to be at the center of any curriculum discussion, our aspiration is that this white paper improves our ability to understand student learning and generates new ideas about how to better define and assess student learning within sociology.

The first section reviews the literature on learning outcomes in sociology and describes prior attempts to define a core in sociology. We then describe efforts to define learning outcomes for the introductory course in sociology at the high school and college levels before summarizing the literature on learning outcomes for the sociology major. We conclude our review with a list of twelve areas of agreement in the literature concerning the sociology curriculum. These twelve areas of overlap indicate what most sociologists think are essential for every college-level sociology student to master. Following the literature review, we present our new sociology matrix, the *Sociological Literacy Framework*, which articulates a set of essential concepts and competencies for both the sociology major and for the introductory course. We then describe and critically evaluate current assessments in sociology. Finally, we conclude with recommendations regarding how a new assessment of student learning in sociology should be constructed.

Literature Review

> The first wisdom of sociology is this—things are not
> what they seem.
>
>   Peter Berger

Debate about critical learning outcomes in sociology has been ongoing for over a hundred years. Concerns about the content and scope of introductory sociology courses can be documented as early as the 1909 American Sociological Society (ASS) business meeting, when Jerome Dowd proposed the first committee to investigate the introductory course and to make a recommendation for standardization for course content that would serve as a guide to sociology instructors. This committee of ten scholars included Charles Horton Cooley, Albion Small, Jerome Dowd (chair), and William Graham Sumner, the ASS president of 1908–1909. Dowd's overarching concern was "that sociology teachers, not researchers or theorists, should be the ones who define the scope of the discipline of sociology" (Howard 2010, 83). The committee had substantial agreement on the larger scope of the introductory course; however, they could not fully agree upon a detailed outline of the course, so they amended their report with their individual course outlines. This lack of full consensus on the specific content of introductory sociology continues to this day, with numerous recent attempts to identify a common core in introductory sociology and in the major.[2]

Some of this lack of consensus is due to the nature of the discipline. DiMaggio (1997, 193), for example, argues that sociology appears to be a generalist field in terms of theory, methodology, and content because "sociologists study so many things in so many ways that as soon as outsiders fix a mental image of the field they encounter instances that seem inconsistent with it."

---

[2] There have been many sessions on a core in sociology at regional and national meetings including Greenwood et al. (2014), Jenkins (2014), Kain (2013), and Zipp (2013). Published literature on the core in sociology will be addressed herein and includes the ASA Task Force (2008), Babbie (1990), Collins (1998), D'Antonio (1983), Davis (1983), Howard, Novak, Cline, and Scott (2014), Keith and Ender (2004), Lenski (1983), Persell et al. (2007), Schwartz and Smith (2010), Wagenaar (2004a), and Wagenaar, Keith, and Ender (2004).

This generality makes it difficult to identify specific content for courses or curricula. DiMaggio goes on to argue: "I believe that sociology *does* have a core: the study of social organization from a comparative perspective" (193). In contrast, Abbott (2000) argues that sociology is an endangered discipline among the social sciences because it is organized around an archipelago of empirical questions concerning work and occupations, race and ethnicity, population, stratification, et cetera.

Collins (1998) argues that the common core of sociology is not a set of texts or ideas, but a distinctive intellectual activity: to see that there is sociology in everything, via what Collins labels the sociological eye. The sociological eye is one's ability to see sociology in everyday life. Sociologists see more than the immediate microsituation; the sociological eye also sees the importance of social structure and the relationships between individuals and the larger society. The sociological eye "sees suggestions of social movements mobilizing or winding down, indications of class domination or conflict, or perhaps the organizational process" (3). According to Collins, it is sociologists' ability to perceive the interrelationships between various social phenomena that makes the discipline distinctive. Kai Erikson (1997, 7) similarly contends that sociologists have a unique way of looking at the social world, what he calls "a distinctive intellectual sensibility" or "a distinctive disciplinary lens." He states, "What differentiates us from other observers of the human scene is the way we look out at the world—the way our eyes are trained, the way our intellectual reflexes are set, the way our imaginations are tuned. Sociologists scan the same landscapes as historians or poets or economists, but we select different details to attend to closely, and we sort them in different ways" (3). Erikson's argument reveals that sociologists often study the same subjects and social phenomena as other disciplines, but see different things. Sociologists observe relationships, social networks, the organization of social structures, or the presence of hierarchies and power.

Other sociologists maintain that the lack of consensus in sociology is due to the structure of the academy. Goldsmid and Wilson (1980), for example, argue that curriculum and course content tend to rely heavily on what has been taught before or on the content of textbooks. In this sense, sociology instruction can be seen as a form of mimicry. As an alternative, Goldsmid and Wilson advocate for sociologists to be more intentional and thoughtful about what the core curriculum is in sociology. They believe that the creation of a common core would provide some minimum standards for the discipline, and it also would be a means to create coherency and structure in departmental curricula. Having shared curricular learning goals and a set of required courses enhances both pedagogy and student learning.

Since 1980, there has been an explosion in the Scholarship of Teaching and Learning (SoTL) research and in studies of the sociology curriculum. For example, Fink (2003) advocates for designing college courses around different types of learning goals, including goals for foundational knowledge, for application, and for integration of subject content. Beyond course content, Fink also wants courses to enhance learning skills and to have additional learning goals that enhance the human dimension and the students' ability to care about what they are learning. Fink's research and that of others is part of a larger pedagogical movement from a teaching-centered approach to a learning-centered approach. Sociologists have been active in this pedagogical movement from its beginning. Hans Mauksch, for example, started the American Sociological Association (ASA) Project on Teaching Undergraduate Sociology more than forty years ago. Berheide (2005) also has been an active participant, and in her research on strengthening the sociology curriculum she argues that these learning goals need to be infused throughout the sociology curriculum and courses sequenced in such a way as to provide study in depth,[3] one of the nine goals of the Association of American Colleges' 1985 *Integrity in the College Curriculum* report.

Our review to this point has largely focused on arguments regarding why sociology is a distinctive discipline and the challenges in defining an agreed upon core. What follows is a review of tangible efforts to develop a core in sociology and explicit learning outcomes for the purposes of teaching and program development. Although no consensus exists across proposals regarding what the specific core of sociology should be, there are key concurrences on a number of learning outcomes to be covered either in the introductory sociology course or in the sociology major. We summarize some of these significant pieces of scholarship and then highlight twelve areas of agreement found within this literature. Delineating these areas of agreement is necessary for the discipline to establish learning outcomes and to create meaningful assessments of those learning outcomes. Moreover, having a defined foundation in sociology will help promote the discipline and the major.

Introduction to Sociology

We will describe efforts to define a sociological core at three different levels of schooling: high school, community (two-year) college, and four-year college. At the high school level, local and state boards of education have largely defined the content of sociology courses. In response to teacher requests for curricular standards in sociology, the American Sociological Association began working on high school

---

[3] Berheide states, "The *Integrity* report defines study in depth as comprehension of a complex structure of knowledge. To achieve this comprehension, the *Integrity* report argues that students need a course of study that exposes them to: (1) a central core of method and theory; (2) a range of topics and variety of analytical tools; (3) a sequence that promotes increasing intellectual sophistication in the discipline; and (4) a means to demonstrate mastery of the discipline's complexity" (2005, 4).

standards as early as 1998 and also worked to establish an advanced placement sociology course in 2001. More recently, the ASA advocated to be included in the National Council of Social Studies' guide, *College, Career, and Civic Life: C3 Framework for Social Studies State Standards*. As a result, in 2013, the ASA released a "Sociology Companion Document" to the *C3 Framework*, which is a set of high school sociology standards. The document identifies four main content areas that should be covered in high school sociology courses: (a) the Sociological Perspective and methods of inquiry; (b) social structure (culture, institutions, and society); (c) social relationships (self, groups, and socialization); and (d) stratification and inequality. Under each of these four domains, four or five learning goals are delineated. Working in parallel with this effort, an ASA Task Force formed to develop the ASA National Standards for High School Sociology, and their recommendations were formally approved by the ASA Council at the national meeting in August 2015.

Some community colleges also have collaborated in identifying a common core of learning outcomes for the Introduction to Sociology course. A central concern for community colleges is having clear articulation agreements with colleges and universities for classes taken at the community college level to be transferable to four-year institutions. One effort at Glendale Community College in Arizona involved sociologists from ten different community colleges who reviewed learning goals in sociology and designed a common course description and outline (Jenkins 2014). The learning goals borrowed heavily from the ASA guide, *Liberal Learning and the Sociology Major Updated* (McKinney, Howery, Strand, Kain, and Berheide 2004, 51–52), which is probably the most cited curricular document in sociology.[4] McKinney et al. outline twelve

---

[4] The earlier version of this document was written by Wagenaar in a 1991 *Teaching Sociology* article, "Goals for the Discipline?" This article became a part of the first edition of the ASA guide: *Liberal Learning and the Major* (1991), edited by Eberts, et al. This 1991 edition was revised by another ASA Task Force in 2004, and it currently is undergoing revision again with the third edition expected in 2017.

broad learning outcomes for the sociology major. In their review of the literature for teaching introductory sociology, Greenwood and Howard (2011, 9) acknowledge the widespread use of the ASA guide *Liberal Learning and the Sociology Major* (Eberts et al. 1991; McKinney et al. 2004), and they argue that while outcomes for *the major* have been established and revised, no such universal standards exist for *introductory sociology*.

At the four-year college level, D'Antonio (1983) argues for defining a core and describes his colleagues' reluctance to define a common curriculum in the introductory sociology course, including suggestions that to do so would violate academic freedom. Despite this resistance, D'Antonio states that "there is a body of knowledge that can be identified as the core of sociology, which can be introduced to the student at the introductory level. It embodies theories, methods, and findings from research based on these theories and using these methods" (169). D'Antonio creates a core set of topics for introductory sociology that emphasizes three areas: theorists and their theories, sociological concepts (including social organizations, social inequality, socialization, and social change), and methodology.

Two other articles attempting to define a core for introductory sociology that appeared in the same edition of *Teaching Sociology* as D'Antonio's article are by Davis (1983) and Lenski (1983). Davis (1983) argues for organizing introductory sociology courses around empirical scientific findings, which were true, easily demonstrated, thought provoking, and illustrative of the sociological perspective. Davis also prefers causal models, and he demonstrates his teaching model for introductory sociology using data from the National Opinion Research Center (NORC) on what he labels *five well-established research results*. In contrast, Lenski (1983) argues the introductory course should utilize a historical and comparative framework and focus on the three structural domains of sociology at the micro (e.g., individuals and relationships), meso (e.g., communities and organizations), and macro levels (e.g., social institutions, culture, ideologies). These two approaches have been criticized for overemphasizing social structure and quantitative methodologies (Reinharz 1986).

In 2004, a special issue of *Teaching Sociology* returned to this conversation about a core in sociology. The lead article by Wagenaar (2004a) reports his findings from a survey of 301 sociologists and their views regarding which skills, topics, and concepts they see as central to the introduction to sociology course and to the sociology curriculum overall. Wagenaar created a list of seventy-two items that were grouped into the following ten categories: sociological perspective; theory; methods and statistics; differences, inequality, and stratification; social structure and institutions; culture and social change; individual and society; applied sociology; values and commitments; and skills. Wagenaar found that at least six items from these ten categories overlap between the lists of critical concepts and skills sociologists attribute to the introductory course and to the sociology curriculum overall: the sociological imagination, social stratification, sociological critical thinking, social structure, think like a sociologist, and how to use and assess research. Wagenaar also found some differences in what sociologists think are critical categories for the introductory course and for the major (e.g., for the introductory course, the concepts of culture and socialization are rated particularly highly). Wagenaar's results reveal that, although there is some overlap between learning outcomes for the introductory course and for the major, there is little agreement among sociologists about the presence of a core in the field of sociology. No single item in Wagenaar's survey exceeds the threshold of 10 percent among all respondents. However, the overlap does indicate a few areas of agreement among sociologists about a possible list of core concepts, topics, and skills for sociology. He concludes that identifying this sociology core will not only strengthen the introductory students' grounding in the discipline but will also increase the majors' study-in-depth experience (2004a, 17).

Persell, Pfeiffer, and Syed's (2007) research provides a systematic comparison of earlier studies that tried to identify key concepts and content in sociology, including Wagenaar's previously discussed study. They also interviewed forty-four leaders in sociology to learn their views of a sociological core. Their findings indicate a consensus around nine major themes for introductory sociology: (a) the social part of sociology, or learning to think sociologically; (b) the scientific nature of sociology; (c) complex and critical thinking; (d) the centrality of inequality; (e) a sense of sociology as a field; (f) the social construction of ideas; (g) the difference between sociology and other social sciences; (h) the importance of trying to improve the world; and (i) the important social institutions in society. These nine themes are a useful point of comparison between a number of studies, and many can be found in the following list of twelve domains. Persell and her colleagues note that it is ironic that many of the sociology leaders they interviewed were not teaching introduction sociology, nor had they taught undergraduates for some years. However, their views of the introductory course did not differ much from those found in the SoTL scholarship or from those sociologists who were recipients of the Distinguished Contributions to Teaching Award in sociology. Thus, there appears to be some agreement among sociology leaders and teaching-focused publications about what students should understand after taking an introductory course in sociology.

In 2008, the ASA Task Force on a College Level Introduction to Sociology Course published their course outline and learning goals for studying introductory sociology. The summary course outline has nine topics: the sociological perspective; research methods; culture; socialization; social organization; social inequalities; deviance and conformity; social institutions; and social change. This grouping of topics is common in introductory textbooks and syllabi that use a survey approach to teaching sociology. Many sociologists assume we have a core because of these common topics found in introductory texts. However, some departments have rejected the survey model and are pursuing alternatives, such as in-depth case studies (Schwartz and Smith 2010) or thematically focused courses. Howard et al. (2014), for example, described an effort to evaluate student learning across twelve thematically focused introductory sociology courses. They first enumerated a core set of skills and concepts to be covered in four main areas: a sociological perspective; sociological theory; research methods; and key concepts in sociology. A twenty-question multiple-choice assessment was created and administered to students at the beginning and end of the semester. Students made significant learning gains on all four dimensions, with the greatest gains coming in *sociological theory*. Howard et al. conclude their assessment, albeit limited, does demonstrate considerable learning gains in the four main areas in a thematic introductory sociology class, and they advocate for more discussion and agreement on key learning outcomes for sociology.

The Sociology Major

Many scholars also have articulated learning outcomes for the sociology major. These frameworks often describe knowledge, attitudes, and skills that sociology majors should be able to demonstrate after finishing their undergraduate education. For example, McKinney et al. (2004) offers a comprehensive list of skills sociology majors should be able to demonstrate. McKinney and her colleagues on the ASA Task Force list twelve items that cover sociological concepts, theories, and skills. The authors maintained that these learning outcomes are not to be prescriptive, but rather, they should be used as a guide or model to help sociology departments design their own curricula in accordance with their mission statements and student populations. Some departments may choose to emphasize six of the learning outcomes, whereas others try to emulate more. For example, Lowry et al. (2005) provide the learning outcomes for the sociology major for four different schools (California State University at Fresno, Central Michigan University, Roanoke College, and Skidmore College). While still showing variation, this small sample reveals substantial overlap in learning outcomes for the sociology major.

We were particularly interested in whether or not distinctions were made between learning outcomes for the introductory sociology course versus learning outcomes for the sociology major. Wagenaar's (2004a) study is the only one to compare the learning outcomes for the sociology major with those for the introductory course. Wagenaar found that sociologists agreed that both the students in the introductory course and in the major should be able to explain the sociological imagination, social stratification, and social structure. Both groups of students also should be able to identify sociological critical thinking, to think like a sociologist, and be able to know how to use and assess research. But for the sociology major, deeper knowledge and skills need to be demonstrated, especially skills related to methods and statistics. According to Wagenaar, and we concur, sociology majors should be able to emphasize the interplay of theory and methods and to demonstrate their ability to theorize, conduct sociological research, and show greater complexity of thinking.

Two final documents we reviewed in the literature on creating a core in sociology are the UK Quality Assurance Agency for Higher Education's (QAA) benchmark statement for sociology (2007) and the Australian Sociological Association's (TASA) "Sociology: Threshold Learning Outcomes" (2012). The first document, written for the QAA by the British Sociological Association, provides sociology programs in the United Kingdom with a guiding set of learning outcomes for the bachelor's degree in sociology. Although much more comprehensive than any of the U.S. reports on sociological learning outcomes, it includes substantial overlap with prior attempts to identify fundamental sociological skills and knowledge. In particular, the QAA delineates learning outcomes in the following areas: knowledge of sociology as a unique discipline, sociological concepts and principles, and skills specific to sociology. It also includes numerous general skills graduating college seniors should be able to demonstrate that are quite broad and not specific to the sociology major (e.g., making reasoned arguments, learning and studying skills, and group work skills).

The second document was published more recently in 2012, and it reflects the work of the Australian Sociological Association (TASA), which responded to a governmental charge that disciplines in higher education in Australia must define learning outcomes as part of their *quality assurance activities*. Using discipline experts from across Australia, TASA developed *threshold learning outcomes* or "the minimum outcomes that graduates of bachelor degrees with majors in sociology are expected to have achieved at the completion of their course of study" (TASA 2012, 2). Of interest here is how TASA organizes the sociology threshold learning outcomes (TLOs) into three primary domains: knowledge and understanding; skills; and engagement. Contained within these three domains is a total of seven specific threshold learning outcomes: demonstrate an understanding of sociological concepts; demonstrate an understanding of sociological theories; demonstrate an understanding of research processes; apply concepts and theories; evaluate sociological scholarship; develop arguments using evidence; and communicate sociological ideas and knowledge to both specialist and non-specialist audiences. These Australian sociology learning outcomes parallel nicely the work done in the United States and in the United Kingdom.

Our literature review suggests that although sociologists have struggled to agree upon a core, and even though it can be difficult to see consensus within the discipline concerning the introductory course and the sociology major, many concepts and themes are consistent across several frameworks. We found the following twelve areas of overlap:

1. The unique perspective of sociology
2. The fact that sociology is a science
3. A sense of sociology as a field or as a discipline
4. The importance of theory in forming sociological thinking and research

5. The centrality of social inequality
6. The importance of social structure
7. The relationship between self and society
8. The concept of culture
9. The concept of social change
10. Complex and critical thinking skills
11. Other skills such as writing, oral skills, technological literacy
12. The importance of trying to improve the world

This strong degree of overlap between the many different frameworks and typologies that we reviewed provides an important road map. The Sociological Literacy Framework that we propose builds on this overlap, organizing these different areas of agreement into a concise set of essential concepts and competencies. Importantly, the framework is sufficiently broad in ways that will enable sociologists to make progress in conceptualizing how college learning in the introductory sociology course and in the sociology major could be measured.

The Sociological Literacy Framework: Essential Concepts and Competencies for the Sociology Major

The literature review and discussions from the MCL sociology faculty panel indicate that there is sufficient overlap in various frameworks to enumerate a reasonable number of broad learning outcomes for the introductory sociology course and for the sociology major. Our synthesis of this material led us to create the Sociological Literacy Framework, which summarizes and describes a set of essential concepts and competencies for the sociology major. The framework has two broad categories that organize learning outcomes for sociology. The first category, labeled the *Sociological Perspective*, contains five essential concepts that are central to the discipline of sociology. They should be introduced in the introductory sociology course and then explored in depth as the student proceeds through the major. In addition to having an understanding of these essential sociological concepts, students also need to develop and apply disciplinary competencies. Thus, the second category, labeled the *Sociological Toolbox*, contains six essential competencies that sociology majors should master. Table 4.1 offers a brief overview of the Sociological Literacy Framework.

In addition to intersecting well with the U.S. literature on learning outcomes in sociology, the Sociological Literacy Framework dialogues well with the United Kingdom's benchmark statement for sociology (QAA 2007), and the Australian Sociological Association's threshold learning outcomes (TASA 2012). Although we present the concepts and competencies of the framework separately, undergraduates should nevertheless learn them in a fully integrated fashion, with each supporting and augmenting

Table 4.1 Brief Overview of the Sociological Literacy Framework

The Sociological Perspective (Essential Concepts)	The Sociological Toolbox (Essential Competencies)
The Sociological Eye: Sociology as a distinctive discipline	**Apply Sociological Theories to Understand Social Phenomena** (Theory)
Social Structure: The impact of social structures on human action	**Critically Evaluate Explanations of Human Behavior and Social Phenomena** (Evaluation)
Socialization: The relationship between the self and society	**Apply Scientific Principles to Understand the Social World** (Sociology as a Science)
Stratification: The patterns and effects of social inequality	**Evaluate the Quality of Social Scientific Methods and Data** (Methodological Practice)
Social Change and Social Reproduction: How social phenomena replicate and change	**Rigorously Analyze Social Scientific Data** (Quantitative and Qualitative Data Literacy)
	Use Sociological Knowledge to Inform Policy Debates and Promote Public Understanding (Public Skills and Citizenship)

the other. In our view, what makes sociology *exceptional* is its perspective (i.e., the essential concepts that students learn), but what makes it *valuable* is the knowledge and skills that students gain and can integrate together. Accordingly, what makes sociology distinctive is the *sui generis* of the major or the combination of the items in the Sociological Literacy Framework, not the individual items on their own.[5] Sociologists understand the social world by using both theory and evidence to pose and answer important questions about society. Concepts and compétencies are used together in sociological research, and students should recognize this integration in their courses and in their knowledge and application of sociology outside of the classroom.

The Sociological Perspective: Essential Concepts

The Sociological Perspective consists of five essential concepts that reflect larger organizing themes that lay the foundation of critical undergraduate knowledge in sociology. Each concept is a shorthand label or starting point for the overarching principles that underlie both the introductory sociology course and the sociology major. Taken together, these essential concepts and related themes provide an organizational model for what knowledge is expected in the college-level sociology curriculum. These essential concepts illustrate how sociologists view the social world and how sociology contributes to our understanding of the human experience. Below each essential concept is briefly summarized with a description of related themes and topics.

The Sociological Eye

The first essential concept in the Sociological Perspective is the *sociological eye*, a term we adopted from Randall Collins (1998). Sociology students should be able to delineate the major theoretical

---

[5] Thank you to Diane Pike for this insight on an earlier draft.

frameworks and distinctive assumptions on which our discipline is founded and that differentiate it from other social sciences. Topics related to this concept include: the founding theoretical traditions (Marx, Weber, Durkheim, and Mead); a critique of rational choice as the primary explanation of human behavior; and an introduction to the *sociological imagination* and the *social construction of everyday life*, two constructs that facilitate understanding of how social forces affect individuals and how actions of individuals both constitute and are shaped by daily life.

Social Structure

Students of sociology should also be able to describe social structure and how structural forces affect human action and social life at the micro, meso, and macro levels of society. More specifically, sociology students should be able to distinguish important social institutions in society that make up the social structure, and how they affect individuals and each other. In addition, students should be able to differentiate the processes through which social roles and statuses, relationships, social groups, formal organizations, and social networks influence human thought and action. Students should recognize how hierarchy, power, and authority operate across these structural contexts. Finally, students should be able to provide examples of these concepts related to social structure in multiple historical and cultural settings.

Socialization

Students of sociology should be able to explain the relationship between the self and society, particularly how the self is socially constructed and maintained at multiple levels of society. Related topics include the processes and agents of socialization; the role of culture in shaping human thought and action; the operation of social norms, including the study of social control, anomie, and deviance; the power of the self-fulfilling prophesy; and the role of human agency in describing behavior. Finally, students should be able to explain concepts and theories that illustrate how the self and social interaction influence the larger society and social structure.

Stratification

The essential concept of stratification comprises the different forms of social inequality in human societies and the processes through which they are established and operate. Related critical topics include the theories of social stratification; the structure of inequalities of power, status, income, and wealth; the distinction between social and economic mobility and how ascriptive and meritocratic traits are related to each; and the impact of changes in the opportunity structure on inequality and social mobility. Additionally, students should be able to identify structural patterns of social inequality and their effects on groups and individuals, and explain the intersections of race, social class, gender, and other social factors at both the macro level and micro level of society.

Social Change and Social Reproduction

Sociology students also should be able to identify the social processes underpinning social change and describe how demographic and other types of social change affect individuals and social structures. More specifically, students should be able to explain how social structures change as a result of social forces, including the actions of social groups through social movements and collective action; the impact of macro level economic and social changes such as industrialization, secularization, and globalization; and struggles over social institutions that are linked to social and economic development and mobility. A critical component of social change is *social reproduction*, which emphasizes the basic processes of how social structures reproduce themselves from generation to generation in cultural, social, political, and economic terms.

Table 4.2 summarizes all five essential concepts that form the Sociological Perspective.

Table 4.2 The Sociological Perspective: Five Essential Concepts

Essential Concept	Significance (Students Will . . .)
The Sociological Eye	Recognize key theoretical frameworks and assumptions on which the discipline is founded and differentiated from other social sciences.
Social Structure	Articulate what sociologists mean by *social structure* and how structural forces affect human action and social life at the micro, meso, and macro levels.
Socialization	Explain the relationship between the self and society and how the self is socially constructed and maintained at multiple levels.
Stratification	Identify how social structures create and reproduce different forms of social inequality in human society through specific processes, and interpret empirical patterns and effects of social inequality.
Social Change and Social Reproduction	Comprehend how social structures reproduce themselves across generations but also how social change occurs in cultural, social, political, and economic terms.

The Sociological Toolbox: Essential Competencies

The six essential competencies in the Sociological Toolbox are the skills that we think sociology students should be able to demonstrate at different points in the sociology curriculum. For example, in introductory courses these skills are introduced, in intermediate courses these skills are developed and applied, and in advanced courses they are particularly emphasized. By the time sociology majors graduate, they should have developed mastery of these skills.

Apply Sociological Theories to Understand Social Phenomena

Sociology students should be able to move beyond folk explanations of social phenomena and instead invoke evidence-based theories of sociological phenomena. Sociology students should be able to demonstrate how to apply sociological theories and concepts to the social world around them by doing the following: using the sociological imagination to analyze social problems in context and to generate and evaluate solutions; and by applying other sociological theories and concepts to social phenomena, both locally and globally.

Critically Evaluate Explanations of Human Behavior and Social Phenomena

Sociology students should be able to describe the role of theory in building sociological knowledge and evaluate the limitations of different theoretical frameworks. This essential competency provides students with the tools to critically evaluate claims about the social world by identifying and appraising assumptions underlying theory construction and social policy, deductively deriving theories from assumptions, inductively reasoning from evidence to theoretical conclusions, and effectively using sociological theories and evidence to suggest real-world solutions to social problems.

Apply Scientific Principles to Understand the Social World

Sociology students should not only be able to describe the role of social research methods in building sociological knowledge, but be able to identify major methodological approaches and the design of doing research including sampling, measurement, and data collection. Students should learn to conduct and critique empirical research through the articulation of the effective use of evidence, the generation of research questions or hypotheses from sociological theories and concepts, and the recognition of the limits of the scientific method in understanding social behavior.

Evaluate the Quality of Social Scientific Methods and Data

Sociology students should be able to critically assess the empirical sociological research of others and be able to identify the assumptions and limitations underlying particular research methodologies in sociology. The particular characteristics that sociologists use to evaluate the quality of research methods and data sources include operationalizing concepts into measurable variables; learning the importance of precision, reliability, and validity of data sources; and understanding the distinctions between probability and non-probability samples.

Rigorously Analyze Social Scientific Data

Students should be able to articulate and apply disciplinary standards for data analysis and also delineate the differing goals, strengths, and limitations of different modes of analysis. These methodological skills should include an ability to fathom basic descriptive and inferential statistics and the importance of statistical and experimental controls for making causal claims when analyzing data. Students also should be able to evaluate multiple representations of data in public discourse. The ability to evaluate statistical information and analyses is central to the quantitative literacy of sociology students.

Use Sociological Knowledge to Inform Policy Debates and Promote Public Understanding

We want sociology students to be able to use all of the essential concepts and competencies of the Sociological Literacy Framework to engage with and have an impact upon the world in which they live and work. This last competency is not solely the ideal of using sociological education to develop better citizens, but in addition, it covers a broad range of abilities and potential applications for sociology students, including being able to express sociological ideas in a clear and coherent manner, in both written and oral communication, to the general public. Sociology students also should be able to demonstrate informational, technological, and quantitative literacy. This essential competency suggests that sociology students should understand the kinds of work sociologists do, including an awareness of how sociology is used in clinical and applied settings, and the value of sociological knowledge and skills in the workplace. Additionally, students should be aware of public sociology and be able to use and understand the value of sociological theories and knowledge when participating in public discourse and civic life. This essential competency effectively parallels one of the goals of LEAP, Liberal Education and America's Promise, which argues that learning outcomes are essential for success in life, civil society, and work in the 21st century.[6]

Table 4.3 describes the six essential competencies that make up the Sociological Toolbox in the Sociological Literacy Framework.

Uses of the Sociological Literacy Framework

Taken together, these five essential concepts and six essential competencies create a Sociological Literacy Framework that can be modified and applied in a variety of academic settings. The model distinguishes between learning outcomes that demonstrate what

---

[6] LEAP promotes essential learning outcomes that include: "1) broad knowledge of culture, science and society, as well as competence in specific fields; 2) intellectual and practical skills, such as inquiry and analysis; critical and creative thinking; written and oral communication; quantitative literacy; information literacy; teamwork and problem solving; 3) studies and experiences related to democratic and global citizenship and intercultural competence; and 4) integrative, applied and adaptive learning" (LEAP 2015).

Table 4.3 The Sociological Toolbox: Six Essential Competencies

Essential Competency	Significance	Proposed Learning Outcome
Apply Sociological Theories to Understand Social Phenomena	Sociology provides concepts and theories that reveal hidden patterns in the social world.	Students will be able to identify how sociological concepts and theories relate to everyday life.
Critically Evaluate Explanations of Human Behavior and Social Phenomena	Sociology provides the tools to critically evaluate claims about the social world.	Students will possess a critical lens for understanding human behavior and societies.
Apply Scientific Principles to Understand the Social World	Sociology is an evidence-based discipline.	Students will articulate the importance of evidence and scientific methods for explanations of social phenomena.
Evaluate the Quality of Social Scientific Methods and Data	Sociology requires high-quality research methods and data to describe and explain social phenomena.	Students will be able to identify the characteristics of high-quality data and methods in sociological research.
Rigorously Analyze Social Scientific Data	Sociology relies on scientifically valid methodologies to analyze data.	Students will identify disciplinary standards for both the qualitative and quantitative analysis of data.
Use Sociological Knowledge to Inform Policy Debates and Promote Public Understanding	Sociological research can create a more knowledgeable citizenry and serve as a resource for policymakers.	Students will use their sociological knowledge and skills to engage with and impact the world around them.

students should be able to comprehend, and what they should be able to do. The framework is flexible and easily adaptable by sociology faculty and departments with different strengths, interests, and emphases. It sets a clear target that faculty can use in developing their courses while preserving pedagogical autonomy in the classroom.

The main goal of the Sociological Literacy Framework is to catalyze a change in how students think about social phenomena by learning and applying sociological concepts, theories, and skills that enable them to view the social world as a sociologist does. It provides an essential set of concepts and skills that will help to train students how to think critically from a sociological perspective. With this goal in mind, the framework also is designed to help instructors and departments develop and organize introductory, required, and advanced courses. We want to provide sociology programs with a set of ideas and guidelines to begin or further conversations about the curriculum and when certain concepts or skills should be introduced. We also want sociology programs to think about how courses are linked together or sequenced across the undergraduate major, and how learning in sociology can increase in depth over time. Sweet, McElrath, and Kain's (2014) research on the coordinated curriculum suggests that a structured curriculum with linked learning goals will facilitate the achievement of performance outcomes. Thus, the framework will bring coherence and consistency across students' course work, and it also will help their instructors target, teach, and develop more of these learning outcomes within and across sociology programs at different colleges and universities.

The essential concepts and competencies that we present in the Sociological Literacy Framework are intentionally broad and open-ended so that they can be appropriately tailored for different courses. The introductory course should provide students with exposure to the main perspectives of sociology (essential concepts or themes) and introduce the basic skills (essential competencies) that the framework delineates. In addition, since Bain (2004) argues that learning goals should foster deep-learning and practical application, we see our framework as helping to support developmental logic and deep learning within the major. Different courses within the sociology major may drill down and provide students with greater depth and exposure to a subset of themes and skills within the framework. As students progress through the sociology major, they gain greater competency in each learning outcome. Moreover, this approach to learning focuses on learning as a process; subsequent courses will extend and multiply knowledge and skill acquisition. Advanced courses within the major should give students more opportunities to develop and practice specific skills in the toolbox. Ideally, sociology programs can use the Sociological Literacy Framework to ensure that many (or most) of the dimensions are covered by a diverse array of courses within the major. The framework also is a scaffold on which instructors can begin to overlay specific sociological content in their courses. This underlying scaffold will help provide cohesion to courses and readings based on the potentially disparate, seemingly disconnected array of facts that sociologists produce with their research in different subfields. In sum, this framework can be used to enhance teaching, learning, and assessment.

Essential Concepts and Competencies for the Introductory Course

The Sociological Literacy Framework lists essential concepts and competencies that we would expect students to demonstrate at the completion of a major in sociology. But what might we expect students in the introductory course itself to learn, and how does that relate to the goals for the major? Our literature review and the MCL Sociology faculty panel identified learning outcomes for the introductory course that were similar to those for the sociology major. For example, the faculty panel agreed on six major learning outcomes for the introductory course, which we incorporated into the Sociological Literacy Framework:

1. Identify and apply major theoretical paradigms to social problems.
2. Recognize and apply the sociological imagination.
3. Interpret empirical patterns and the effects of social inequality.
4. Obtain working definitions of key concepts.
5. Explain the process of the scientific method and be able to identify different methods of data collection.
6. Articulate how sociology views the world distinctively from or similarly to other social sciences.

In addition, the MCL Sociology faculty panelists reaffirmed the importance of the introductory sociology course because it is often the only course in sociology that many college students will take. As such, they want this course to convey a basic understanding of the essential concepts and competencies that are fundamental to the discipline. Achieving this goal can be a challenge, however, because of the diversity of approaches in teaching introductory sociology at the college level. Two primary teaching models for the introductory course are *the survey textbook model*, where the focus is on content and teaching a list of topics rather than on teaching skills, and *the problem-solving model*, where the focus is on teaching critical thinking skills. Similar to arguments made by Greenwood and Howard (2011), several faculty panelists emphasized the importance of teaching both concepts and skills in the introductory course by introducing a few concepts or the vocabulary of sociology and then assigning different types of materials to apply those concepts. For example, some faculty members assign readings from newspapers, empirical case studies, or even pieces of fiction, and then ask students to apply their sociological learning to those readings. Still others organize their introductory course around specific themes, such as those found in Joel Charon's *Ten Questions: A Sociological Perspective* (2013). Each of these approaches can incorporate the essential concepts and competencies found in the Sociological Literacy Framework.

A related concern about the introductory course taught at most colleges and universities is that this course often is seen as serving two different functions. As McKeever (2014) argues, the first is as a service course to the college or university, as it commonly fulfills distribution requirements being satisfied by first- or second-year undergraduates. As such, it might be the only opportunity for students to encounter the discipline. For that reason, the emphasis of the introductory course is often on trying to get a general sense of the discipline across in at least a minimal fashion. Theoretical and methodological complexity tends to be simplified so that content, perspective, and some sense of method can be communicated. The second purpose of the introductory course is as the first interaction with the discipline for future majors, nearly all of whom do not realize they will be majors when they sign up for the course. For such students complexity is something they will encounter in subsequent courses. Consequently, we often spend time in subsequent courses undermining some of the material from introductory sociology when we reproblematize certain content and conclusions on theoretical or empirical grounds.

Regardless of teaching approach or purpose of the introductory sociology course at the college level, the same essential concepts and competencies that are identified for the sociology major in the Sociological Literacy Framework are applicable to the introductory course. Research supports this dual emphasis on concepts and skills: The American Sociological Association's Integrating Data Analysis (IDA) project argues for data analysis to be brought into the sociology curriculum in a manner that is "early, often, and sequenced." Hillsman and Vitullo (2014) report that 40 percent of the students in the twenty departments that participated in the 2005 NSF-sponsored IDA project used data analysis modules as first year students. After the data analysis modules, students stated that they felt less fearful about working with numbers; they understood that sociology is a science, not just based on opinions; and they saw how important it was to base new social services on empirical data.

Hillsman and Vitullo (2014) further argue that, in today's technologically enhanced world, there is a wealth of accessible data on the Internet that students in introductory classes can use to discover evidence of concepts in empirical data. We agree with their assertion and think that bringing the empirical basis of the discipline squarely into introductory courses supports the kind of learning-centered, inquiry-based pedagogies that have been shown to improve learning outcomes that are called for in this white paper. Thus, the essential competencies in the Sociological Literacy Framework should be introduced in the introductory course. To be sure, we would not expect students to have fully developed their expertise in applying scientific principles to understand the social world or their ability to evaluate the quality of social scientific data or to be able to rigorously analyze social scientific data until they completed their sociology major. These methodological skills should be introduced, but mastery is accomplished as the student takes more sociology courses beyond the introductory level.

Finally, the ability to interpret findings and to collect data and conduct basic analysis are valuable skills strongly linked to employment opportunities for sociology majors. Students in introductory courses are potential majors who are increasingly concerned about their future employment and need to know that a degree in sociology can lead to interesting and rewarding careers (Eagan, Lozano, Hurtado, and Case 2013). Students in the major need to have a solid understanding of the kind of work sociologists do and of the value of their sociological knowledge and skills in the workplace. Sociology majors often use the skills they learn in social service agencies, consulting firms, market research firms, and nonprofit organizations, just to name a few. Employers also are seeking college graduates who can demonstrate a broad range of skills, including the ability to deal with complexity (Hart Research Associates 2013). As a discipline that attracts many underrepresented minority and first generation college students, curricular content that explicitly makes the connection between the major and the skills employers' value can be seen as a social justice issue. The last essential competency in the framework's Sociological Toolbox makes this point: Sociology students and majors should be able to apply their sociological knowledge and skills to life outside of the classroom and to life after college.

Current Assessments of Student Learning in Sociology

In 2005, the ASA Task Force on Assessing the Undergraduate Sociology Major issued a report to provide guidance to departments on assessing student learning. In the report, Lowry et al. (2005) argue that the most critical reason that sociology departments should assess academic majors and programs is because it is a constructive method to enrich student learning. In addition, academic program assessment enables faculty to make a conceptual distinction between *teaching* and *learning* that has the potential to greatly enhance both. Lowry et al. advocate for sociology faculty to have serious discussions about what we want our students to learn and to achieve. Sociologists Atkinson and Lowney (2014) similarly argue that one of the most critical stakeholders in assessment is the student. They state, "We owe them [the students] the best, most cohesive process of introducing them to the discipline we love and then gradually but consistently deepening their analytical, theoretical, and problem-solving skills, as they advance through the degree requirements" (194). They also provide a guide to help departments design an assessment protocol and offer several examples of program assessment tools, including portfolios, major writing assignments, and pre–post measures.

The ASA Task Force report on assessment also includes many useful examples of departmental practices that are—and should be—used to measure student learning within the sociology major, such as (a) direct measures of learning, such as capstone courses, course-embedded assessments, student portfolios, and departmentally developed or nationally normed tests; and (b) indirect measures of learning, such as surveys and focus groups of current students and alumni, surveys of employers and graduate schools, and external reviews. All the practices described in the report can be tremendously helpful to individual sociology programs and departments as they critically evaluate their own practices and student learning outcomes. In the rest of this section, we will focus in particular on assessments that have the potential to allow for comparisons of student learning outcomes across institutions and over time.

The two large-scale standardized assessments that are used most widely to measure sociological knowledge and reasoning are the Major Field Test (MFT) conducted by the Educational Testing Service (ETS) and the Psychological, Social, and Biological Foundations of Behavior (PSBFB) section of the Medical College Admissions Test (MCAT) conducted by the Association of American Medical Colleges (AAMC). ETS reported aggregated results for 2,543 examinees (in 110 postsecondary institutions) who took the MFT in sociology from September 2012 to May 2014 (ETS 2014). In contrast, roughly 85,000 people take the MCAT each time it is offered (although each sitting often includes individuals who have taken the exam at least once in the past) (AAMC 2015).

The MFT for sociology is designed as an end-of-program assessment that measures the discipline specific skills and knowledge of sociology majors. The MFT was designed to be shorter and less difficult than the now-defunct GRE in sociology, with the population of interest being all sociology majors rather than only those with an interest in attending graduate school (Szafran 1996). ETS describes all of its major field tests as measuring "the mastery of concepts, principles, and knowledge expected of students at the conclusion of a major" (ETS 2012). Although the exam assesses factual knowledge, ETS also argues that the MFT measures "students' abilities to analyze and solve problems, understand relationships, and interpret material" (ETS 2012). The MFT is designed to help academic departments evaluate student learning for the purpose of self-study by providing individual-level scores that can be aggregated to the department level.

The MFT for sociology is a two-hour multiple-choice exam with 140 questions. Some questions are stand-alone measures, and others are divided into question sets based on graphs, data, and diagrams provided for test takers on the exam. In describing the MFT for sociology, ETS states that most questions "require knowledge of specific sociological information, but the test also draws on the student's ability to interpret data, to apply concepts and ideas, and to analyze sociological data, theories and relationships, deductively and inductively" (ETS 2012). ETS identifies thirteen content areas for the exam: general theory; methodology and statistics; criminology and deviance; demography and urban sociology; organizations; race, ethnicity, gender; social change; social institutions; social psychology; social stratification; critical thinking; gender; and global. The last three areas (critical thinking, gender, and global) are described by ETS as "integrated into the entire [MFT]," which suggests that numerous questions may be designed to test multiple, overlapping content areas.

ETS divides the MFT in sociology into two main sections, each with its own subscore: core sociology (described as "general theory and methodology and statistics"), and critical thinking. The observed correlation between these two subscores among examinees is very high ($r = .85$), which indicates that students' scores on the two sections are very strongly associated with each other

(ETS 2014). A total score as well as subscores for core sociology and critical thinking can be estimated for each individual student. Subscores in nine additional content areas (general theory; methodology and statistics; criminology and deviance; social stratification; race, ethnicity, gender; social psychology; gender; and global) can be estimated, but these scores are only valid at the department level and are not available for individual students, due to the smaller number of questions in each area (ETS 2014).

ETS provides fifteen sample questions from the MFT on the ETS website, and the questions cover a wide range of substantive topics within sociology (ETS 2003). Although ETS (2003) provides a caveat that the questions should not be considered "representative of the entire scope of the test in either content or difficulty," it is possible to make some generalizations about the types of questions that appear on the MFT. All the sample items are stand-alone questions (as opposed to question sets). Many of the questions depend on an examinee's background knowledge of key concepts, sociological terminology, or factual knowledge. For example, one question asks, "A person who sells drugs in order to become wealthy best fits which of Merton's modes of adaptation to anomie?" Clearly, prior knowledge of the concept of anomie is necessary to determine the correct response ("Innovator"). One can reasonably deduce this correct answer, but only if one has prior knowledge of the core concept. Another sample question is much more narrowly focused on factual knowledge: "Which of the following Supreme Court decisions most significantly improved the legal status of African Americans in the United States?" The examinee is given five possible responses, each of which is the title of a Supreme Court case (*Brown v. the Topeka Board of Education* is the correct response). This item solely evaluates specific factual knowledge and is completely divorced from sociological reasoning. Other questions focus on specific research findings: "Research has shown that a bystander is most likely to help a person in distress if [correct response: there are no other bystanders present]."

Once again, there is little to no reasoning involved in determining the correct response to this question; it is solely a test of factual knowledge. Finally, two of the fifteen sample questions (one on factorial designs, and another on the difference between a sample and a population) were completely divorced from sociological content; neither question required any knowledge of sociology to be answered correctly.

The PSBFB section of the MCAT shares similarities with but also differs from the MFT in assessing sociological knowledge and skills. The AAMC describes the PSBFB section of the MCAT as measuring a student's understanding of "the ways psychological, social, and biological factors influence perceptions and reactions to the world; behavior and behavior change; what people think about themselves and others; the cultural and social differences that influence well-being; and relationships between social stratification, access to resources, and well-being" (AAMC 2015, 1). This section of the MCAT consists of fifty-nine questions, for which examinees are given ninety-five minutes to answer. Roughly 30 percent of the content for the PSBFB is sociological, 65 percent is psychological, and 5 percent is biological. According to the AAMC, this section of the MCAT tests knowledge and concepts that are typically taught in a first-semester psychology or sociology course.

There are several important contrasts between the MFT and MCAT's PSBFB. First, the main purpose of the MCAT's PSBFB is fundamentally different from the MFT: The MFT is largely designed for program evaluation, and the MCAT is used exclusively as a tool to make relative comparisons among students to determine admission to medical school. Consequently, whereas the MFT provides overall scores and subscores for both programs and students, the PSBFB of the MCAT does not provide subscores that specifically describe an examinee's sociological knowledge (since it comprises only 30 percent of this section of the exam). In addition, when compared with the MFT, the PSBFB is designed as an assessment of the learning that occurs in an introductory sociology course, rather than the full major. Relatedly, unlike the MFT, the MCAT assesses a population of students who are not expected to be sociology majors but rather those who have likely taken an introductory sociology course or another entry-level sociology course for students planning to apply to medical school.

The overall scope of the sociological content of the MCAT's PSBFB is considerably more circumscribed than the MFT. There is a strong emphasis on social psychological theory and research on the PSBFB, with questions on the following content areas: social processes that influence human behavior, self-identity, social thinking, and social interactions (AAMC 2015, 18–25). Additional content areas include understanding social structure (theoretical approaches, social institutions, and culture), demographic characteristics and processes, and social inequalities (26–31). Methodology and statistics are not explicitly described as *sociological content* on the MCAT, but there is ample representation of this knowledge and skill set in the PSBFB. In short, the MCAT has less breadth in content relative to the MFT and our own Sociological Literacy Framework.

MCAT examinees also are commonly asked to reach a specific conclusion based on a graph or table that is provided in the PSBFB section. For example, one sample question includes a graph describing how mortality rates (on the y-axis) change by age (on the x-axis) for individuals with different marital statuses (e.g., continuously married, divorced, never married). Examinees are given a series of statements and asked to identify which statement was unsupported by the graph. Other questions provide examinees with specific research questions ("researchers were interested in whether early mental health issues were associated with later educational attainment") in which they are asked to identify independent, dependent, and mediating variables. As with the MFT, these tests of methodological and statistical skills and knowledge are often independent of background knowledge in sociology.

In other words, even though the content of these examples is sociological, the knowledge needed to answer these questions could be
learned in many other natural and social science disciplines.

The MCAT's PSBFB relies exclusively on question sets rather
than the kinds of stand-alone questions that make up the bulk of
the MFT. Examinees are given one or two paragraphs that describe
a research topic, a research question, and occasionally some specific published research studies. A table or graph is typically also
included as part of the question set. Four multiple-choice questions follow the information that is provided. The questions often
isolate specific theories and concepts, and examinees are typically
asked to apply their knowledge to concrete examples. For example, they are presented with an example of a study that examined
whether individuals who experience mental health problems are
more likely to drift to a lower social status as adults. The question
requires the examinee identify which concept best describes this
pattern ("social mobility"). Other questions require examinees to
identify which theory (e.g., functionalism, conflict theory, symbolic interactionism) best describes a given relationship or pattern.
Interestingly, although the format differed, the MFT and MCAT
both assessed examinees' familiarity with many of the same theories and concepts that are typically taught in introductory sociology courses.

Future Assessments

The MFT and MCAT clearly have some strengths. Both assessments identify some key content areas and skills that overlap with
our proposed Sociological Literacy Framework. Numerous items
on these assessments measure whether students possess core knowledge (in the form of major theories and basic methodology), and
they also assess the breadth of student learning across several major
subfields in the discipline. The MFT and MCAT both have items
that are well suited to measure fundamental skills and knowledge

that should be taught in an introductory sociology course, and each exam could be a useful starting point for a new assessment designed for that purpose.

However, both assessments also share several important weaknesses and limitations, particularly when we consider assessing learning within the major. First, neither assessment adequately measures the ability of test takers to *reason sociologically*. Most questions on the MFT are recall questions that measure a student's background knowledge; students are rarely asked to apply the theories and knowledge that they have learned to solve intellectual problems using a sociological perspective. Several sociology faculty on the MCL panel expressed concern that the MFT is too driven by specific content and uses too much specialized technical language (jargon). For example, the *Brown* question on the MFT could be reworked to measure whether students can think sociologically about *how change happens* in societies. Students who can apply different sociological theories to make sense of *Brown's* impact on society and can incorporate the role of institutions, social structure, culture, and human agency in an explanation of social change are demonstrating sociological reasoning. Future assessments of student learning must allow examinees an opportunity to demonstrate these important abilities. Second, the MFT and MCAT do a very poor job of measuring the depth and specialized character of students' sociological skills and knowledge. Consequently, neither assessment is well suited toward measuring how much sociology majors learn within the major. The MCAT is fairly well aligned to the curriculum for an introductory sociology course and consequently does not provide many opportunities for students to demonstrate the depth of their learning. The MFT includes material that might be learned in some advanced and specialized courses, but these questions typically involve the basic recall of information (e.g., the *Brown* and bystander effect questions), and they do not provide students with an opportunity to demonstrate the overall breadth and depth of their knowledge.

Finding a good balance between the breadth and depth of student learning is important, particularly in a broad field like sociology, where the curriculum and required coursework for the major can vary greatly across departments. The large diversity of subfields and specialty areas within the discipline can be viewed by some as posing a major challenge in developing a valid assessment of learning outcomes among sociology majors. The American Sociological Association, for example, currently has fifty-two sections, each of which is organized around the substantive interests of its members. However, even the largest sociology departments struggle to teach courses in more than a small minority of these areas. In addition, undergraduate majors commonly take specialized courses in several different areas. Thus, although sociology majors are learning *essential* concepts and competencies, they also are learning *specialized* knowledge and skills that will be difficult to measure with a standardized assessment. Recognizing this challenge, we argue that we do not need to measure—and could never measure—everything students learn. What we need and want to measure are the essential concepts and competencies that are found in all fields and subfields of sociology (e.g., the concepts and competencies that we articulate in the Sociological Literacy Framework).

We propose five ways to move beyond the limitations of current assessments of learning in sociology. First, a valid assessment for measuring learning within the major should be designed to cover content that is normally presented in courses that are required in most typical undergraduate programs: introductory sociology, sociological theory, research methods, and statistics. Key concepts, theories, skills, and knowledge that should be mastered in these four courses should be identified and incorporated into the new assessment. Since the MFT and MCAT cover some of this material, both of these assessments serve as useful building blocks for a new assessment. However, an improved assessment should require that students demonstrate that they can *apply* their knowledge and skills to solve sociological problems. Both multiple-choice questions and written essays can evaluate students' abilities as sociological problem solvers.

Second, a new assessment of sociological learning should include an essay or open-ended component that would provide flexibility in allowing students to demonstrate the depth of their learning and the more specialized knowledge that they have acquired. Written responses also would allow students to demonstrate their ability to reason sociologically as described above. Indeed, many of the MCL Sociology faculty panelists favored the essay format of the Collegiate Learning Assessment (CLA) because it emphasizes problem solving, synthesizing information, and constructing an argument using critical thinking skills. Wagenaar (2004b, 233) also advocates for an essay-type of assessment instrument over a multiple-choice instrument because it would better assess "the integrated nature of the ideal sociology curriculum more fully and accurately, testing in a more authentic manner students' abilities to think sociologically." A sociology assessment would have to be focused centrally on sociological problems and questions. For example, examinees could be provided with an essay prompt regarding changes in gender inequality in the United States during the 20th century. The prompt could be structured so that it is possible for students to use different theories and content knowledge in their response. A student who has expertise in social movements could build an argument using theories and research from that area, while another who has expertise in the family could use a different perspective on the same question.

The main disadvantages of including open-ended responses in an assessment are increased costs for the training and labor to grade each response, issues related to ensuring high levels of intercoder reliability, and the length of time required for students to take the assessment. Administering the written component of the assessment to only a subsample of examinees could reduce these costs. In developing a new assessment tool, assessment designers also should pay close attention to the correlation between the subscores for multiple-choice and essay responses. Even though our intuition is that essay responses measure different knowledge and skills than multiple-choice questions, it is an open question that can and should be addressed with empirical analyses of data.

Third, although a new assessment should measure essential knowledge and skills for all students, customizable test modules could measure the depth of students' knowledge in specific sub-areas, based on departmental areas of strength and specialization. For example, a department that has an area of emphasis in the sociology of culture (or perhaps has a concentration or required course work in that area) could select a culture module for inclusion in the assessment. This module would have a greater number of questions in the subfield of cultural sociology, and it would measure students' specialized knowledge within this area. The modular approach would enable departments to better align the assessment with their course offerings and enhance the sensitivity of the measurement instrument to the depth of student learning.

Fourth, the MCL Sociology faculty panel agreed that future assessments of learning in sociology should measure *growth* in student knowledge and abilities. Therefore, any new assessment should allow for valid comparisons between pretest and posttest scores. For the introductory course, comparable scores at the beginning and end of the course are needed, whereas for the major, students' knowledge should be assessed after declaring the major and then again upon completing the major. The focus on test score gains makes it especially important to create assessments that account for possible floor and ceiling effects. In particular, the posttests for the introductory course and the major should differ in both content and difficulty since we expect that students will learn much more in the major than in the introductory course.

Fifth, the American Association for Higher Education has argued that we need to think about learning and assessment as multifactorial processes (Astin et al. 1992; Pike 2014). Therefore, we advocate measuring student learning at multiple points in the teaching process and utilizing several instruments of assessment. We also want these tools to help foster active learning among our students. The MCL Sociology faculty panel similarly agreed that a new assessment should serve the best interests of faculty and students, and not lead to faculty teaching to the test in college classrooms. Several panelists argued that the primary purpose of a new instrument should be to improve teaching and learning. If that is the case, departments might be a more appropriate unit of analysis than the individual student. The unit of analysis is an important issue to consider in designing the assessment because it has implications for how the test is designed. In other words, if student level data are not needed, matrix sampling could be used to create a test with greater breadth, higher reliability, and a lower overall burden on each examinee.

Conclusion

For many years, sociologists have debated important questions regarding teaching and learning in our discipline: What features of our discipline are distinctive from other social sciences? What skills and knowledge should our students be learning? How can we best measure how much our students are learning? Our review of the literature and our discussions with the MCL Sociology faculty panel strongly suggest that, as a discipline, we have made significant progress toward answering these questions. Our goals in this white paper have been to document this progress and to suggest how sociology can move forward as a discipline in establishing a shared framework to articulate learning outcomes and devising valid assessments to measure these outcomes.

After reviewing the research literature on the sociology curriculum, we found substantial overlap in the numerous typologies that describe what students in an introductory course and sociology majors should be learning. The Sociological Literacy Framework is a synthesis of these prior efforts that succinctly

summarizes five essential concepts and six essential competencies that can be introduced to sociology students in introductory
courses, reinforced in other classes, and mastered by sociology
majors. It is designed to be a flexible tool for faculty as they design
their courses and continually revise and rethink curricula for the
major. Indeed, the framework is a starting point for deeper conversations among faculty within sociology programs and departments regarding learning outcomes and how they can devise and
arrange curricular offerings that are aligned with those outcomes.
The Sociological Literacy Framework also can serve as a useful
resource for test makers, external reviewers, and accrediting bodies. The framework should not be used by any of these entities
as a checklist, but instead we hope it will be a useful anchor for
understanding the choices that departments have made in setting
learning outcomes for students.

There have been many efforts to describe the foundational
knowledge and competencies that sociology students should be
learning, but there has been less discussion and progress regarding
how instructors, departments, researchers, and professional organizations (e.g., the American Sociological Association) can measure the knowledge and skills that sociology students are learning.
Assessment can serve many different purposes. Every year, students
in thousands of courses are assessed by their instructors for the purpose of assigning letter grades. Instructors have been tremendously
creative in devising course-embedded assessments to measure their
students' intellectual growth during a semester (Diamond 2008;
Lowry et al. 2005; Persell and Mateiro 2014). These local assessments are essential ingredients to successful teaching because
they define for students the content and skills that they should be
learning. They also provide direct feedback to students regarding
their progress toward meeting those goals. However, these course-
embedded assessments are not well suited for the broader goals
of measuring variation in student learning across classes, across
and between departments, and over time. This statement is not

a critique of these assessments; they were not created with those purposes in mind, nor should they have been.

This white paper has shown that sociology lacks an assessment that adequately measures students' progress toward mastering the essential concepts and competencies that we describe in the Sociological Literacy Framework. Although a standardized assessment should be only one of several tools that departments use to measure student learning (Lowry et al. 2005), it is a weighty and necessary tool that can allow departments to compare their progress with their peers and to their students' performance in past years. Departments can benefit from a valid and reliable standardized assessment tool, and researchers can also use this instrument to measure factors that are correlated with student learning in postsecondary education. It also would allow them to measure, for example, whether discipline-specific knowledge and skills in the field of sociology have long-term effects on labor market, civic, and other adult outcomes. Finally, the American Sociological Association also can use data from such an assessment to evaluate how well the discipline is serving its undergraduate population.

We reviewed the two most widely administered standardized assessments in sociology—the ETS Major Field Test and the Psychological, Social, and Biological Foundations of Behavior section of the MCAT—and described their strengths and limitations. We argued that a new assessment instrument is needed, and made specific recommendations regarding how such an assessment should be designed. In our view, students must be allowed to demonstrate both the depth and breadth of their learning. This objective is a great challenge given the breadth of topics covered and methodologies used in sociology. However, we believe that these challenges are surmountable, and we hope that future research can identify concrete strategies for resolving these tensions.

We close by encouraging sociology faculty and teachers to consider Fazzino's argument (2014) for *passionate pedagogy*—teaching that demonstrates an emotional transparency about the love of teaching, or what Van Auken (2012) calls *intellectual excitement*. Sociology is a prominent and exciting subject to teach, and we should convey our passion for our discipline to our students. Our aim is that the proposed Sociological Literacy Framework helps instructors and departments build rigor, coherence, and continuity into their courses and curriculum and that new assessments can measure students' growth toward mastering the learning outcomes that are central to our discipline.

References

Abbott, Andrew. 2000. "Reflections on the Future of Sociology." *Contemporary Sociology* 29, no. 2: 296–300.

American Association for the Advancement of Science (AAAS). 2011. *Vision and Change in Undergraduate Biology Education: A Call to Action*. Washington, DC: AAAS Press.

American Association of Medical Colleges (AAMC). 2015. "What's on the MCAT 2015 Exam? Psychological, Social, and Biological Foundations of Behavior." https://www.aamc.org/students/ download/374014/data/mcat2015-psbb.pdf

American Sociological Association. 2013. "Sociology Companion Document for the C3 Framework." Pages 73–76 in *College, Career, and Civic Life: C3 Framework for Social Studies State Standards*. Washington, DC: American Sociological Association.

American Sociological Association. 2015. "ASA National Standards for High School Sociology." Washington, DC: American Sociological Association.

ASA Task Force on a College Level Introduction to Sociology Course. 2008. "College-Level Sociology Curriculum for Introduction to Sociology." Washington, DC: American Sociological Association.

Association of American Colleges. 1985. *Integrity in the College Curriculum*. Washington, DC: Association of American Colleges.

Astin, Alexander W., Trudy W. Banta, K. Patricia Cross, Elaine El-Khawas, Peter T. Ewell, Pat T. Hutchings, Theodore J. Marchese, Kay M. McClenney, Marcia Mentkowski, Margaret A. Miller, E. Thomas Moran, and Barbara D. Wright. 2003, 1992. "Principles of Good Practice for Assessing Student Learning." *AAHE Bulletin* 45 (4).

Atkinson, Maxine P., and Kathleen S. Lowney. 2014. *In the Trenches: Teaching and Learning Sociology*. New York: W.W. Norton.

Babbie, Earl. 1990. "The Essential Wisdom of Sociology." *Teaching Sociology* 18, no. 4: 526–30.

Bain, Ken. 2004. *What the Best College Teachers Do*. Cambridge, MA: Harvard University Press.

Berger, Peter L. 1963. *Invitation to Sociology: A Humanistic Perspective*. Garden City, NY: Doubleday.

Berheide, Catherine White. 2005. "Searching for Structure: Creating Coherence in the Sociology Curriculum." *Teaching Sociology* 33, no. 1: 1–15.

Calhoun, Craig, Ed. 2007. *Sociology in America: A History*. Chicago: University of Chicago Press.

Charon, Joel M. 2013. *Ten Questions: A Sociological Perspective*, 8th ed. Belmont, CA: Wadsworth/Cengage.

Collins, Randall. 1998. "The Sociological Eye and Its Blinders." *Contemporary Sociology* 27, no. 1: 2–7.

Curtis, John W. 2015. "Bachelor's Degrees in Sociology, 1987–2013." Unpublished table compiled for the American Sociological Association. Washington, DC: American Sociological Association.

D'Antonio, William. 1983. "Nibbling at the Core." *Teaching Sociology* 10, no. 2: 169–85.

Davis, James A. 1983. "Five Well-Established Research Results That I Think Are Probably True, Teaching in Introductory Sociology, and Worth Teaching." *Teaching Sociology* 10, no. 2: 186–209.

Diamond, Robert M. 2008. *Designing and Assessing Courses and Curricula: A Practical Guide*, 3rd ed. San Francisco, CA: John Wiley and Sons, Inc.

DiMaggio, Paul. 1997. "Epilogue." In *Sociological Visions*, edited by Kai Erikson, 185–215. Lanham, MD: Rowman and Littlefield.

Duncan, Arne. 2015. "Toward a New Focus on Outcomes in Higher Education." Press release of Secretary Arne Duncan's Speech at the University of Maryland-Baltimore County by Department of Education, July 27.

Eagan, Kevin, Jennifer B. Lozano, Sylvia Hurtado, and Matthew H. Case. 2013. *The American Freshman: National Norms—Fall 2013*. Los Angeles, CA: Higher Education Research Institute, UCLA.

Eberts, Paul, Carla B. Howery, Catherine W. Berheide, Kathleen Crittenden, Robert Davis, Zelda Gamson, and Theodore C. Wagenaar. 1991. *Liberal Learning and the Sociology Major: A Report to the Profession*. Washington, DC: American Sociological Association.

Educational Testing Service (ETS). 2003. "Major Field Test in Sociology: Sample Questions." https://www.ets.org/Media/Tests/MFT/pdf/mft_samp_questions_sociology.pdf

Educational Testing Service (ETS). 2012. "Major Field Test in Sociology: Test Description." https://www.ets.org/s/mft/pdf/mft_testdesc_sociology_4imf.pdf

Educational Testing Service (ETS). 2014. "2014 Major Field Test Comparative Data Guide: Major Field Test for Sociology." https://www.ets.org/s/mft/pdf/acdg_sociology.pdf

Erikson, Kai. 1997. "Prologue: Sociology as a Perspective." In *Sociological Visions*, edited by Kai Erikson, 3–16. Lanham, MD: Rowman and Littlefield.

Fazzino, Lori L. 2014. "Passionate Pedagogy and Sociology." *Teaching/Learning Matters*, Newsletter of the American Sociological Association Section on Teaching and Learning, Spring.

Fink, L. Dee. 2003. *Creating Significant Learning Experiences: An Integrated Approach to Designing College Courses*. San Francisco: Jossey-Bass.

Goldsmid, Charles A., and Everett K. Wilson. 1980. *Passing on Sociology: The Teaching of a Discipline*. Washington, DC: American Sociological Association.

Greenwood, Nancy A., Carol A. Jenkins, and Diane Pike. 2014. "Toward Developing a Core Content in Introductory Sociology: Ideas for Building Consensus within the Discipline." Session 82. Midwest Sociological Society Meeting, April 3-6, 2014. Omaha, Nebraska.

Greenwood, Nancy A., and Jay R. Howard. 2011. *First Contact: Teaching and Learning in Introductory Sociology*. Lanham, MD: Rowman and Littlefield Publishers.

Hart Research Associates. 2013. *It Takes More than a Major: Employer Priorities for College Learning and Student Success.* Washington, DC: AAC&U.

Hillsman, Sally T., and Margaret Weigers Vitullo. 2014. "Comments on First Draft of White Paper." Unpublished notes.

Howard, Jay R. 2010. "Where Are We and How Did We Get Here? A Brief Examination of the Past, Present, and Future of the Teaching and Learning Movement in Sociology." *Teaching Sociology* 38: 81–92.

Howard, Jay R., Katherine Novak, Krista M. C. Cline, and Marvin B. Scott. 2014. "Another Nibble at the Core: Student Learning in a Thematically-Focused Introductory Sociology Course." *Teaching Sociology* 42: 177–186.

Jenkins, Carol. A. 2014. "The 'Core'—Introduction to Sociology at a Community College." Paper presented at the Midwest Sociological Society meetings in Omaha, NE, April 3–6.

Kain, Ed. 2013. Handout from "Teaching the Core of Sociology—or Not! What Should Introductory Students Know?" ASA Annual Meeting, New York City, August.

Keith, Bruce, and Morten G. Ender. 2004. "The Sociological Core: Conceptual Patterns and Idiosyncrasies in the Structure and Content of Introductory Sociology Textbooks, 1940–2000." *Teaching Sociology* 32, no. 1: 19–36.

LEAP. 2015. "LEAP at a Glance" handout. Washington, DC: Association of American Colleges and Universities.

Lenski, Gerhard. 1983. "Rethinking the Introductory Sociology Course." *Teaching Sociology* 10, no. 2: 153–168.

Lowry, Janet Huber, Carla B. Howery, John P. Myers, Harry Perlstadt, Caroline Hodges Persell, Diane Pike, Charles H. Powers, Shirley A. Scritchfield, Cynthia M. Siemsen, Barbara Trepagnier, Judith Ann Warner, and Gregory L. Weiss. 2005. *Creating an Effective Assessment Plan for the Sociology Major.* Report of the ASA Task Force on Assessing the Undergraduate Sociology Major. Washington, DC: American Sociological Association.

McKeever, Matthew. 2014. "Comments on First Draft of White Paper." Unpublished notes.

McKinney, Kathleen, Carla B. Howery, Kerry J. Strand, Edward L. Kain, and Catherine White Berheide. 2004. *Liberal Learning and the Sociology Major Updated: Meeting the Challenge of Teaching Sociology in the Twenty-First Century*. Washington, D.C.: American Sociological Association.

Persell, Caroline Hodges, and Antonio E. Mateiro. 2014. "Assessing Strategies for Teaching Key Sociological Understandings." In *The Scholarship of Teaching and Learning in and Across Disciplines*, edited by Kathleen McKinney, 114–131. Bloomington: University of Indiana Press.

Persell, Caroline Hodges, Kathryn M. Pfeiffer, and Ali Syed. 2007. "What Should Students Understand after Taking Introduction to Sociology?" *Teaching Sociology* 35: 300–314.

Quality Assurance Agency for Higher Education (QAA). 2007. *Subject Benchmark Statement for Sociology*. Gloucester, UK: QAA.

Reinharz, Shulamit. 1986. Book review of *Teaching Sociology: The Quest of Excellence*, edited by Frederick L. Campbell, Hubert M. Blalock, and Reece McGee. *Journal of Higher Education* 57, no. 4: 445–448.

Schwartz, Michael, and R. Tyson Smith. 2010. "Beyond the Core: The Hot Topic(al) Alternative to the Survey-Based Introduction to Sociology Course." *American Sociologist* 41, no. 3: 249–276.

Sweet, Stephen, Kevin McElrath, and Edward L. Kain. 2014. "The Coordinated Curriculum: How Institutional Theory Can Be Used to Catalyze Revision of the Sociology Major." *Teaching Sociology* 42: 287–297.

Szafran, Robert. 1996. "The Reliability and Validity of the Major Field Test in Measuring the Learning of Sociology." *Teaching Sociology* 24: 92–96.

Taylor, Paul, Kim Parker, Richard Fry, D'Vera Cohn, Wendy Wang, Gabriel Velasco, and Daniel Dockterman. 2011. *Is College Worth It? College Presidents, Public Assess, Value, Quality, and Mission of Higher Education*. Report of the Pew Research Center. Washington, DC: Pew Social & Demographic Trends.

The Australian Sociological Association (TASA). 2012. "Sociology: Threshold Learning Outcomes." Hawthorne, Victoria: Australian Sociological Association.

Van Auken, Paul. 2012. "Maybe It's Both of Us: Engagement and Learning." *Teaching Sociology* 41, no. 2: 207–215.

Wagenaar, Theodore C. 1991. "Goals for the Discipline?" *Teaching Sociology* 19, no. 1: 92–95.

Wagenaar, Theodore C. 2004a. "Is There a Core in Sociology: Results from a Survey." *Teaching Sociology* 32, no. 1: 1–18.

Wagenaar, Theodore C. 2004b. "Assessing Sociological Knowledge: A First Try." *Teaching Sociology* 32, no. 2: 232–238.

Wagenaar, Theodore C., Bruce Keith, and Morten G. Ender, Eds. 2004. Special Issue on the Core in Sociology. *Teaching Sociology* 32, no. 1: 1–42.

Zipp, John. 2013. "Approaching a Common Core in Sociology." Draft document presented at the ASA Annual Meeting in New York City, August 9–12.

5

Measuring College Learning in Communication

Nancy Kidd
National Communication Association

Trevor Parry-Giles
National Communication Association

Steven A. Beebe
Texas State University

W. Bradford Mello
Saint Xavier University[1]

This contribution focuses on learning outcomes and assessment in the discipline of communication. Building on a history of the discipline, as well as some more recent efforts to articulate learning outcomes for students of communication, the authors describe a set of five essential concepts (social construction, relationality, strategy, symbolism, and

[1] The authors thank the other members of the MCL Communication faculty panel (Walid Afifi, University of Iowa; Timothy Barney, University of Richmond; Pat Ganer, Cyprus College; Joseph Mazer, Clemson University; Kevin Meyer, Illinois State University; and Ken Sereno, University of Southern California), LaKesha Anderson, Lynn Disbrow, Wendy Fernando, Jon Hess, David Marshall, Paul Schrodt, and Meg Tucker for their helpful feedback on drafts of this paper.

adaptability) and seven essential competencies (engage in communication inquiry; create messages appropriate to the audience, purpose, and context; critically analyze messages; demonstrate self-efficacy; apply ethical communication principles and practices; utilize communication to embrace difference; and influence public discourse). Following a discussion of essential concepts and competencies, the authors present an overview of existing learning outcomes assessments in communication and articulates a vision for the future of assessment in the discipline.

Introduction

In November 1914, on an unseasonably warm Chicago day, seventeen speech teachers voted to formally sever ties with the National Council of Teachers of English and form their own association, the National Association of Academic Teachers of Public Speaking.[2] In so doing, these teachers declared that the study and teaching of communication was distinct from other disciplines, deserving of its own institutional and intellectual legitimacy as a discipline within the context of American higher education. Over the next century, this vision flourished; communication is now firmly established as a course of both undergraduate and graduate study in colleges and universities across the United States and around the world. At its foundation, communication focuses on how people use messages to generate meanings within and across various contexts and is the discipline that studies all forms, modes, media, and consequences of communication through humanistic, social scientific, and aesthetic inquiry.

The academic study of communication dates back centuries. For the ancients, communication was the study of rhetoric—the art of persuading others through public speaking and oratory; they

---

[2] After several interim name changes, the National Association of Academic Teachers of Public Speaking is now the National Communication Association.

believed that understanding rhetoric was critical for every citizen's education. As the ancient Greek rhetorician Isocrates wrote in his famous *Antidosis*, "Because there has been implanted in us the power to persuade each other and to make clear to each other whatever we desire, not only have we escaped the life of wild beasts, but we have come together and founded cities and made laws and invented arts; and, generally speaking, there is no institution devised by man which the power of speech has not helped us to establish." Throughout many centuries of rhetorical study as a liberal art, Isocrates's words have served as an enduring reminder of the power of communication, and the contemporary academic discipline of communication continues to promote its effective and ethical practice.

The classical study of rhetoric as a liberal art migrated to U.S. colleges and universities; Harvard University has long had an endowed chair in rhetoric and oratory (the Boylston Chair), for example, and one of the first professors in that position, John Quincy Adams, authored a two-volume collection of *Lectures on Rhetoric and Oratory* in 1810. The development of the communication discipline in the United States owes much to this classical tradition. The mid-20th-century expansion and evolution of the discipline, furthermore, owes much to the emergent interest in the social sciences that flowered in the post–World War II period. Perplexed by the power of communication to move entire populations toward fascism and violence in Europe and Asia, communication scholars turned to social scientific methods as a means to understand audiences and message effects. As the research focus of some communication scholars shifted, so, too, did the curriculum in many communication departments. Joining the courses in public speaking, British and American public address, rhetorical theory, radio speaking, and the like were new offerings in interpersonal communication, mass communication effects, and persuasion and social influence. Along with studies of great orators and their rhetoric, graduate students began producing dissertations that experimentally tested the power and reach of mass-mediated communication and that surveyed large audiences for their attitudes toward political communication, for example.

Amid all of these disciplinary and scholarly changes, communication scholars and teachers retained their appreciation for the role and influence of communication across all aspects of public and private life. They continue to embrace the ubiquity of communication and are mindful of the inherent value of communication to meaningful citizenship. Emerging from the democratic impulse embodied in 19th- and 20th-century progressivism, this is the pedagogical foundation of the discipline. Communication cuts across contexts and situations; it is the relational and collaborative force that strategically constructs the social world. Knowledge and understanding of communication and strong communication skills allow people to create and maintain interpersonal relationships; employers in all sectors seek employees with strong communication skills; and society needs effective communicators to support productive civic activity in communities.[3]

Historical Perspectives on Learning Outcomes in Communication

Emerging as it did from programs in English literature and criticism, early efforts to articulate the discipline's agenda were often responsive to the prevailing disciplinary orthodoxies of the day from the parent discipline. Research efforts in the history and criticism of oratory (as a form of literature), studies of dramatic performance, and studies of speech composition and debate dominated the field,

---

[3] This introductory section is excerpted from *The Role of the Communication Discipline on Campus and Beyond*, a publication of the National Communication Association's Learning Outcomes in Communication project (NCA Copyright © 2015 National Communication Association. All rights reserved.).

alongside work in speech pathology and vocal physiology (Wool-bert 1920). Over the span of the 20th century, the domains of communication research shifted and expanded; research explored the full range of human communication—messages and texts, mass audiences and isolated individuals, public opinion and message effects, media technology and channels of interaction—across contexts broad and narrow in scope. Today, the National Communication Association (NCA) has nearly fifty interest groups defined by the substantive areas of focus of the scholars and teachers who affiliate with them. Typically, these groups reflect the delineation of the scope of the discipline's inquiry: the broad-ranging contexts, channels, media, and practices wherein human beings engage in the symbolic exchange of meaning. At the same time, communication scholars maintain a focus on the *core* of the discipline, or how people create and use messages to generate meanings within and across various contexts.

Scholars of teaching and learning in communication have historically occupied a pivotal place in the discipline, reflective of its genesis in the skilled delivery of important content. "Our profession has a long tradition of valuing instruction as well as research," noted Ruth Anne Clark, one of communication's most dedicated scholars of teaching and learning, "and part of the obligation of being a good instructor is to consider carefully what the students are learning" (2002, 396). Clark argued that "we need to carefully scrutinize our instructional practices and rigorously assess the learning outcomes" (396).

Clark's 21st-century commentary is consistent with the discipline's long-term commitment to teaching and learning and their enhancement. As a newly established discipline in the early 20th century, the primary concern for communication scholars and teachers was the institutional and academic credibility of the discipline's research and teaching. At the time, few institutions housed departments of speech or communication; most instruction in communication was limited to a public speaking course. The first speech teachers, thus, sought to both understand the extent and nature of communication instruction in the United States and sketch out a preliminary sense of what the new major would entail. In 1916, MacLeod published a survey of forty colleges and universities that revealed just seventeen departments with majors in speech around the nation. At the same time, MacLeod's survey identified many speech teachers working in assorted departments to teach an increasing number of speech courses.

By 1932, while speech departments were growing nationwide, "comparatively few institutions so far require Speech courses for graduation," reported Weaver (1932, 611), based on his review of 356 college and university course catalogs. Fewer than half of the colleges and universities studied by Weaver offered a major in speech. Hargis (1950) surveyed 522 course catalogs and discovered that 272 colleges and universities offered a speech major. Students in those majors graduated with course work that was primarily focused on public address and oratory, speech science (or speech pathology), voice and diction, and drama/theater. Seifrit's (1961) duplication of Hargis's study found 303 speech majors across 564 colleges and universities. Courses for the major, according to Seifrit, typically clustered around public address, drama/theater, and speech science. A century after MacLeod conducted her original survey, there are 806 communication departments in colleges and universities around the United States that confer at minimum a bachelor's degree.[4]

Owing to the discipline's foundation in public speaking instruction, an ongoing dilemma for communication scholars of teaching and learning is the bifurcation of instruction between communication skills and communication knowledge/theory. Differentiation of public speaking instruction from other courses in the English

---

[4] In addition, there are currently more than five hundred community colleges nationwide that offer courses and/or degrees in communication, journalism, or related programs.

curriculum required a sensibility about the course that conferred to it academic legitimacy—postsecondary instruction in speech also needed to be meaningfully different from nonacademic speech instruction available from elocutionists and others. As such, early speech teachers debated the proper role of *content* in the public speaking curriculum.

Offering a clear prescription for how to infuse substance into the public speaking curriculum, Hunt argued that "the problem of content . . . should be recognized and dealt with as an integral part of instruction in public speaking" (1922, 256). If the sole province of public speaking is oratorical form and rhetorical organization, Sandford suggested, "public speaking is indeed a provincial field" (1922, 364). Without such a focus on substance, he argued, the public speaking curriculum is bankrupt and students will indulge "the general triviality of speech subjects and the superficial treatment usually accorded to them" (371). James O'Neill, one of the discipline's founders and the first president of NCA, identified this discussion of form versus content as "vital" to the emerging discipline, because the answer to the question would determine "the very existence of courses and departments devoted to the instruction of public speaking" (1923, 26). O'Neill warned against going too far down the path of focusing exclusively on content when he concluded that "they would, apparently, give courses in public speaking for the primary purpose of teaching philosophy and economics—not public speaking" (30). The tension between public speaking as form and the content of public speeches, as it relates to effective teaching and curriculum design, lingers in discussions of learning outcomes in communication.

In 1936, O'Neill penned an article reflecting upon changing circumstances in higher education and the consequences of such changes for speech instruction. The most significant change facing higher education, he remarked, was the "change from emphasis on the dissemination of knowledge, to emphasis on the development of power, ability, attitudes, habits" (1936, 183). Acknowledging this shift, O'Neill concluded, means "the acceptance of the essential philosophy of speech education for the last twenty years in the United States," or that "the great objective of education cannot rightly be expressed in terms of knowledge gained or truth learned, but only in terms of abilities perfected, of powers developed. Real education results not so much in a state of mind as in a habit of mind" (184).

O'Neill's celebration of the pragmatic value of higher education is reflected today in the attempt to articulate, across all disciplines, the essential concepts and competencies that define meaningful learning outcomes. O'Neill did not reject or minimize the importance of knowledge and truth in higher education. Instead, he suggested that knowledge and truth taught solely for their own sake are insufficient for a complete, 20th-century system of higher education. Students and society demand more: "It is not a status arrived at," O'Neill wrote, "but a force generated. Not the knowledge that is learned, but what one can do with knowledge is what counts" (1936, 184). For communication, as with other disciplines, this quest is an existential one; the discipline is defined, essentially, by the concepts and competencies learned by its students, and the discussion about learning outcomes for the communication curriculum has proceeded apace for decades. Clearly defined concepts and competencies for the discipline of communication allow scholars and teachers to articulate the value of the discipline for improving personal, professional, and civic life to a wide range of audiences, from students to parents and from employers to legislators.

One marker of academic and intellectual legitimacy, the early speech teachers believed, was the continued inclusion of speech in the core curriculum of college and universities, required of all students. Part of the rationale for such incorporation relied on an evolving sense of learning outcomes for an individual college graduate; a vision of this evolution was articulated by O'Neill when he suggested that higher education was experiencing "a change of focus from the subject to the student" (1936, 183). O'Neill placed communication at the center of this shift: "Speech activities are the capstone of educational experiences in which activity replaces passivity on the part of the student. Speech activity, in public or in private, is the finished product, the final test of competence, in the use of knowledge" (186).

Echoing the sensibilities toward higher education articulated by O'Neill, the College Committee on Problems of Speech Education, formed by what was then called the National Association of Teachers of Speech (now NCA), sought to provide guidance for speech teachers as they planned curriculum and taught classes. As reported by Anderson (1943), speech programs ought to achieve certain learning outcomes: (a) teach students to think by teaching them to "face facts," organize thought, reason logically, and research facts thoroughly; (b) improve the social attitudes of students by provoking a sense of civic responsibility, by participating in local and civic events, and by achieving emotional balance; (c) broaden and intensify appreciation of speech as a social force and of the ethical dimensions of speech; (d) teach the rhetorical, psychological, and physiological theories of speech; and (e) direct the development of visible and audible techniques of speech through instruction in articulation, diction, and so on. These learning outcomes offer an initial foray by a core group of speech faculty to respond to the pressing demands of the time, to "help a teacher in any type of college face and think through the fundamental problems involved in providing the most effective Speech program" (354).

Noting that World War II "precipitated a veritable downpour of books and articles dealing with education," a Harvard University committee issued a 1945 report entitled "General Education in a Free Society." The report was widely circulated and contained a lengthy section highlighting the value and importance of communication for general education. The report identifies four main characteristics for effective general education: "to think effectively, to communicate thought, to make relevant judgments, to discriminate among values" (Harvard Committee 1945, 65). Within older higher education curricula, the committee noted, "rhetoric was a normal part of the curriculum." "Rhetoric to us suggests oratory," the report continued, "and today we are suspicious of or at least indifferent to oratory. Yet the art of rhetoric meant the simple skill of making one's ideas clear and cogent; it did not necessarily mean high-flown speeches" (68). As if to resurrect communication and its place in general education, the committee concluded that "language needs to be neither high learning nor high literature in order to be communication. What we have in mind is the language of the businessman writing a plain and crisp letter, of a scientist making a report, of a citizen asking straight questions, of human beings arguing together on some matter of common interest" (69). Communication scholars took note of this set of learning outcomes for the discipline and offered analyses of the role of communication in general education in light of the Harvard report, concluding, as Hunt did, that the report offered "a new background for our demand for the good man skilled in speaking" (Hunt 1949, 276; see also Harrington 1952; Klapper et al.1949).

The midcentury focus on effective teaching and curricular design intensified as communication programs witnessed tremendous growth in the post–World War II years. Such growth accompanied the expansion of both higher education in general and the focus and purpose of the discipline's research. One initiative, introduced as a resolution at the 1957 Speech Association of America (now NCA) convention, called for a standardized curriculum to be accredited by the organization for all speech programs. Skinner (1961) reported that, based on a national survey, almost 70 percent of department chairs opposed such a standardized curriculum. Conferences about the nature and scope of the discipline, in rhetoric and the social sciences, respectively, which were held in the late 1960s and early 1970s, reflected the concerns about a standardized curriculum. Both the Wingspread Conference about the prospects of rhetorical study (Bitzer and

Black 1971) and the New Orleans Conference (Kibler and Barker 1969) about the conceptual frontiers of social scientific study in Communication, though mostly focused on research and graduate education, argued for a broader, more inclusive vision for the discipline and for the courses and material that members of the discipline taught. More than a decade later, a more narrowly defined task force offered guidelines for curricula and program design for speech and theater teacher education programs. These guidelines also were articulated as what would now be called learning outcomes; the first guidelines urged that programs develop curricula to allow a student "to develop personal communication skills and theater performance competencies and attitudes in order to become a facilitator of learning" (Joint Task Force of the Speech Communication Association and American Theatre Association 1975, 354).

Discussions of curriculum and program design in communication and other disciplines throughout the mid-20th century culminated in the National Taxonomy Project, which sought to "provide a classification of educational subject matter that currently exists from pre-elementary through post-doctoral studies" (McBath and Jeffrey 1978, 182). This project, begun in 1975, was conducted by the National Center for Education Statistics. By 2000, it culminated in the Department of Education's *Classification of Instructional Programs* (CIP). Communication Studies was defined in the CIP as "a program that focuses on the scientific, humanistic, and critical study of human communication in a variety of formats, media, and contexts" (U.S. Department of Education 2000, III–32).[5]

---

[5] In contrast, Communications Technologies programs were defined as "[i]nstructional programs that prepare individuals to function as equipment operators, support technicians, and operations managers in the film/video, recording, and graphic communications industries" (U.S. Department of Education 2000, III-36).

By century's end, scholars of teaching and learning in communication focused primarily on conceptualizing effective learning outcomes in two realms: the introductory, general education course in communication and the development of "communication competency" among communication majors. A 2015 survey found that the vast majority of colleges and universities across the United States require some form of the introductory course in communication (Morreale, Myers, Backlund, and Simonds). That translates into an estimated 1.3 million students in the United States taking one of these courses each year (Beebe 2013). Over the span of several decades, via various conferences, task forces, and seminars, communication scholars and teachers articulated and delineated a series of skill-based competencies for college and university students, often in conjunction with national educational assessment efforts. Most of the skills derived from these efforts found delivery to college students via the introductory communication course, whereas some other skills, labeled as "advanced," are taught to students in the communication major, usually in advanced public speaking courses or in courses on small group communication, discussion and debate, interviewing, or conflict resolution. These initiatives and the skill-based competencies they generated are detailed in an NCA publication, *Speaking and Listening Competencies for College Students* (Morreale, Rubin, and Jones 1998). The growth and refinement of the introductory course prompted the formation of a task force in 2013 charged with delineating the core competencies expected as learning outcomes from the course (Engleberg, Disbrow, Katt, Myers, O'Keefe, and Ward 2013). The Engleberg et al. work was an extension of the efforts from the late 20th and early 21st centuries to demarcate a clear sense of learning outcomes for the general education communication course.

The other domain of contemporary discussions of learning outcomes in communication focuses on the development of "communication competency" in students, particularly at the upper levels of communication course work and within the communication major. Drawn primarily from the work of Spitzberg (1983, 2000, 2006), communication competence is based on a learner's possession of three things: knowledge, motivation, and skill. These three components of competent communication mirror the three domains of learning: cognitive, affective, and behavioral learning. For communication to be "competent" in each of the three learning domains, it should be effective, appropriate, satisfying, and efficient; evidence verisimilitude (fidelity or accurate understanding); and achieve the intended task.

Alongside the focus on the communication major and the development of communication competence, the 2000 Hope College Conference released a report on the preferred curriculum for the communication major. This report delineated eight competencies to emerge from the communication major: (a) understanding of multiple theoretical perspectives and diverse intellectual underpinnings in communication as reflected in its philosophy or history; (b) competency in effective communication with diverse others; (c) competency in presentation, preferably in more than one format; (d) competency in analysis and interpretation of contemporary media; (e) competency in reflective construction and analysis of arguments and discourse intended to influence beliefs, attitudes, values, and practices; (f) competency in systematic inquiry (the process of asking questions and systematically attempting to answer them, and understanding the limitations of the conclusions reached); (g) competency in analysis and practice of ethical communication; and (h) competency in human relational interaction (Report of the Hope College Conference 2000).

The NCA's 2015 Learning Outcomes in Communication (LOC) project, funded by Lumina Foundation, was driven by a team of thirty faculty members[6] from diverse institutions around the country who were charged with answering the question, "What should a student with a communication degree know, understand, and be able to do?" using "Tuning." Tuning "is a process by which faculty in different fields of study determine discipline-specific desired learning outcomes for their subject area through consultations with one another, colleagues on other campuses, students, alumni, and employers" (Institute for Evidence-Based Change 2015). Tuning involves a set of iterative steps including identifying essential learning outcomes, mapping career pathways, consulting stakeholders, honing core competencies and learning outcomes, and implementing locally (Lumina Foundation 2015b). It is an open process,

---

[6] The following group has worked together on this project from 2013 to the present: Betsy Bach, University of Montana; Philip Backlund, Central Washington University; Timothy Ball, James Madison University; Kristen Berkos, Bryant University; David Bodary, Sinclair Community College; Jonathan Bowman, University of San Diego; Leila Brammer, Gustavus Adolphus College; Timothy J. Brown, West Chester University; Kerry Byrnes, Collin College; Theresa Castor, University of Wisconsin–Parkside; Melissa Chastain, Spalding University; Rebecca Curnalia, Youngstown State University; Deanna Dannels, North Carolina State University; Lynn Disbrow, Huntingdon College; Qingwen Dong, University of the Pacific; John Frederick, University of North Carolina–Charlotte; Elizabeth Goering, Indiana University–Purdue University Indianapolis; Kandace Harris, Clark Atlanta University; Patricia Hernandez, California Baptist University; Brad Love, University of Texas at Austin; Jimmie Manning, Northern Illinois University; Chad McBride, Creighton University; W. Bradford Mello, Saint Xavier University; Claire Procopio, Southeastern Louisiana University; Armeda Reitzel, Humboldt State University; Mary Toale, State University of New York–Oswego; Shawn Wahl, Missouri State University; Sara Weintraub, Regis College; Cindy White, University of Colorado–Boulder; and Kesha Morant Williams, The Pennsylvania State University–Berks. David Marshall, Associate Director, Tuning USA at the Institute for Evidence-Based Change, expertly facilitated this process.

driven by interaction with and among stakeholders, which broadens discussions while preserving faculty control over the end results. It started in Europe in 2000 and has been used around the world since then. First introduced in the United States in 2009, American Tuning projects thus far have mostly been state based, with only the American Historical Association and NCA engaging in national disciplinary efforts (Lumina Foundation 2015a).

The LOC work is not about accreditation or standards; it is not about administrators or teaching evaluations; and it is not about achieving specific results. It is a faculty-driven effort that is about deep reflection on teaching and learning, with a focus on students. It is designed to prompt thoughtful conversations about curriculum and course development in ways that make sense on individual campuses, with respect both to the discipline itself and to how communication fits into general education. There is no one-size-fits-all implementation strategy for a Tuned discipline. Tuning allows for the clear articulation of what a graduate knows, understands, and is able to do with a degree in a particular discipline to a wide range of stakeholders including students, parents, employers, and campus administrators, among others.

Essential Learning Outcomes for the Communication Major

Process

The communication strand of the Measuring College Learning (MCL) project was carried out concurrently with the complementary LOC Tuning project. The LOC project sought to address the question: What should a student with a communication degree know, understand, and be able to do? The MCL project focused on differentiating between concepts (know and understand) and competencies (do), with an eye toward translating learning outcomes into a measurement and assessment strategy. Like the LOC project, MCL was faculty-driven, but with a smaller team and a less formal process. As the respective conversations converged, it seemed sensible for this white paper to provide an integrated view drawing from the work of both groups of faculty members. To provide an integrated list of essential concepts and competencies for this paper, we mapped the results of both efforts onto each other. The majority of the LOC project's learning outcomes were competencies, and the competencies identified by the MCL faculty panel easily mapped onto the LOC competencies, though the ways they were articulated differed slightly.

The concepts and competencies described in this paper are based on the combined discussions of the LOC and MCL teams. The language is in large part drawn directly from the LOC document; however, it is not identical, and ideas from the MCL faculty panel are fully incorporated. It is important to note that this list is not meant to be fixed or prescriptive. It is meant to prompt thoughtful consideration, with an expectation of revision as appropriate over time and place. This is a starting point for curricular design and, eventually, for measurement.

As articulated, communication scholars and teachers have been carefully considering appropriate learning outcomes for the major since the inception of the discipline. Although this question has certainly led to debate about which specific outcomes best reflect the core of the discipline, there seems to be consensus that, fundamentally, communication is about how people use messages to generate meanings within and across various contexts. With that assumption in mind, a graduate should know, understand, and be able to do the following upon completion of a communication degree.

Concepts: What Should a Communication Graduate Know and Understand?

Social Construction

Communication, as a discipline, is predicated on the theory of knowledge that attends to jointly constructed understandings of the world.

This theory holds that understanding and meaning emerge in coordination with other human beings and is dependent on language as a fundamental system for the construction of meaningful reality.

Relationality

Communication is inherently transactional and collaborative; as a human behavior, to communicate is to engage with others, share meaning, make arguments, speak and listen, and transact together in a state of consubstantiality. A fundamental concept, then, of communication is relationality, or how and why relationships form and are developed among communicating individuals, groups, and audiences.

Strategy

Communication is primarily an intentional activity. The communication graduate knows and understands that competent communication requires strategy and intention. It involves the capacity to read and interpret contexts and situations to readily tailor and develop messages. For centuries, scholars and teachers have theorized strategies for effective, intentional communication, and knowledge of those theories and concepts is essential.

Symbolism

While all disciplines use and involve language and other symbols, symbolism as a concept occupies a core place in communication. Communication graduates study and understand the theories behind the semiotic formation of meaning; they explore the capacity of symbols to socially construct reality, form relationships, and express strategic intention. Symbolism infuses every aspect of the communication transaction.

Adaptability

Immutable truths and certain knowledge do not constitute a palpable dimension of communication study. One concept, though, is immutable—that communication and communicators are adaptable. The knowledge that communication behaviors must change, and the theories that explain such adaptation (e.g., in different contexts, cultures, and communities), are fundamental to the communication discipline.

Competencies: What Should a Communication Graduate Be Able to Do?

Engage in Communication Inquiry

Communication graduates should be able to interpret, evaluate, and apply communication scholarship. They should be able to formulate questions appropriate for communication scholarship and engage in communication scholarship using the research traditions of the discipline. In addition, communication graduates should be able to differentiate between various approaches to the study of communication and contribute to scholarly conversations appropriate to the purpose of inquiry. For example, a communication graduate ought to be able to formulate a communication-based research problem about the impact of social media on the development of family relationships, review the scholarly literature about social media and family relationship formation, explore and select relevant theories and concepts that explain the connections between social media and family dynamics, and offer specific, fully theorized means to study and explain how family communication is influenced by social media use.

Create Messages Appropriate to the Audience, Purpose, and Context

Communication graduates should be able to locate and use information relevant to their audiences, purposes, and contexts, and to select and present messages in creative and appropriate modalities and technologies to accomplish communicative goals. In addition, graduates should be able to adapt messages to the diverse needs of different audiences, adjust messages while in the process of communicating, and critically reflect on their own messages after communication events. For example, a communication graduate ought to be able to examine the particularities of a specific political or social activist campaign, audit preexisting campaign messages, and craft new, adapted, relevant campaign messages that are strategically important for the campaign's success.

Critically Analyze Messages

Communication graduates should be able to identify meanings that are embedded in messages, articulate characteristics of mediated and nonmediated messages, recognize the influence of messages, engage in active listening, and enact mindful responses to messages. For example, when communication graduates encounter a commercial advertisement for a new pharmaceutical, they should be able to explain the verbal and visual content of the ad, recognize the argumentative attempts at persuasion that emerge from the ad, actively and critically engage with both the verbal and visual aspects of the ad, and arrive at a considered, mindful response to the ad that is fully and critically informed.

Demonstrate Self-efficacy

Communication graduates should be able to identify barriers that impede communication self-efficacy and perform verbal and nonverbal communication behaviors that illustrate self-efficacy. Graduates should be able to articulate personal beliefs about abilities to accomplish communication goals and evaluate personal communication strengths and weaknesses. For example, when entering into a new interpersonal friendship, a communication graduate should be able to reflectively examine his or her individualized goals and expected outcomes from the friendship, and to enact communication behaviors that will achieve those goals and outcomes. As the friendship proceeds, deepens, or ends, the communication graduate should be able to explore the communication-based reasons for his or her particular behaviors and attitudes toward the friendship.

Apply Ethical Communication Principles and Practices

Communication graduates should be able to identify ethical perspectives, explain the relevance of those perspectives, and articulate the ethical dimensions of communication situations. Graduates should choose to communicate with ethical intention, propose solutions for (un)ethical communication, and evaluate the ethical elements of a communication situation. For example, a communication graduate confronting a hostile workplace environment should be able to assess his or her own and others' communication behaviors within the context of relevant ethical perspectives. From that assessment, the communication graduate should be able to suggest clear and purposeful communication strategies to resolve or mitigate the ethical dilemmas presented in the workplace environment.

Utilize Communication to Embrace Difference

Communication graduates should be able to articulate the connection between communication and culture, recognize and appreciate individual and cultural similarities and differences, and respect diverse perspectives and the ways they influence communication. Graduates should be able to articulate their own cultural standpoints and how they affect communication and worldviews and to demonstrate the ability to be culturally self-aware and adapt their communication in diverse cultural contexts. For example, if a communication graduate were to volunteer as a host for an international exchange student, he or she would be particularly sensitive to the specific cultural similarities and differences that the host student may experience in the United States. As a host, the communication graduate should embrace and communicate about the value of difference in both verbal and nonverbal ways.

This sensitivity would derive from an understanding of the power of communication for intercultural competence.

Influence Public Discourse

Communication graduates should be able to explain the importance of communication in civic life and identify the challenges facing communities and the role of communication in resolving those challenges. Graduates should be able to frame and evaluate local, national, and global issues from a communication perspective and utilize communication to respond to such issues and advocate for courses of action. Communication graduates should be able to empower individuals to promote human rights, dignity, and freedom. For example, when asked to participate in a public meeting about new zoning requirements for the local community, a communication graduate should be able to use his or her educational background to critically assess and evaluate the message and advocacies that are shared at the public meeting and formulate clear, reasonable arguments reflective of his or her own position on the question at hand.

Relationship between Learning Outcomes for the Major and the Introductory Course

The essential competencies and concepts enumerated for the major echo the core that has been articulated for the introductory course, though typically assessment for the introductory course is more heavily focused on competencies than concepts. The *National Communication Association Core Competencies Task Force Report* (Engleberg et al. 2013) articulated seven core competencies for the introductory course: (a) monitor and present your self; (b) communicate ethically; (c) adapt to others; (d) practice effective listening; (e) express messages; (f) explain communication processes; and (g) create and analyze message strategies. Of course, the level of expectation for successful learning is lower for the completion of the introductory course than it is for the completion of the major.

Relationship between Learning Outcomes for Communication and Other Disciplines/General Education

It is noteworthy that communication is often invoked as a generalized skill that is critical to the success of general education and even to successful student learning in other disciplines. Examples of this abound. In the 1994 *Goals 2000: Educate America Act*, signed into law by President Clinton (H.R. 1804), one of the eight National Education Goals (Sec. 102) is "adult literacy and lifelong learning." Among the six objectives under that goal is to increase the "ability to think critically, communicate effectively, and solve problems." The Association of American Colleges and Universities' Liberal Education and America's Promise (LEAP) initiative is organized around twelve essential learning outcomes that "are best developed by a contemporary liberal education." Written and oral communication is one of those learning outcomes (Rhodes 2010).

Among the five other disciplines working on the MCL project, several implicitly or explicitly include communication as part of their essential learning outcomes. Specifically, the authors of the MCL in economics paper include "ability to communicate economic ideas in diverse collaborations" as an essential learning outcome (Allgood and Bayer 2016) while the others include communication skills as relevant to the achievement of a top level competency. Lumina Foundation's Degree Qualifications Profile (DQP), furthermore, provides reference points for what a graduate should know, understand, and be able to do with associate's, bachelor's, and master's degrees, irrespective of the chosen major. The DQP includes five "essential areas of learning," one of which is "intellectual skills." The intellectual skills category is broken down into six subcategories, one of which is "communicative fluency." Lumina Foundation says "the crosscutting intellectual skills define proficiencies that transcend the boundaries of particular fields of study. They overlap, interact with and enable the other major areas of learning described in the DQP" (Lumina Foundation 2014).

We know of no other discipline that is routinely invoked as a generic skill. In addition to the many important and commonly understood reasons to identify and clearly articulate learning outcomes for any discipline, there seems to be an additional imperative for the discipline of communication. Articulation of student learning outcomes is one way to present the broader picture of the communication discipline and its full range of concepts and competencies. It may be productive to have conversations on campuses and among higher education policymakers about how to align the unidimensional "communication competency" with the broader picture of the discipline. It is critical to ensure that there is an understanding of and appreciation for the theoretical basis and essential concepts of the communication discipline, as well as the skills-based dimensions of communication. In addition, the discipline's competencies are far more multidimensional than what is conveyed with a single "communication competency." With a well-articulated, publicly shared articulation of student learning outcomes in communication, we can ensure robust incorporation of communication into the general education curriculum.[7]

Assessment of Student Learning in Communication

The discipline of communication has a long history of thoughtful consideration about what communication graduates should learn. There is a shorter, but still substantial, history of considering how to assess student learning outcomes in communication that

---

[7] This section is adapted from Nancy Kidd, "Reflecting on Experience: The Heart of NCA's Learning Outcomes in Communication Project," *Spectra* 51, November. Copyright © 2015 National Communication Association. All rights reserved.

began in earnest in the 1970s and continues to this day. These efforts were initially formalized at the institutional level with the creation of the NCA Task Force on Assessment and Testing, which ultimately became the NCA Communication Assessment Division (Backlund, Detwiler, Arneson, and Danielson 2010). Since the 1970s, there have been several conferences on communication assessment, and a series of publications have emerged in part from those conferences.

Written in 1979, *Standards for Effective Oral Communication Programs* was an early call for specific assessment approaches including, for example, the use of multiple sources of data and instruments (American Speech-Language-Hearing Association and Speech Communication Association 1979). A subsequent effort led to *Criteria for Evaluating Instruments and Procedures for Assessing Speaking and Listening* in 1986. Among the criteria articulated are the need to focus on demonstrated skill, avoid cultural bias, use familiar situations for test questions, use questions with a range of acceptable responses, be sensitive to time and cost, and ensure reliability and validity. The participants at a 1987 conference built upon this work and advocated for assessing speaking skills through the content of oral speaking performances and student speaking competencies. They further considered strategies for assessment of student learning for listening, and they discussed issues related to training assessors. At the 1988 Flagstaff Conference, participants called for more proactive efforts to develop standardized assessment tools because past efforts had been problematic in a variety of ways, ranging from poor reliability to poor feasibility to cultural bias (Morreale, Moore, Surges-Tatum, and Webster 2007).

Participants at the 1990 NCA-sponsored National Conference on Assessment listed twenty-five recommended criteria for assessing oral communication related to the content, instruments, procedures, frequency, and use of results. For example, assessment of oral communication should include evaluation of knowledge, skills, and attitudes; verbal and nonverbal communication; and competence in more than one communication setting. Instruments for assessing oral communication should describe degrees of competence. There was agreement that no single assessment instrument would likely meet all of the criteria (Morreale et al. 2007).

Over the last several decades, many assessment tools have been developed, but no single tool comprehensively addresses student learning for the communication major. Most are specialized by context and focused exclusively on assessing performance of competencies. A few illustrative examples follow.

Perhaps the most attention has been paid to evaluation of oral communication skills or public speaking competence. The *Competent Speaker Speech Evaluation Form (CSSEF)* is a valid and reliable standardized instrument for assessing this at the higher education level. Developed in 1990 by a subcommittee of what was then called the NCA Committee on Assessment and Testing (now the Communication Assessment Division), composed of faculty members from twelve campuses, it was the first assessment of its kind. The *CSSEF* articulates eight public speaking competencies, half of which are about preparation and half of which focus on delivery. Three levels of performance are stipulated for each competency for which criteria are specified. Although the authors recognize that knowledge and understanding of concepts might be inferred by the results of the demonstrated behavior, this assessment tool is designed to measure only what one is able to *do*, and only in the context of public speaking.

A more recent effort to assess oral communication skill was undertaken by the Association of American Colleges and Universities through the LEAP initiative. Part of the initiative was the creation of sixteen Valid Assessment of Learning in Undergraduate Education (VALUE) rubrics that align with the LEAP essential learning outcomes. Among them is oral communication,[8] which

---

[8] Also included is written communication, but that is addressed from a disciplinary perspective more closely aligned with English.

focuses on public presentation. Developed by a team of faculty and tested on campuses, the oral communication rubric focuses on five categories for evaluation of a public presentation, including organization, language, delivery, supporting material, and central message. A four-point evaluation scale is used to describe how each level of achievement should appear to evaluators (Rhodes 2010).

First introduced by Spitzberg and Hurt in 1987, the *Conversation Skills Rating Scale (CSRS)* is used to evaluate the effectiveness and appropriateness of communication in the context of interpersonal conversation. This scale uses twenty-five behavioral and five general impression items and has demonstrated validity and reliability. There are five levels of performance, but "it is the philosophy of the assessment approach . . . that competence be considered an inherently socially anchored, evolutionary, and subjective phenomenon" (Spitzberg 2007, 4). Hence, specific performance criteria are not articulated.

An assessment tool for participation in task-oriented small group discussions has also been developed. Beebe, Barge, and McCormick's (1995) *Competent Group Communicator* is an assessment tool that rates student problem-oriented, solution-oriented, discussion-management, and relational competencies in group communication. Criteria for assessing performance of each of ten competencies are provided, with specified expectations for excellent, adequate, inadequate, or not used.

In addition to tools that are designed to assess communication skills in specific contexts, effort has also been made to assess communication apprehension and willingness to communicate. The primary tools to assess each of these were developed by McCroskey. They are written self-reports that have been tested for reliability and validity. Both tests have total scores and context-specific subscores. The *Personal Report of Communication Apprehension-24* focuses on assessing one's fear of communicating with a twenty-four-item test, and *Willingness to Communicate* uses a twenty-item test, twelve of which are scored (McCroskey 2005; Morreale 2007).

More limited measures of communication knowledge have also been developed. These have tended to be more localized. For example, at the University of Minnesota–Crookston, a 100-item multiple-choice WebCT test is completed as a pretest and posttest in the required speech course, and at George Mason University five questions are used across different courses to measure student understanding of communication concepts (Hay and Garland 2010).

A more integrated approach is Spitzberg's (2011) *Interactive Media Package for Assessment of Communication and Critical Thinking (IMPACCT©)*, which is an online survey of communication skills designed for self- and peer-reporting. It combines several assessments, most of which were designed for this purpose, including the Conversational Skills Rating Scale, interpersonal competence, computer-mediated communication competence, group and leadership competence, public speaking competence, and communication quality. This assumes that motivation, knowledge, and skill are relevant to an integrated view of communication competence across contexts. Spitzberg indicates that new competencies can be integrated into IMPACCT© in the future, which seems worthy of consideration as we think through ways to measure the essential learning outcomes described in this white paper.

Although Spitzberg's recent work begins to take a more comprehensive view, this brief illustrative summary of existing assessment tools reveals that we need to think more broadly and systematically about measurement to holistically assess student learning in the communication major. Building on what has been done before, the MCL Communication faculty panel recommends extending efforts to the full range of essential concepts and competencies articulated in this paper and considering these learning outcomes across multiple contexts.

That does not imply that a single instrument should be developed for assessing student learning in the major. To the contrary, such an instrument would be unlikely to lend itself well to assessment of the communication major, given the breadth of disciplinary contexts. Instead of a single test, we recommend a pluralistic approach, with complementary measures that together serve to assess student learning in an integrated fashion. Some of the assessment tools could be standardized and others nonstandardized. The value of having some standardization is the ability to compare results over time and place. The MCL project in particular advocates for the development of psychometrically rigorous and high-quality standardized assessment measures that would be designed to move beyond multiple-choice testing of content knowledge. Rather, students would be assessed with a range of items, including open-ended questions that require students to demonstrate mastery of concepts and competencies in practice. These standardized assessments would be voluntarily adopted and used in conjunction with other indicators of student learning outcomes.

Starting with the concepts and competencies articulated earlier in this paper, a logical next step is to focus on measurement of learning outcomes. This effort would involve surveying existing assessment strategies, identifying gaps vis-à-vis the list of learning outcomes and relevant contexts, and creating new tools to fill those gaps. The goal of this work would be to develop multiple measures for each learning outcome, and multiple tools across the endeavor that can be used nationally.

For such a national effort to be successful, the same values used for the Tuning project would need to be applied. This effort, for example, would need to be faculty driven and based on an assumption that implementation would ultimately be flexible enough for adaptation to particular campus contexts. A similar process would also need to be used. For example, an iterative model that incorporates stakeholder feedback would be productive. Assessment is fundamentally about the improvement of teaching and learning, but other stakeholders such as employers and parents also have an interest in student learning in communication. Gathering and understanding their feedback as part of the development of an assessment strategy for the major would help ensure that selected measures are easy to understand and useful for those external parties. Sensitivity to multiple audiences for the results of these assessments would allow us to serve as better advocates for the discipline while improving teaching and learning. A highly publicized, national effort in which measures and measurement tools are identified, developed, and integrated would undoubtedly enhance the assessment of student learning in the major across the country and increase the likelihood of evaluating learning across schools and over time.

There is a nascent measurement effort that is reflective of a desire to measure learning outcomes and also demonstrates one additional measurement approach that can be usefully pursued as part of this broader effort, among others. Spearheaded by the National Institute for Learning Outcomes Assessment (NILOA), communication faculty members are developing classroom-based assignments for assessment purposes. NILOA has begun sponsoring assignment workshops, or charrettes, involving intensive evaluation by groups of faculty of assignments designed to address specific learning outcomes. Suggestions for improving the assignments are provided to those who designed them. NILOA argues that there are several important reasons to use assignments for assessment purposes, including the fact that assessment is embedded in the classroom, faculty are the assessors, and students are more likely to take seriously assignments rather than external assessments. The idea is to develop assignments that link the central task to specific desired learning outcomes, explicitly state how results of the task should be communicated, and provide clear direction regarding the level of evidence required for an effective response. NILOA suggests using rubrics to evaluate the design (Hutchings, Jankowski, and Ewell 2014). Assignment design is just one potentially fruitful avenue for filling in some of the gaps currently facing the communication discipline with respect to assessing student learning for the major.

NCA is currently collecting examples of the use of learning outcomes on different campuses. Short of, or in conjunction with, a national assessment review, NCA can also collect measurement efforts on specific campuses to facilitate a more comprehensive accounting of the approaches currently in use. Those approaches that render positive programmatic outcomes could be offered as exemplars.

Conclusion

"An important means of ensuring that our efforts supporting instructional improvement are moving in the right direction," noted Ruth Anne Clark, "is the careful assessment of what students are learning" (2002, 403). In support of Clark's admonition, and mindful of the communication discipline's long-standing commitment to the enhancement of teaching and learning, this white paper has sought to locate contemporary learning outcomes and assessment initiatives within the long trajectory of the discipline. From that foundation, we have articulated a set of essential concepts and competencies emergent from hours of faculty discussion and careful work in both the LOC and MCL projects. We ultimately suggest that the communication discipline must embrace the vision of multiple assessment avenues to effectively assess student learning in the communication major and in the individual communication classroom.

It is important for all members of the discipline to think about what they can do as individual faculty to facilitate support for, and development of, robust assessment efforts. It is no less important for departments to collectively consider these issues. At present, there are pressing external and internal imperatives for assessment. Accreditors, higher education administrators, legislators, and parents, for example, all want evidence of student learning in the communication discipline. Although this can be perceived as top-down imposition, it may be more productive to think of it as providing an opportunity to reinforce the value of a communication degree. Assessing student learning in communication is, however, fundamentally for the purpose of improving teaching and learning.

References

Allgood, Sam, and Amanda Bayer. 2016. "Measuring College Learning in Economics." In *Improving Quality in American Higher Education: Learning Outcomes and Assessments for the 21st Century*, edited by Richard Arum, Josipa Roksa, and Amanda Cook. San Francisco: Jossey-Bass.

American Speech-Language-Hearing Association and Speech Communication Association. 1979. "Standards for Effective Oral Communication Programs." *Spectra* 15: 3.

Anderson, Hurst R. 1943. "Rethinking the College Speech Curriculum." *Quarterly Journal of Speech* 29, no. 3: 354–359.

Backlund, Phil, Timothy J. Detwiler, Pat Arneson, and MaryAnn Danielson. 2010. "Assessing Communication Knowledge, Skills, and Attitudes." In *A Communication Assessment Primer*, edited by Phil Backlund and Gay Wakefield, 1–14. Washington, DC: National Communication Association.

Beebe, Steven A. 2013. "It's a Wonderful Discipline." Presidential Address to annual meeting for the National Communication Association, Washington, DC, November 23.

Beebe, Steven A., J. Kevin Barge, and Colleen McCormick. 1995. "The Competent Group Communicator: Assessing Essential Competencies of Small Group Problem Solving." Paper presented at the annual meeting of the Speech Communication Association, San Antonio, TX, November 18-21.

Bitzer, Lloyd F., and Edwin Black. 1971. *The Prospect of Rhetoric: Report of the National Development Project*. Englewood Cliffs, NJ: Prentice-Hall.

Clark, Ruth Anne 2002. "Learning Outcomes: The Bottom Line." *Communication Education* 51, no. 4: 396–404.

Engleberg, Isa, Lynn Disbrow, James Katt, Scott Myers, Patricia O'Keefe, and Susan Ward. 2013. *National Communication Association Core Competencies Task Force Report*. Washington, DC: National Communication Association.

Goals 2000: Educate America Act. 1994. http://www2.ed.gov/legislation/GOALS2000/TheAct/index.html

Hargis, Donald E. 1950. "The General Speech Major." *Quarterly Journal of Speech* 36, no. 1: 71–76.

Harrington, Elbert W. 1952. "On General Education." *Quarterly Journal of Speech* 38, no. 3: 345–347.

Harvard Committee. 1945. *General Education in a Free Society*. Cambridge, MA: Harvard University Press.

Hay, Ellen A., and Michelle Epstein Garland. 2010. "Assessing Communication as Part of General Education." In *A Communication Assessment Primer*, edited by Phil Backlund and Gay Wakefield, 107–116. Washington, DC: National Communication Association.

Hunt, Everett L. 1922. "Adding Substance to Form in Public Speaking Courses." *Quarterly Journal of Speech* 8, no. 3: 256–265.

Hunt, Everett L. 1949. "Rhetoric and General Education." *Quarterly Journal of Speech* 35, no. 3: 275–279.

Hutchings, Pat, Natasha A. Jankowski, and Peter T. Ewell. 2014. *Catalyzing Assignment Design Activity on Your Campus: Lessons from NILOA's Assignment Library Initiative*. Urbana, IL: University of Illinois and Indiana University, National Institute for Learning Outcomes Assessment (NILOA).

Institute for Evidence-Based Change (IEBC). 2015. "Tuning USA: Tuning and the Degree Qualifications Profile." http://www.iebcnow.org/OurWork/Tuning.aspx.

Joint Task Force of the Speech Communication Association and American Theatre Association. 1975. "Guidelines for Speech Communication and Theatre Programs in Teacher Education." *Speech Teacher* 24, no. 4: 343–364.

Kibler, Robert J., and Larry L. Barker. 1969. *Conceptual Frontiers in Speech-Communication: Report of the New Orleans Conference on Research and Instructional Development*. New York: Speech Communication Association.

Kidd, Nancy. 2015. "Reflecting on Experience: The Heart of NCA's Learning Outcomes in Communication Project." *Spectra* 51:4.

Klapper, Paul, et al. 1949. "A Symposium on Rhetoric and General Education." *Quarterly Journal of Speech* 35, no. 4: 419–426.

Lumina Foundation. 2014. *"The Degree Qualifications Profile."* http://degreeprofile.org/.

Lumina Foundation. 2015a. "Appendix B: The DQP and Tuning." In *The Degree Qualifications Profile*. http://degreeprofile.org/read-the-dqp/appendix-b/.

Lumina Foundation. 2015b. *What is Tuning?* http://degreeprofile.org/press_four/wp-content/uploads/2014/12/What-is-Tuning.pdf

Macleod, Alice W. 1916. "Majors and Credits in Public Speaking." *Quarterly Journal of Speech* 2, no. 2: 149–152.

McBath, James H., and Robert C. Jeffrey. 1978. "Defining Speech Communication." *Communication Education* 27, no. 3: 181–188.

McCroskey, James C. 2005. *An Introduction to Rhetorical Communication*, 9th ed. Englewood Cliffs, NJ: Prentice Hall.

Morreale, Sherwyn P., Ed. 2007. *Assessing Motivation to Communicate: Willingness to Communicate and Personal Report of Communication Apprehension*, 2nd ed. Washington, DC: National Communication Association.

Morreale, Sherwyn P., Michael Moore, Donna Surges-Tatum, and Linda Webster, Eds. 2007. *The Competent Communication Speaker Speech Evaluation Form*. Washington, DC: National Communication Association.

Morreale, Sherwyn P., Scott A. Myers, Phil M. Backlund, and Cheri J. Simonds. 2015. "Study IX of the Basic Communication Course at Two- and Four-Year U.S. Colleges and Universities: A Re-examination of our Discipline's 'Front Porch.'" *Communication Education*: DOI 10.1080/03634523.2015.1073339.

Morreale, Sherwyn P., Rebecca B. Rubin, and Elizabeth Jones. 1998. *Speaking and Listening Competencies for College Students*. Washington, DC: National Communication Association.

National Communication Association. 2015. *The Role of the Communication Discipline on Campus and Beyond*. Washington, DC: National Communication Association.

O'Neill, James M. 1923. "Speech Content and Course Content in Public Speaking." *Quarterly Journal of Speech* 9, no. 1: 26–52.

O'Neill, James M. 1936. "Speech in the Changing Curriculum." *Quarterly Journal of Speech* 22, no. 2: 183–186.

Report of the Hope College Conference on Designing the Undergraduate Curriculum in Communication. 2000. Washington, DC: National Communication Association.

Rhodes, Terrel. 2010. *Assessing Outcomes and Improving Achievement: Tips and Tools for Using Rubrics.* Washington, DC: Association of American Colleges & Universities.

Sandford, William P. 1922. "The Problem of Speech Content." *Quarterly Journal of Speech* 8, no. 4: 364–371.

Seifrit, William C. 1961. "The General Speech Major: Ten Years Later." *Speech Teacher* 10, no. 1: 35–40.

Skinner, Ted. 1961. "A Study of Speech Major Requirements." *Speech Teacher* 10, no. 4: 302–303.

Spitzberg, Brian H. 1983. "Communication Competence as Knowledge, Skills, and Impression." *Communication Education* 32, no. 3: 323–329.

Spitzberg, Brian H. 2000. "What Is Good Communication?" *Journal of the Association for Communication Administration* 29, no. 1: 103–119.

Spitzberg, Brian H. 2006. "Preliminary Development of a Model and Measure of Computer-mediated Communication (CMC) Competence." *Journal of Computer-Mediated Communication* 11, no. 2: 629–666.

Spitzberg, Brian H. 2007. *The Conversational Skills Rating Scale: An Instructional Assessment of Interpersonal Competence.* Washington, DC: National Communication Association.

Spitzberg, Brian H. 2011. "The Interactive Media Package for Assessment of Communication and Critical Thinking (IMPACCT©): Testing a Programmatic Online Communication Competence Assessment System." *Communication Education* 60, no. 2: 145–173.

Spitzberg, Brian H., and Thomas H. Hurt. 1987. "The Measurement of Interpersonal Skills in Instructional Contexts." *Communication Education* 36, no. 1: 28–45.

U.S. Department of Education, National Center for Education
    Statistics. 2000. *Classification of Instructional Programs—2000:
    (NCES 2002–165)*. Washington, DC: U.S. Government Printing
    Office.

Weaver, J. Clark.1932. "A Survey of Speech Curricula." *Quarterly
    Journal of Speech* 18, no. 4: 607–612.

Woolbert, Charles Henry. 1920. "Report of the Committee on
    Research." *Quarterly Journal of Speech* 6, no. 3: 59–72.

6

Measuring College Learning in Biology

Clarissa Dirks
The Evergreen State College

Jennifer K. Knight
University of Colorado Boulder

This contribution offers an overview of prior efforts to articulate and measure learning outcomes in biology, presents a streamlined set of essential learning outcomes for undergraduate biology education, and offers a set of recommendations for the improvement of learning outcomes assessment in the discipline. To generate a set of essential learning outcomes, the authors synthesized across a number of existing learning outcomes frameworks. The resultant framework contains five essential concepts (evolution, information flow, structure and function, pathways and transformation of matter and energy, and systems) and six essential competencies (model, apply quantitative reasoning, engage in argument from evidence, engage in scientific inquiry and experimental design, analyze and evaluate data, and appreciate and apply the nature of science). The authors' discussion of assessment in biology begins with a description of existing assessment tools and others under development, and concludes with a set of principles to guide the development of future biology assessments.

Introduction

The call for reforming science education by enhancing student engagement, providing faculty development opportunities in pedagogy, and overhauling science curricula has been made in many national reports, including *Bio2010: Transforming Undergraduate Education for Future Research Biologists* (NRC 2003), *Scientific Foundations for Future Physicians* (AAMC and HHMI 2009), *Vision and Change in Undergraduate Biology Education* (AAAS 2011), and the *President's Council of Advisors on Science and Technology* report (EOP 2012). These reports and many others emphasize the need for recruiting students to be science majors and for retaining them in these disciplines to ensure a scientifically trained future workforce in the United States. Also needed are highly creative leaders capable of dealing with the challenges presented by a more globalized and economically competitive world. To this end, it is imperative that we create a scientifically literate society, one that embraces science as an important endeavor and supports science literacy as vital to the overall well-being and success of our country. To achieve these goals, biology education should be transformed to better align with them.

Biology is a broad and ever-changing discipline composed of many subdisciplines with diverse and far-reaching applications. Students interested in studying how to conserve the planet's species, fight cancer, treat infections caused by multiresistant microorganisms, develop better biofuels, increase crop yields, treat and prevent genetic diseases, stop the spread of infectious pathogens, or predict local and global changes due to climate instability would all most likely enroll in a college biology course. Therefore, it is not surprising that many students arrive at college with the intention to major in a subdiscipline of biology and will enroll in an introductory biology course before graduation. Given the importance that the study of biology has to students, their institutions, and society, it is crucial that we continue to improve science education through teaching and learning research, faculty development, and curricular reform.

One important step in reforming biology curricula is for faculty to clearly articulate and agree upon the essential concepts and competencies that all biology majors or majors in a subdiscipline of biology must know and be able to do upon graduation. If faculty shared this common vision, then new teaching materials, creative classroom and laboratory activities, and assessments could be designed, thus positively impacting biology students. Moreover, faculty development programs could be better focused if there were a more united view of biology concepts and competencies. Unfortunately, it is difficult to achieve faculty consensus regarding goals for biology courses, given the diverse nature of the discipline. After students complete their introductory biology courses, they commonly focus on a specific area or subdiscipline such as microbiology, cell and developmental biology, ecology, biochemistry, or molecular and cellular biology. Biology departments also employ faculty whose doctoral training and research are equally diverse. As a consequence, individual faculty and thus biology departments are likely to come to different decisions about the goals of any given introductory biology course and the goals of the major.

Despite these challenges, establishing goals for both introductory courses and biology majors has recently received considerable attention. In this paper, we focus in particular on the *Vision and Change in Undergraduate Biology Education* (2011) effort, a collaborative project spanning more than five years involving academic scientists, educators, students, and administrators. This work was significant not only because of the sheer number of participants but also because it has significantly impacted administrators and faculty across the nation. In addition, national agencies such as the American Association for the Advancement of Science (AAAS), National Science Foundation (NSF), and Howard Hughes Medical Institute (HHMI) initiated and supported the project. Discussions began in 2007 with more than two hundred biologists and stakeholders from around the country. In 2009, the conversations continued with an additional five hundred people, including students, faculty, and administrators. Ultimately, the 2011 *Vision and Change* publication articulates critical core concepts and competencies and makes numerous pedagogical recommendations for improving undergraduate biology education. An additional conference in 2013 continued the work and resulted in another publication devoted to implementing change (AAAS 2015). Additional work by science educators has continued to work on better defining the essential concepts and competencies for the subdisciplines of ecology, physiology, and molecular biology (Brownell, Freeman, Wenderoth, and Crowe 2014). Others have used the *Vision and Change* report as a guiding document to begin developing concept inventories and other assessments (see, e.g., Couch, Wood, and Knight 2015 and the BioMAPS project).

Other organizations have identified key concepts and skills for undergraduate biology. For example, the College Board has articulated essential concepts and competencies required for the success of incoming science majors (College Board 2009, 2012), whereas the Association of American Medical Colleges and Howard Hughes Medical Institute have outlined such a document for those who are graduating from college and will enter medical school (AAMC and HHMI 2009). Organizations that deliver high-stakes exams such as the Graduate Record Examination (GRE) subject test in biology and the Medical College Admission Test (MCAT) have also impacted curricula at colleges and universities since student success on these tests is often required for continued education in biology-related disciplines.

Despite these national-level conversations and publications, it is clear that not a single document for introductory biology or the biology major has been widely adopted by faculty teaching undergraduates. To address these unresolved needs, as part of the Measuring College Learning (MCL) project, we have (a) reviewed previous efforts that attempt to describe essential concepts and competencies for introductory biology and the major; (b) used numerous resources to compile a detailed list of essential concepts and competencies for biology; (c) created a matrix demonstrating, with examples, how the learning expectations for concepts and skills can be articulated together; (d) described current instruments designed to measure biology learning outcomes; and (e) outlined the future of assessment instruments aimed at measuring essential concepts and competencies in the biology discipline. Our efforts build upon the foundational work of others and our in-depth conversations with the MCL Biology faculty panel[1] and have been guided by the unifying principle that biology is an experimental science. The discipline of biology is changing so rapidly that concepts are not as enduring as skills. Thus, emphasis should be placed on deepening students' concept knowledge through skill acquisition and mastery. We realize that our final product is not comprehensive and is certainly subject to continued discussion and debate.

Literature Review

In this section, we provide a review of the sources that have previously attempted to articulate essential concepts and competencies, and associated learning outcomes, for biology undergraduates. We have organized the review into sections that focus on student

---

[1] The MCL Biology faculty panel included the following individuals: Cynthia Bauerle (Howard Hughes Medical Institute), Sara Brownell (Arizona State University), Clarissa Dirks (The Evergreen State College), Chris Kaiser (Massachusetts Institute of Technology), Jennifer Knight (University of Colorado, Boulder), Susan Singer (National Science Foundation), Michelle Smith (University of Maine), Nancy Songer (Drexel University), Gordon Uno (University of Oklahoma), William Wood (University of Colorado, Boulder), and Robin Wright (University of Minnesota).

learning immediately prior to, during, and after college because each of these impact how college faculty define learning outcomes in biology. Only the most recent and pertinent reports and publications are considered, particularly those that have had some traction with biology faculty. This organizational structure is meant to provide a comprehensive overview of the many stakeholders impacted by and ultimately influencing decisions about teaching and learning in undergraduate biology education.

Concepts and Competencies for K–12 Students

The National Research Council (NRC), the National Science Teachers Association, the American Association for the Advancement of Science, and Achieve (an independent nonprofit organization) worked together to create an important K–12 document called the Next Generation Science Standards (NGSS), published in 2013. These standards were designed to serve as a framework for describing a progression of performance expectations through K–12 levels that emphasize critical thinking in science. The development process included an initial development of a framework by the NRC, A Framework for K–12 Science Education (2012), which articulated the science that K–12 students should know and is grounded in research on student learning. The NGSS were then developed collaboratively with states and other stakeholders in science, science education, higher education, and industry and were designed to blend science practices with disciplinary core ideas. For example, a performance expectation might blend the science practice of constructing explanations with the disciplinary core idea of interdependent relationships in ecosystems. Although the framework is broad, one area that is well addressed, and mostly missing in other reports, is the focus on critical thinking. The intention of the framework is to increase the coherence of K–12 science education through the emphasis on these multidimensional standards (e.g., practices blended with concepts) at each grade band (K–2, 3–5, 6–8, and 9–12) and in sequences across grades and grade bands. The framework was designed for state school systems and has been implemented in a handful of states, with several others adopting new standards that have a similar spirit and emphasis on blended or multidimensional standards.

Whereas the Next Generation Science Standards provide guidelines for K–12, the Advanced Placement (AP) biology curriculum and College Board Standards for College Success are directed at students transitioning from high school to college. The AP program consists of both courses and examinations in different areas, including biology. College faculty and AP teachers design the courses and exams, aiming to provide high school students with opportunities for college-level work. A tremendous amount of effort goes into making sure that the concepts and skills taught in AP courses and measured by AP exams align with college-level standards. A relatively high score on an AP exam earns students credit, placement, or both at most colleges and universities and is therefore an important driver of which concepts and competencies are taught in high school science courses. In 2009, the College Board, which also provides Advanced Placement programs and the SAT, generated the College Board Standards for College Success. Like the Next Generation Science Standards, the standards in this pre-AP document consist entirely of standards that blend science practices with disciplinary core ideas. These standards were designed for the first two years of high school (i.e., the science concepts and practices just prior to Advanced Placement courses or university-level coursework).

Interestingly, the essential concept knowledge for biology described in the Next Generation Science Standards, AP biology curriculum, and College Board Standards for College Success are nearly identical, although the emphasis differs. Although NGSS broadly addresses science, technology, engineering, and mathematics (STEM) disciplines, not just biology, all three of these publications organize biology concepts into broad headings, such as cell structure or evolution, which are either identical or clearly overlap with the five *Vision and Change* concept categories that will be discussed in detail later. The documents also provide knowledge statements (called either essential knowledge or enduring understandings) under these broader headings and articulate performance expectations or learning outcomes that are more detailed than the broader essential knowledge statements. The reported essential biology competencies, also referred to as skills and practices, are also congruent among these reports for K–12 and are presented as practices blended with concepts (in NGSS in particular). They are further supported in the literature by validated assessments aimed to measure them (Dillashaw and Okey 1980). The level at which the learning outcomes and skills are described in these documents is strikingly similar to, or in some cases even higher than, those described for undergraduate students (Coil, Wenderoth, Cunningham, and Dirks 2010; Gormally, Brickman, and Lutz 2013). Although some overlap in essential concepts and competencies is expected across educational levels, future work should be done to examine the different cognitive levels at which students should be expected to work in high school versus undergraduate biology courses.

Concepts and Competencies for Undergraduates

Compared with K–12, there have been fewer long-term national efforts in higher education aimed at standardizing essential concepts and competencies for biology students. However, in the last several years progress at the college level has been stimulated by *Vision and Change*. Most important, the work around *Vision and Change* has involved broad participation of faculty. For example, in developing the BioCore guide, Brownell et al. (2014) surveyed hundreds of biologists and biology education researchers for their input in developing a more detailed framework of the concepts outlined in *Vision and Change*. The BioCore Guide is a framework for departments to more easily implement the *Vision and Change* goals. Additionally, the Partnership in Undergraduate Life Science Education (PULSE) fellows have created the PULSE Vision and Change rubrics that are meant to assess if departments are success- fully implementing *Vision and Change* in their curricula.

After students graduate with an undergraduate degree in biol- ogy, the GRE subject test in biology and the Major Field Test (MFT) in biology, among others, may be used to assess whether students are ready for more advanced work. The topics selected for these tests serve as a proxy for what the testing organizations and their constituents believe is important for biology students to learn in their undergraduate work. The publicly available descriptions of the biology MFT and GRE, which are intended to measure the performance levels of students graduating from college, articulate nearly identical concept or knowledge statements to those out- lined in the expectations for high school students. Again, more work should be done to better clarify the cognitive levels at which students are expected to work along the continuum of K–12 to undergraduate education.

Progress has been made to define essential concepts for under- graduate biology majors, but very little has been done to artic- ulate the competencies, skills, and practices biology students should learn. Several groups have surveyed life science faculty to identify the skills all students should master by the time they graduate with an undergraduate degree in biology (Coil et al. 2010; Dasgupta, Anderson, and Pelaez 2014), whereas another group has created an assessment tool for measuring general scien- tific literacy skills in the context of biology (Gormally, Brickman, and Lutz 2013). For students graduating with a biology degree, *Scientific Foundations for Future Physicians* (AAMC and HHMI 2009) has presented a thorough list of skills that should be devel- oped by those wanting to enter the medical profession. Not sur- prisingly, the skills identified by the aforementioned groups also overlap with many of the core competencies in *Vision and Change* and the documents described for K–12 education. However, given the ever-changing nature of biology and the importance of developing biology students' skills, it is evident that much more work needs to be done in this area.

In addition to the aforementioned efforts initiated by *Vision and Change*, many others have worked to better define the concepts students need to know in subdisciplines of biology and the skills that introductory students should learn in biology. The many concept inventories (also known as concept assessments) in biology will be discussed further in the current assessments section of this paper. Here, we would simply like to note that the authors of these concept inventories had to identify core concepts to be tested in the concept areas targeted (e.g., molecular and cell biology, genetics, evolution, developmental biology, microbiology, physiology, introductory biology, and plant biology). Collectively, such work has helped to lay the foundation for identifying the essential concepts for the biology major since many inventories address overlapping concepts. For example, questions about evolution or information flow are found on many of these tests.

Finally, although not directly related to articulating core general concepts and competencies for biology, an additional resource is important to mention here. This new resource is CourseSource, a Web-based journal for publishing teaching tools and learning outcomes statements (http://coursesource.org). The learning outcomes for Course Source were constructed in collaboration with professional societies in biology subdisciplines (e.g., Society for Developmental Biology, American Society for Biochemistry and Molecular Biology, American Society for Microbiology, Botanical Society of America, American Society of Plant Biologists, American Society of Cell Biology, and Genetics Society of America). Faculty can use both the outcomes and the published teaching tools to help improve pedagogy. This resource may prove helpful for establishing core sets of learning outcomes, especially at the course level.

Methods for Creating a List of Essential Concepts and Competencies for Biology

Many biology educators have attempted over the past ten years to articulate what is essential for students of biology to learn at both the K–12 and undergraduate levels. The documents that exist for K–12, such as the Next Generation Science Standards and the AP biology curriculum, are exceptionally detailed. Those that have been created specifically for university-level learning tend to be more general if they are describing the content of the biology major and more detailed if describing the content of a particular course. Because the discipline of biology is comprised of many diverse subdisciplines, the principle challenge in articulating essential concepts and competencies for biology as a complete discipline is to assemble a list that is broad enough to accommodate learning outcomes in multiple subdisciplines without being overly detailed.

NOTE: This chapter includes a number of bonus online appendices which can be found on the publisher's website. To access Appendices A-D, go to www.wiley.com/go/arumimproving.

Concepts

One way to understand the general concepts valued by biology faculty is to explore how biology departments communicate their expectations of biology majors. We collected examples of departmental-level learning goals and outcomes from a variety of biology department websites, ranging from community colleges to R1 institutions. The goals shared for departmental majors were typically extremely broad and described both general competencies and general topic areas (For more detailed information, see Appendix A on the publisher's website; accessing instructions are provided above). No departmental website had detailed lists of learning goals intended to capture specific concept-related learning outcomes of the whole major. Those that had detailed lists of learning outcomes (or goals) had them only for individual courses. Thus, it seems the approach of most departments has been not to articulate detailed outcomes for the major but rather to communicate in broad strokes the basic idea of what it means to be a biology major.

On the other hand, publications that have been generated to communicate the goals of K–12 instruction in biology are highly detail oriented. The AP biology curriculum, College Board Standards for College Success, and NGSS provide extensive lists of learning goals and outcomes. The essential concepts described in these documents are nearly identical, just worded slightly differently. In addition, at the topic or highest level of organization, the concepts overlap almost entirely with the five broad concept topics described in *Vision and Change*.

We also examined the concepts described for the MFT and the GRE in biology since we imagined the designers of these assessments would have articulated goals that overlap closely with faculty goals for students graduating with a degree in biology. Rather than providing clear learning outcomes, however, the MFT and GRE test descriptions feature lists of general topics, the percent of the test devoted to each topic area, and a list of the subtopics addressed in each area. The general topics and subtopics addressed by these two assessments are nearly identical to those outlined for AP biology.

Since a great deal of work has already been done in generating learning outcomes that communicate the essential concepts and competencies for the biology major, we have not written a completely new set of essential concepts and competencies here. Rather, we share in this document several compiled lists that we believe most accurately articulate these outcomes for undergraduate biology majors. First, we collected statements of biology concepts from the previously outlined sources and identified areas of overlap. Although these documents use slightly different language to articulate the concept-related learning outcomes, the essential topics overlap almost entirely. Using information from all of these documents, we generated a detailed list of essential concepts for the biology major at each of three levels: broad topics, subtopics, and specific examples of learning outcomes. However, there were too many individual topics and associated learning outcomes articulated in previously published documents to realistically list for the current audience. To try to capture the many subtopics addressed in each of these larger topic areas, a selection of goals and learning outcomes that addressed the concepts most commonly taught at the undergraduate level were collated to illustrate each of the broader themes. (For details, see Appendix B on the publisher's website.) However, we ultimately deemed this list too lengthy as well and created a more streamlined set of outcomes instead (Table 6.1).

To build the list of essential concepts shown in Table 6.1, we chose to focus on two recently published sources specifically addressing university-level biology: one that summarized the core concepts for biology majors (*Vision and Change*) and another that articulated in more detail the overarching principles within the *Vision and Change* core concepts (BioCore Guide). As mentioned previously, the *Vision and Change* document arose from a significant effort over five years and included contributions from many biologists who weighed in on essential biology concepts for undergraduates. Therefore, we present these five core concepts as the highest level of organization for biology concept knowledge. However, although *Vision and Change* outlines what faculty agree are the core concepts at a broad level, it does not include specific subtopic knowledge statements or learning outcomes. The BioCore guide (Brownell et al. 2014) provides more detail under each of the *Vision and Change* topic headings, so we used, with slight editing, the so-called overarching principles of the BioCore guide to further articulate *Vision and Change's* broad topics and finally included sample learning outcomes for each overarching principle. These example learning outcomes were gathered from the more detailed concept statements presented in BioCore, from other sources such as those presented in papers describing the creation of concept inventories (e.g., Couch et al. 2015), and where necessary, were written de novo.

Competencies

As discussed previously, understandings of essential biology competencies are congruent among several well-recognized reports (AP biology curriculum, College Board Standards for College Success, Next Generation Science Standards, *Vision and Change,* and *Scientific Foundations for Future Physicians*) and research publications (Coil et al. 2010; Dillashaw and Okey 1980; Gormally, Brickman, and Lutz 2013). We used these to identify nine main categories of competencies and two categories that bridge concepts and competencies. When reports or publications contained an overlapping competency (which occurred frequently), we used the reference that best articulated the competency or modified the statement for clarity. We parsed statements of competencies that were verbose or in paragraph form into several more clearly measurable outcomes. Some references included laboratory practice or the use of instrumentation related to competencies acquisition; for these competencies, we edited the text such that the learning outcome was more generalizable to any biology class setting. We then reviewed and removed redundant phrasing or learning outcomes and ultimately created an exhaustive list of representative competencies for biology (see Appendix C on the publisher's website). Although this exercise of pulling together detailed articulations of competencies was instructive (primarily because of the extensive overlap among all sources), the list was too detailed to be useful. Thus, we further refined the list using the seven competencies presented in the AP biology curriculum into six competencies that best reflect college-level biology competencies (competencies 3 and 6 were rephrased into a single competency: engage in scientific inquiry and experimental design). The AP biology competencies were the most completely articulated of the lists we examined and over-lapped nearly completely with the MCL faculty panelists' opinions of essential competencies for undergraduate biology majors. We also added an additional set of knowledge statements that falls under the category of nature of science (see Appendix D on the publisher's website).

Essential Concepts and Competencies for the Biology Major

Using the process described above, we were able to generate a distilled list of essential concepts and competencies for biology (Tables 6.1 and 6.2). The committee members overseeing this work unanimously agreed that biology instruction should focus on the experimental nature of biology and that, as emphasized in the NGSS literature, concepts and competencies are inextricably linked. To illustrate this link, we generated a matrix providing examples of how both concepts and competencies can be articulated together in meaningful learning outcomes. Rather than articulating this integration for all of the competencies, we selected the three competencies the group deemed most critical to teach and assess—experimental design, data analysis, and the interdisciplinary nature of science—and paired them with the five essential concepts (Table 6.3). The order of concepts is not meant to be hierarchical, and each box in the matrix is merely a possible exemplar. No one example is intended to be exhaustive or definitive.

Table 6.1 Essential Concepts for Biology

Essential Concept	Definition	Example Learning Outcomes
Evolution: *The diversity of life evolved over time by processes of mutation, selection, and genetic change*	• All living organisms share a common ancestor. • Species evolve over time, and new species can arise, when allele frequencies change due to mutation, natural selection, gene flow, and genetic drift.	• Explain how a specific mutation arose in a population that has undergone a change in its environment and exhibits different traits from its ancestors. • Predict the impact of different factors on the genetic composition of a newly isolated population compared with its parent population.
Information Flow: *The growth and behavior of organisms are activated through the expression of genetic information in context*	• Organisms inherit genetic and epigenetic information that influences the location, timing, and intensity of gene expression. • Cells/organs/organisms have multiple mechanisms to perceive and respond to changing environmental conditions.	• Determine how mutations at different locations within a gene could alter the amino acid sequence and function of the resulting protein. • Predict the contribution of environment versus genetics on the phenotype for a specific trait among individuals in a particular population.
Structure and Function: *Basic units of structure define the function of all living things*	• A structure's physical and chemical characteristics influence its interactions with other structures and therefore its function. • Natural selection leads to the evolution of structures that tend to increase fitness within the context of evolutionary, developmental, and environmental constraints.	• Compare how the properties of water affect the three-dimensional structures and stabilities of macromolecules, macromolecular assemblies, and lipid membranes. • Compare how competition, mutualism, and other interactions are mediated by different organisms' morphological, physiological, and behavioral traits.

Pathways and Transformations of Matter and Energy: *Biological systems grow and change by processes based upon chemical reactions and are governed by the laws of thermodynamics*	• Energy and matter cannot be created or destroyed but can be changed from one form to another. • Energy supports the maintenance, growth and reproduction of all organisms.	• Explain how free energy and entropy contribute to the folding of a protein comprised of polar and nonpolar amino acids. • Explain in energetic terms why reaction rate changes when the reaction is heated or when a specific enzyme is added.
Systems: *Living systems are interconnected and interacting*	• Biological molecules, genes, cells, tissues, organs, individuals, and ecosystems interact to form complex networks that exhibit emergent properties. A change in one component of the network can affect many other components. • Organisms have complex systems that integrate internal and external information, incorporate feedback control, and allow them to respond to changes in the environment.	• Make predictions about how organisms might use negative feedback mechanisms to maintain their internal environment. • Predict whether a biological or physical disturbance to an ecosystem will induce a change in the ecosystem depending on the complex set of interactions within the ecosystem.

Table 6.2 Essential Competencies for Biology

Essential Competency	Definition (Students Will Be Able To...)
Model	Construct, use, reexpress, and revise models and representations of natural and designed objects, systems, phenomena, and scientific ideas in the appropriate context and in formulating their explanation.
Apply Quantitative Reasoning	Reason about relationships between variables (e.g., data, representations, uncertainty, samples) through the lens of ratios, rates, percentages, probability, or proportional relationships when approaching or solving problems or when interpreting results or situations.
Engage in Argument from Evidence	Evaluate the claims, evidence, or reasoning behind currently accepted explanations or solutions to determine the merits of arguments.
Engage in Scientific Inquiry and Experimental Design	Design experiments with appropriate strategies, controls, and alternative approaches.
Analyze and Evaluate Data	Extract information from data and analyze it to discover patterns, critically evaluate conclusions, and generate predictions for subsequent experiments.
Appreciate and Apply the Interdisciplinary Nature of Science	Apply concepts from within biology subdisciplines and outside of biology to interpret biological phenomena.

Table 6.3 Matrix of Learning Outcomes That Blends Essential Concepts with Essential Competencies

		Essential Competencies		
		Engage in Scientific Inquiry and Experimental Design	Analyze and Evaluate Data	Appreciate and Apply the Interdisciplinary Nature of Science
Essential Concepts	Evolution	Design an experiment to measure changes in genetic makeup of a population over several generations.	Determine from graphical representations how the relative reproductive success of genetically distinct individuals affects the overall genetic composition of a population.	Apply the geological principles of cross-cutting and superposition to fossils in different strata to infer common ancestry.
	Information Flow	Design a series of experiments to determine whether a mutation in a gene alters gene expression by affecting transcriptional, post-transcriptional, or post-translational regulation.	Interpret results from a Northern blot to predict what kinds of mutations could be responsible for altering gene expression and contributing to disease phenotypes.	Compare and contrast how different organisms respond to wavelengths of light and how this results in modulation of gene expression.

(continued)

Table 6.3 (*Continued*)

		Essential Competencies		
		Engage in Scientific Inquiry and Experimental Design	Analyze and Evaluate Data	Appreciate and Apply the Interdisciplinary Nature of Science
Essential Concepts	Structure and Function	Design an experiment that would enable one to classify a newly discovered single-celled organism as eukaryote, bacteria, or archaea.	From their structures, predict which solutes will be able to diffuse spontaneously through a pure phospholipid bilayer membrane and which will require transport by membrane associated proteins.	From structures of amino acids, make predictions about where they would be found in a folded protein based on their chemical properties.
	Pathways and Transformations of Energy and Matter	Create a diagram that illustrates the flow of matter and energy during growth and cellular activities, and identify appropriate experimental analyses at different points to determine measurable outputs.	Given thermodynamic and kinetic data about a biochemical reaction, predict whether it will proceed spontaneously and the rate at which it will proceed.	Explain the transformations of energy between the plucking of a note on a guitar to the time a singer registers the note played.
	Systems	Design an experiment to identify the feedback points that operate in a system that exhibits homeostasis.	Using diagrammatic representations of feedback loops, make predictions of how organisms could use such mechanisms to maintain their internal environment.	Design a quantitative model that represents the exchange of molecules between an organism and its environment.

Essential Concepts and Competencies for the Introductory Biology Course

Articulating concept-related learning outcomes for introductory biology courses can be a daunting task in part because such courses are not at all uniform in the concepts they cover. Departments may offer an introductory course focused primarily on molecular and cell biology, ecology, or a general introductory biology, in which molecular and cell, ecology, genetics, and some physiology are all addressed. Some introductory courses are a single semester, whereas others are two semesters. Usually, the concepts covered in an introductory course reflect the overall specialization of the department—the department may be a general biology department, or it may be an ecology or molecular biology department. As a consequence of this diversity, it is unlikely that any one set of content outcomes would be adopted by all departments or all instructors of introductory biology. In fact, this diversity is likely one reason for the development of many new concept inventories that address components of introductory biology, for example: molecular and cell (Shi et al. 2010); genetics (Smith, Wood, and Knight 2008); meiosis (Kalas et al. 2013); natural selection (Anderson, Fisher, and Norman 2002); genetic drift (Price et al. 2014); and evo-devo (Perez et al. 2013). A similar issue exists for assessments designed to measure progression through or completion of the major. Aside from the standardized GRE and MFT, only one tool designed for college seniors is currently available (Couch et al. 2015), although others are in progress (e.g., the BioMAPS project). Since there is no typical introductory biology course, Table 6.4 shows an example set of essential concepts for a course that focuses on molecular and cell biology, an emphasis of many biology departments. This list could be modified for courses with slightly different emphases or expanded for courses that are more general.

Table 6.4 Concept Learning Outcomes for an Introductory Molecular and Cell Biology Course

Learning Outcomes (Students Will Be Able To. . .)
Outline the theory of evolution, citing evidence that supports it and properties of organisms that it explains.
Contrast the features that distinguish viruses, bacteria, archaea, and eukaryotic cells.
Recognize structures of the four major classes of building block molecules (monomers) that make up cellular macromolecules.
Compare how the properties of water affect the three-dimensional structures and stabilities of macromolecules, macromolecular assemblies, and lipid membranes.
Given the thermodynamic and kinetic characteristics of a biochemical reaction, predict whether it will proceed spontaneously and the rate at which it will proceed.
From their structures, predict which solutes will be able to diffuse spontaneously through a pure phospholipid bilayer membrane and which will require transport by membrane associated proteins.
Outline the flow of matter and energy in the processes by which organisms fuel growth and cellular activities, and explain how these processes conform to the laws of thermodynamics.
Using diagrams, demonstrate how the information in a gene is stored, replicated, and transmitted to daughter cells.
Describe how the information in a gene directs expression of a specific protein.

Although the biology concepts taught in introductory biology are diverse, the same six science competencies that we articulated in Table 6.2 are universally described by instructors as critical for students to learn in almost any kind of biology course, including introductory biology. Thus, we do not think there is value in writing an additional set of competencies just for introductory biology. We note, however, that students will likely achieve competencies at a lower level as they are completing introductory biology compared with their level of competency when they are completing a major in biology.

A Note on Majors Versus Nonmajors

There are generally three kinds of introductory biology courses offered to undergraduates: those intended for biology majors only; those for nonmajors only; and those for the two populations combined. Many colleges and universities offer introductory biology courses that are taken both by majors and by other students who are fulfilling science distribution requirements, even when such a course is described as required for biology majors. This combination of majors and nonmajors presents a dilemma because such an introductory biology course may be the only science course the nonmajors take during their entire college experience. However, for those intending to major in biology, the introductory course is a foundation for the rest of the biology courses that follow. Thus, even though scientific literacy is often mentioned as a critical component of a student's undergraduate experience, no matter their major, nonmajors may not get the kind of specialized exposure that might be required for them to establish scientific literacy if they are taking courses designed specifically for nonmajors. This dilemma is worth considering as assessment tools for introductory biology are planned and developed.

Current Assessments of Student Learning in Biology

Because high-quality, meaningful assessments are difficult and time-consuming to create, most standardized assessments used to measure biology concept knowledge have traditionally been multiple-choice exams focused on details rather than concepts, principally developed by organizations such as the College Board, Educational Testing Service (ETS), and Association of American Medical Colleges. These standardized assessments often come with a financial cost to the students who take them or the departments that administer them. Unfortunately, this model has unintended consequences for underserved students who have significant financial burdens. Since many of these exams measure college readiness for biology or mastery of concepts and skills taught in biology and are used for entry into college science courses or graduate school, respectively, this model may eliminate many talented students from the discipline.

However, in the past eight years, many biology faculty have been working to develop well-tested and reliable assessment instruments designed to measure conceptual understanding of a diverse set of biology topics at the undergraduate level. These faculty-developed concept inventories (or assessments) differ from many prior individual department-level assessments because they have been rigorously developed to specifically test known student incorrect ideas (i.e., common misconceptions), and evaluated for reliability and evidence of validity. In this section we focus our discussion on both the standardized assessments created by large organizations, and on the more recently developed concept assessments, emphasizing those that have been used by colleges and universities across the country. We also highlight assessments that may serve as useful tools in the future or as foundational work for creating a more comprehensive assessment instrument.

Concept Assessments

The AP biology exam aims to measure the concept knowledge and skills of students who have taken a high school AP biology course, which is designed to be equivalent to an introductory biology course in college. The exam assesses many of the essential concepts and competencies that many efforts, including *Vision and Change*, have highlighted as important for biology students. It contains mostly multiple-choice questions that are machine scored and a substantial number of free-response questions that are scored with rubrics by educators; the free-response question scores are weighted and combined with the scores from the multiple-choice section. Students who achieve a top score of 4 or 5 on the AP biology exam may be awarded college credit depending on the colleges or universities they attend.

The GRE subject test in biology has been administered since the early 1990s and is intended to measure test takers' potential for success with graduate-level study in biology. The strictly multiple-choice exam is based on concept categories but does contain a number of grouped sets of questions that are based on descriptions of laboratory and field situations, diagrams, or experimental results. Therefore, the exam does test a subset of the essential competencies we discussed in the previous section. The exam is often used by departments and programs to assess a student's ability for graduate work in biology.

The MFT in biology is an exam designed to assess graduating students' "mastery of concepts, principles and knowledge" in undergraduate-level biology (ETS 2014, 1). Similar to the GRE subject test in biology, but certainly not as comprehensive, the biology MFT assesses student learning of concepts. It also has question groups that are based on experimental design or analysis of data from lab or field scenarios. Similar to the biology GRE, some of the concept topics and skills are aligned with the essential concepts and competencies already outlined. The test consists of 150 multiple-choice questions. Though not widely used, some departments administer the biology MFT to gather data for the purposes of instructional improvement or to satisfy external data reporting requirements from accreditors or other agencies.

Biologists and biology education researchers have recently added to the assessments available by designing instruments that address either certain course topics or individual courses taken by biology majors. These assessments are sometimes referred to as concept inventories because they inventory what a student knows and is able to do shortly after instruction. Although most consist of all multiple-choice questions, several have incorporated two-tiered, multiple true–false, and free-response questions, or a mix of these types along with multiple-choice questions. These inventories have been designed by faculty for faculty use and do not have any associated fees—they are typically published in journals or are made freely available online.[2] Some concept assessments are relatively broad and intended to be used at the beginning and end of a course to measure learning gains as a consequence of instruction. Thus, instruments like the Biology Concept Inventory (Garvin-Doxas and Klymkowsky 2008), the Introductory Molecular and Cell Biology Assessment (Shi et al. 2010), and the Genetics Concept Assessment (Smith, Wood, and Knight 2008) along with several others cover many topics and learning outcomes. Other instruments have been designed to address a smaller number of concepts in more detail, such as the Concept Inventory of Natural Selection (Anderson, Fisher, and Norman 2002), the Diffusion and Osmosis Diagnostic Test (Odom and Barrow 1995), the Host-Pathogens Interactions (Marbach-Ad et al. 2009), and a suite being developed at University of British Columbia (http://q4b.biology.ubc.ca/concept-inventories/).

Recently, a group has begun to develop a suite of assessments intended to measure progression through the major. These assessments use the multiple true–false format and are not tied to any one course but rather consist of a suite of concepts that students would be exposed to throughout their career as biology majors. This project, Biology-Measuring Achievement and Progression in Science (BioMAPS), will ultimately produce a general biology assessment and tools for majors that are more physiology, ecology, and evolution focused. A molecular biology–focused assessment, the Molecular Biology Capstone Assessment, has already been published (Couch et al. 2015). The BioMAPS tools also attempt to more explicitly integrate competencies with concepts than do most previous concept assessments.

----

[2] To view a list of existing concept inventories as of 2014, visit http://go.sdsu.edu/dus/ctl/cabs.aspx.

Published work on some of these faculty-developed concept assessments has helped to reveal or support previous reports of common student difficulties at both introductory and advanced levels (Couch et al. 2015; Smith and Knight 2012). Understanding these difficulties is essential for any further assessment development. However, although there are now many choices for faculty who are interested in measuring students' conceptual learning, no one instrument has been chosen to be the representative measurement tool.

Competency Assessments

Rigorously designed instruments that specifically measure the essential competencies, skills, and practices of undergraduate biology students remain woefully lacking. One of the first such instruments for measuring students' skills was the Test of Integrated Process Skills (TIPS) for Secondary Students (Dillashaw and Okey 1980). TIPS is an instrument designed to measure science students' abilities in data analysis and graphing. TIPS contains some biology-based examples. Up until the development of a biology-specific equivalent, TIPS was appropriate for assessing college freshmen who were biology majors (Dirks and Cunningham 2006). However, TIPS assesses only a narrow range of essential competencies and is incapable of measuring the true range of abilities among introductory biology students. A more recent assessment designed for undergraduate biology is the Test of Science Literacy Skills (Gormally et al. 2013), which focuses on scientific inquiry and working with and using data. This assessment is designed to measure basic scientific literacy, and thus while valuable for measuring general biology education students' literacy, it may not be challenging enough for biology majors. Two additional assessments, the Rubric for Experimental Design (Dasgupta et al. 2014) and the Experimental Design Assessment Test (Sirum and Humberg 2011), specifically assess students' knowledge of experimental design and are targeted to the level of biology majors. These more recently developed tools are excellent resources, but biology faculty have had difficulty implementing them in large-scale biology classes because they are time consuming to administer and analyze. Thus, as is true of concept assessments, although several different instruments could be used to assess essential competencies, biology lacks a comprehensive, universally adopted set of assessments.

Future Assessments in Biology: Blending Competencies and Concepts

Assessing the essential conceptual knowledge and competencies of undergraduate biology students requires a diverse suite of tools capable of measuring a dynamic range of student abilities. Appropriate instruments would be able to distinguish novices from more advanced students both in the depth of their concept knowledge and their competency with biology skills. Although some assessments would measure concepts and competencies that all biology students should learn, others should be tailored to one of the many subdisciplines of biology to reflect their more specific concepts and skills. For example, a molecular biology major would need to know how to read the output from a DNA microarray experiment whereas an ecology major would need to know the difference between a point transect and a line transect and when to use them in field studies. Biology assessments should not only measure critical concepts and competencies, they should also be developed using the most commonly accepted principles of assessment design. Assessments should measure what they intend to measure and be equitable among groups taking the test. Test format, scoring, and interpretation of results are inextricably linked components of assessments. Given that assessment is a practice and a process that may impact curriculum and teaching, these different aspects of assessment require a great deal of attention when designing any instrument (NRC 2001). In this section we discuss assessments most suitable for measuring the core concepts and competencies of biology students.

Assessing biology competencies can be much more challenging than assessing concept knowledge, and test format can strongly impact what kinds of competencies can be measured. Being able to recognize the components of a good experiment is different than designing a novel experiment given a particular scenario. Thus, the creativity that goes into good experimental design is not easily measured with certain test formats, such as multiple-choice tests. The same can be true for other important skills in biology, such as model building and argumentation. Questions that require students to apply their knowledge and creative skills can measure students' ability to be flexible in how they approach interpreting and solving a problem: these questions cannot be multiple choice but rather should be open-ended.

On the other hand, some skills, such as interpreting graphs or making inferences from data, can be measured adequately with multiple-choice questions. Furthermore, not all assessments can be comprised of only open-ended responses due to the difficulty of collecting and analyzing data from such responses. Scoring multiple-choice tests takes far less time and resources compared to scoring open-ended tests. Also, because multiple-choice questions have only one correct answer, the scoring cannot be biased. On the other hand, open-ended questions, which are most often graded by hand, can lead to biases and mismatches between intended and actual measures (Baxter and Glaser 1998). Given that students come to college with a variety of life experiences that influence their thinking and learning, the answers they provide to questions requiring complex answers will be diverse and present challenges for analysis. Thus, because all assessment questions have caveats associated with them, comprehensive tests for measuring concepts and competencies in biology should be based on a variety of question formats (multiple-choice, multiple true–false, open-ended, and two-tiered) and the specific skill measured in each question should dictate which format is selected.

Assessments designed to measure concepts and competencies in biology should also be able to assess the progression of students from novice to master. Determining where a student is at several points along a learning continuum is more useful than just a snapshot of their abilities at any given time. Therefore assessments should be designed to capture a range of abilities within a class or a larger group of students. For example, a rubric designed to score an open-ended question would have a list of items that a student would have demonstrated if they had mastered the concept or skill tested. The same rubric would also show that a novice or intermediate student would have addressed only one or a few of the items, respectively, in their answer. Similarly, multiple-choice tests can be iteratively designed to provide different questions along a difficulty scale—students who progress along the scale are capable of answering more difficult questions about the same concept or skill as they move toward mastery. This is the premise of the adaptive nature of the GRE subject test in biology: When students correctly answer a question they are given a more difficult question, but if they get it wrong they are given an easier question; this continues until the end of the test and their final score is based on an overall ability score along a range of abilities. So as mentioned previously, the interpretation of test results is based on the scoring method and the overall test design. The complex link between concepts and skills in biology will require assessments that are capable of effectively measuring the intersection of these domains along ability continuums.

One potentially useful tool for understanding student thinking is computer-assisted analysis of student writing. Lexical analysis software (Weston et al. 2015) and machine learning programs (Nehm, Ha, and Mayfield 2012) have both recently been leveraged to help analyze student writing about essential biology concepts. If such tools can be perfected, assessment of student thinking will be more robust because creative lines of thought required for more cognitively challenging tasks could potentially be measured rather than only the forced choices dictated by multiple-choice assessments.

A well-designed set of assessments for measuring student progression toward mastery of the essential concepts and competencies in biology is only one step toward improving learning in these areas. How the data are interpreted and used to improve instruction and curriculum is another critical component for enhancing student learning of biology. Good assessments can inform biology faculty about their teaching practices, but they will need support and development opportunities in order to implement the kinds of changes that will improve student learning.

Conclusion

In this paper, we have reviewed the current status of learning outcomes and assessment in undergraduate biology, focusing in particular on learning outcomes for biology majors and how they are currently being assessed. We have reviewed the outcomes articulated in the K–12 literature, which sets the stage for entering undergraduate biology students, and noted the similarities between concepts and competencies typically addressed in introductory biology and those which are typically addressed in high school biology courses. We have also described the current sets of learning outcomes that exist for undergraduate biology majors and the assessment tools, both standardized tests and faculty-developed concept assessments, that have been developed to assess students' achievement of these outcomes. In our research and discussions, we have agreed that biology is an experimental science and that it should be taught and learned with that idea in the forefront. Accordingly, future outcomes and assessments should emphasize the integration of concepts and competencies. To envision how this would manifest, we demonstrate how learning outcomes can be written such that concepts and competencies are articulated together.

All stakeholders in this endeavor should focus on teaching and assessment that merges the process of science with the concepts of biology. Although good assessments can inform biology faculty about their teaching practices, faculty will need support and development opportunities to implement changes that improve student learning. Thus, ultimately, administrators and faculty will benefit from collaborating to assess biology programs and curriculum, as well as pedagogy and student learning. Many faculty who have embraced the process of articulating learning outcomes and creating better assessment tools still emphasize learning detailed concepts at low cognitive levels and miss the opportunity to blend concepts and practices. Administrators can help improve teaching by providing the resources necessary to help instructors develop assessments that will better test science process skills such as reasoning, data analysis, problem solving, and experimental design in concert with essential concepts. Such collaboration between administrators and faculty will help make tangible the goal of advancing the depth of student learning by focusing instruction on merging concepts and competencies.

NOTE: On the publisher's website you'll find additional information, including more sample learning outcomes. To access this bonus online material, go to www.wiley.com/go/arumimproving.

References

American Association for the Advancement of Science (AAAS). 2011. *Vision and Change in Undergraduate Biology Education: A Call to Action*. Washington, DC: AAAS Press.

American Association for the Advancement of Science (AAAS). 2015. *Vision and Change in Undergraduate Biology Education: Chronicling Change, Inspiring the Future*. Washington, DC: AAAS Press.

Anderson, Dianne L., Kathleen M. Fisher, and Gregory J. Norman. 2002. "Development and Evaluation of the Conceptual Inventory of Natural Selection." *Journal of Research in Science Teaching* 39: 952–978.

Association of American Medical Colleges (AAMC) and Howard Hughes Medical Institute (HHMI). 2009. *Scientific Foundations for Future Physicians*. Washington, DC: AAMC. http://www.aamc.org/scientificfoundations.

Baxter, Gail P., and Robert Glaser. 1998. "Investigating the Cognitive Complexity of Science Assessments." *Educational Measurement: Research and Practice* 17, no. 3: 37–45.

Brownell, Sara, Scott Freeman, Mary P. Wenderoth, and Alison Crowe. 2014. "BioCore Guide: A Tool for Interpreting the Core Concepts of Vision and Change for Biology Majors." *CBE—Life Sciences Education* 13: 200–211.

Coil, David, Mary Pat Wenderoth, Matthew Cunningham, and Clarissa Dirks. 2010. "Teaching the Process of Science: Faculty Perceptions and an Effective Methodology." *CBE—Life Sciences Education* 9: 524–535.

College Board. 2009. *Science: College Board Standards for College Success*. https://professionals.collegeboard.com/profdownload/cbscs-science-standards-2009.pdf.

College Board. 2012. *Advanced Placement Biology: Course and Exam Description*. http://media.collegeboard.com/digitalServices/pdf/ap/ap-biology-course-and-exam-description.pdf.

Couch, Brian A., William B. Wood, and Jennifer K. Knight. 2015. "The Molecular Biology Capstone Assessment: A Conceptual Assessment for Upper-Division Molecular Biology Students." *CBE Life Sciences Education* 14: 1–11.

Dasgupta, Annwesa, Trevor R. Anderson, and Nancy Pelaez. 2014. "Development and Validation of a Rubric for Diagnosing Students' Experimental Design Knowledge and Difficulties." *CBE Life Sciences Education* 13, 265–284.

Dillashaw, F. Gerald, and James Okey. 1980. "Test of Integrated Process Skills for Secondary Students." *Science Education* 64: 601–608.

Dirks, Clarissa, and Matthew Cunningham. 2006. "Enhancing Diversity in Science: Is Teaching Scientific Process Skills the Answer?" *CBE Life Science Education* 5, no. 3: 218–226.

Educational Testing Service (ETS). 2014. "ETS Major Field Test for
    Biology: Test Description." https://www.ets.org/mft/about/concept/
    biology.

Executive Office of the President (EOP). 2012. *Engage to Excel:
    Producing One Million Additional College Graduates with Degrees
    in Science, Technology, Engineering, and Math.* Washington, DC:
    The President's Council of Advisors on Science and Technology.
    http://www.whitehouse.gov/sites/default/files/microsites/ostp/pcast-
    executive-report-final_2–13–12.pdf.

Garvin-Doxas, Kathy, and Michael W. Klymkowsky. 2008.
    "Understanding Randomness and Its Impact on Student Learning:
    Lessons Learned from Building the Biology Concept Inventory
    (BCI)." *CBE Life Sciences Education* 7: 227–233.

Gormally, Cara, Peggy Brickman, and M. Lutz. 2013. "Developing a Test
    of Scientific Literacy Skills (TOSLS): Measuring Undergraduates'
    Evaluation of Scientific Information and Arguments." *CBE—Life
    Sciences Education* 11: 364–377.

Kalas, Pamela, Angie O'Neill, Carol Pollock, and Gulnur Birol. 2013.
    "Development of a Meiosis Concept Inventory." *CBE Life Sciences
    Education* 12: 655–664.

Marbach-Ad, Gili, Volker Briken, Najib M. El-Sayed, Kenneth
    Frauwirth, Brenda Fredericksen, Steven Hutcheson, …, and Ann C.
    Smith. 2009. "Assessing Student Understanding of Host Pathogen
    Interactions Using a Concept Inventory." *Journal of Microbiology
    Education* 10: 43–50.

National Research Council (NRC). 2001. *Knowing What Students Know:
    The Science and Design of Educational Assessment.* Washington, DC:
    National Academy Press.

National Research Council (NRC). 2003. *Bio2010: Transforming
    Undergraduate Education for Future Research Biologists.* Washington,
    DC: National Academy Press.

National Research Council (NRC). 2012. *A Framework for K–12
    Science Education: Practices, Crosscutting Concepts, and Core Ideas.*
    Washington, DC: National Academy Press.

Nehm, Ross, Minsu Ha, and Elijah Mayfield. 2012. "Transforming
    Biology Assessment with Machine Learning: Automated Scoring of

Written Evolutionary Explanations." *Journal of Science Education and Technology* 21: 183–196.

Next Generation Science Standards (NGSS). 2013. "Next Generation Science Standards." http://www.nextgenscience.org/next-generation-science-standards.

Odom, Arthur L., and Lloyd H. Barrow. 1995. "Development and Application of a Two-Tier Diagnostic Test Measuring College Biology Students' Understanding of Diffusion and Osmosis After a Course of Instruction." *Journal of Research in Science Teaching* 32: 45–61.

Perez, Kathryn, Anna Hiatt, Gregory K. Davis, Caleb Trujillo, Donald P. French, Mark Terry, and Rebecca M. Price. 2013. "The EvoDevo CI: A Concept Inventory for Gauging Students' Understanding of Evolutionary Developmental Biology." *CBE Life Sciences Education* 12: 665–675.

Price, Rebecca M., Tessa C. Andrews, Teresa L. McElhinny, Louise S. Mead, Joel K. Abraham, Anna Thanukos, and Kathryn E. Perez. 2014. "The Genetic Drift Inventory: A Tool for Measuring What Advanced Undergraduates Have Mastered about Genetic Drift." *CBE Life Sciences Education* 13: 65–75.

Shi, Jia, William B. Wood, Jennifer M. Martin, Nancy A. Guild, Quentin Vincens, and Jennifer K. Knight. 2010. "A Diagnostic Assessment for Introductory Molecular and Cell Biology." *CBE Life Sciences Education* 9: 453–461.

Sirum, Karen, and Jennifer Humburg. 2011. "The Experimental Design Ability Test." *Bioscience: Journal of College Biology Teaching* 37, no. 1: 8–16.

Smith, Michelle K., William B. Wood, and Jennifer K. Knight. 2008. "The Genetics Concept Assessment: A New Concept Inventory for Gauging Student Understanding of Genetics." *CBE Life Sciences Education* 7: 422–430.

Smith, Michelle K., and Jennifer K. Knight. 2012. "Using the Genetics Concept Assessment to Document Persistent Conceptual Difficulties in Undergraduate Genetics Courses." *Genetics* 191: 21–32.

University of British Columbia. 2015. "QB4 Concept Inventories." http://q4b.biology.ubc.ca/concept-inventories.

Weston, Michele, Kevin C. Haudek, Mark Urban-Lurain, and John
    Merrill. 2015. "Examining the Impact of Question Surface Features
    on Students' Answers to Constructed-Response Questions on
    Photosynthesis." *CBE Life Sciences Education* 14: 1–12.
Williams, Kathy S., and Erilynn T. Heinrichsen. 2014. "Concept
    Inventories/Conceptual Assessments in Biology (CABs): An
    Annotated List." San Diego State University Center for Teaching
    and Learning. http://go.sdsu.edu/dus/ctl/cabs.aspx.

7

Measuring College
Learning in Business

Jeffrey Nesteruk
Franklin and Marshall College

Sara Beckman
University of California—Berkeley

This contribution articulates a forward-thinking vision for undergraduate business education, the largest major in the United States. This vision is undergirded by a commitment to fundamental business knowledge and skills, emergent business trends, and the integration of learning across multiple domains and is reflected in the chapter's framework of essential concepts (business and society; globalization; strategy; system dynamics; consumer engagement; and transparency, disclosure, and metrics) and competencies (mastery of diverse thinking styles; ethical judgment; informational and technological literacy; and management, teaming, and cross-cultural competence). After an overview of a range of existing assessment tools, the authors articulate a set of principles that should guide the development of future measures of student learning in business. In particular, the authors emphasize the importance of continuous and incremental assessment that takes advantage of technology-enhanced data gathering capabilities.

> The genius of democratic capitalism . . . is that new norms of economic behavior are likely to emerge from executives and entrepreneurs, workers and consumers, money managers and bankers who find the courage to demand something better of themselves and others.
>
> —Steven Pearlstein, *Washington Post*[1]

Introduction

In this white paper, we seek to describe the concepts and competencies business schools and programs must develop in their students if they are to tap the *genius of democratic capitalism* that Steven Pearlstein envisions. To do so, our educational institutions of business must both respect established domains of business knowledge and recognize how distinctive emerging trends will reframe and reconfigure such knowledge. In a world that is transforming itself with ever-greater rapidity, business education must be more intentionally transformational. It must develop in its students a renewed sense of their own agency in ultimately shaping the context in which business operates.

Our work here reflects our sense of the importance of this subject. Business is the largest undergraduate major in the United States today. Although the major's ready ties to the career aspirations of today's students undoubtedly contribute to its popularity, the contemporary significance of this field has much deeper roots. Fueled by the reach of globalized markets and the power of an ever-expanding digitalized environment, the influence of commerce is far-reaching and profound. This means the study of business today has value not only for those seeking professional opportunities but also for those desiring insight into the contemporary forces at work in our world. Commerce enters intimately

---

[1] Steven Pearlstein, "Can We Save American Capitalism?" *Washington Post*, August 31, 2012.

into the dynamics of our lives, affecting the way we think, play, consume, perceive, and relate to each other. Understanding business thus sheds a critical light on the broader societal choices we are making and the world we are creating.[2]

Accompanying the increasing influence of business practices throughout society is the growing academic richness of business as a field of study. Multiple academic disciplines contribute to the study of business today, and the number of such disciplines is increasing. Sociologists, political scientists, and philosophers may now find a professional home along with scholars of management, finance, operations, and marketing in contemporary business schools and programs. Indeed, there are renewed calls for bringing more generally the values and perspectives of liberal education to the study of business. As the authors of the Carnegie Foundation's recent Business, Entrepreneurship, and Liberal Learning (BELL) Study put it, "Business and liberal learning must be woven together to prepare students for their professional roles and work and also to prepare them for lives of social contribution and personal fulfillment" (Colby, Erlich, Sullivan, and Dolle 2011, 2). A rich description of business schools that have taken on this integration is provided in *Rethinking Undergraduate Business Education*, which opens with the question "What does it mean to think and live like an educated person?" (ix).

Given the increasing influence of business practices throughout society and the growing richness of business as an academic field of study, we have taken special note here of the future directions for business education. Trends ranging from globalization to Big Data to new business-and-society relationships are changing our practice and understanding of business. Increased focus on

---

[2] Take, for instance, the trend toward increasingly collaborative consumption, which is creating new business opportunities (e.g., Airbnb, Uber), changing the ways our goods-making supply chains will work (e.g., more leasing or renting, less ownership), and altering consumer behavior.

business analytics, new approaches to framing and solving problems spawned by a recent focus on design thinking, and the ability
to customize learning through a variety of technologies are changing business schools. This new world will need to engage not only
the admirers of business but also its critics. If we are, as Michael
Sandel (2012) put it, moving from a market economy to a market
society, this will require in business education greater self-reflection
and thoughtfulness. Such evolving trends in business need to be
part of our understanding of the expected learning outcomes and
assessment approaches used for the business major.

To preview our argument regarding these trends, we highlight
four central ideas that must inform business education if students
are to understand and engage the professional environment they
are entering. These central ideas involve having (a) a richer conception of how business is nested in society; (b) a more robust
and multidimensional understanding of globalization; (c) a more
sophisticated and nuanced appreciation of business analytics and
technology; and (d) a greater engagement of cognitive diversity
in business thinking. Rooting business students' education in
these four central ideas will serve students well in navigating the
global workspaces (physical, social, virtual, or otherwise) they will
inhabit. They will be best prepared to confront the question that
marks this contemporary moment in business: as we continue to
generate more information about more things, will we have the
knowledge to understand the meaning of this information and the
wisdom to use this knowledge well?

In this white paper, our discussion of learning outcomes for
the business major revolves around two broad areas: concepts and
competencies. Concepts are the models and frameworks business
professionals draw upon in their problem framing and solving work.
Competencies are the skills and dispositions required by individuals in business in making their professional choices. It is worth noting that business differs from a number of other disciplines in that
it draws from a wide range of disciplines itself, each of which has its

own set of learning outcomes. Rather than replicate learning out-comes from the underlying disciplines (e.g., economics, statistics, psychology, sociology), we focus here on the business concepts and competencies that integrate those underlying disciplines, describing learning outcomes that reflect what business graduates will have to do as they apply what they have learned in their work after graduation.

Through an iterative process that took into account prior efforts to define learning outcomes for business undergraduates as well as the expert opinions of a diverse group of business faculty,[3] we generated a set of *essential* concepts and competencies for the study of business in the 21st century. Such essential concepts and competencies reveal a broad, even if ultimately contestable, consensus regarding what business students should understand and be able to do by the time they graduate. They thus offer an opportunity both to engage a diverse group of faculty and to design effective assessment tools that faculty will be open to using.

We begin with a brief description of our approach to generating a set of essential concepts and competencies for the study of business in the 21st century. Next, we summarize some of the prior efforts to articulate learning outcomes for business undergraduates. Following

---

[3] The MCL Business faculty panelists were Sara Beckman (University of California–Berkeley), Thomas Calderon (University of Akron), Lynn Doran (Georgetown University), Anne Greenhalgh (University of Pennsylvania), Doug Guthrie (George Washington University, Apple Inc.), Kathleen Krentler (San Diego State University), Kathy Lund Dean (Gustavus Adolphus College), Jeffrey Nesteruk (Franklin & Marshall College), Claire Preisser (Aspen Institute), Robert Reid (Association to Advance Collegiate Schools of Business), Paige Reidy Soffen (The Aspen Institute), Scott Romeika (University of Pennsylvania), William Sullivan (Wabash College), Karen Tarnoff (East Tennessee State University), and Lynn Wooten (University of Michigan–Ann Arbor).

that, we propose a new set of learning outcomes for undergraduate business education in the 21st century, ones that draw on the emerging trends we see. In the final sections, we discuss the current state and future direction of learning outcomes assessment in undergraduate business education.

Methods

Any discussion of the learning outcomes desirable in a business major needs to be grounded in some conception of excellence regarding business practice, some sense, even if underdeveloped initially, of what it means to do business well. We thus began by bringing together a panel of business faculty drawn from a diverse group of institutions for a series of conversations about the current state and future direction of undergraduate education in business. We saw our charge as developing our conception of business excellence by articulating an explicit and structured set of learning outcomes essential to the study of business.

In our initial brainstorming sessions, we found that a general consensus regarding the learning outcomes for a major in business readily came to the fore. We grouped the learning outcomes that emerged under the two general headings of concepts (ideas and understandings) and competencies (skills and abilities).

We then subjected the results of our brainstorming sessions to two additional levels of critical scrutiny. First, we compared the outcome of our discussions to the results of prior prominent efforts to articulate learning outcomes for the business major. Second, we examined emerging trends within the contemporary business world and explored their significance for the future of business studies.

Drawing on our discussions and this review, we generated a set of essential concepts and competencies for the business major.

These concepts and competencies constitute a significant core for what business students should know and be able to do. What we articulate differs from prior efforts in that it points to the necessary recalibration of such concepts and competencies in the future business environment that is now emerging, and suggests more thoughtful integration of materials across the disciplines around which our delivery of content is generally organized at present.

Although we believe that articulating essential concepts and competencies as we have done is valuable for faculty in reflecting upon their work and for external stakeholders in understanding the worth of the business major, we acknowledge any discussion of this sort is complex, nuanced, and ultimately contestable. This is especially true because of business's status not as a discrete discipline, but as a field of study illuminating a multifaceted practice. To begin with, the expectations of the roles individuals occupy are not uniform across the domains of business. The risk-taking we so readily admire in an entrepreneur might be inappropriate, indeed suspect, in a corporate accountant. Secondly, the academic disciplines— from finance to marketing to organizational behavior—within business programs draw on different models and frameworks, some of which are in tension with each other. The notion of self that undergirds a finance class often differs from the conception of self that emerges in an organizational behavior course. Thirdly, the larger purpose of business is itself contested terrain. In what ways should corporations serve their shareholders? In what ways should corporations serve the larger society in which they exist? Indeed, what is the role of the broad range of organizations, from nonprofits to government agencies to NGOs, which now more routinely draw upon business models and expertise? Nonetheless, such complexity and nuance should not deter but rather encourage us to engage students' and faculty's interaction with and reflection on these different perspectives, highlighting and probing their ethical choices.

Prior Efforts to Articulate Learning Outcomes for Business Undergraduates

We are certainly far from the first to have examined learning outcomes for business students, and we wish here to highlight some features of such previous efforts. Work by the Association to Advance Collegiate Schools of Business to establish curriculum content standards (AACSB 2013) and by the United Kingdom's Quality Assurance Agency for Higher Education to create the Subject Benchmark Statement for General Business and Management (QAA 2007) stands out for its comprehensive coverage of business learning outcomes. Here we provide a brief summary of that work, clustered into two categories: concepts and competencies.

Concepts: Business Contexts and the Core Disciplines of Business

Because roughly 20 percent of all undergraduate students major in business, and because business organizations are increasingly tapped to play an integral role in our society, preparing students to participate in business implies preparing them at some level to participate in society more broadly. Thus, there is a need to have them understand elements of the broader context in which they will work.

The AACSB standards succinctly suggest that business students should have knowledge of the "economic, political, regulatory, legal, technological, and social contexts of organizations in a global society," whereas the UK QAA (2007, 2) adds that the effects of these upon "strategy, behavior, management and sustainability of organizations" must be understood at the "local, national and international levels." In our discussion of essential concepts for 21st-century business education, we build on the notion of business context, suggesting that students be taught to be more thoughtful about the role of business in society, and about the personal role they have in determining how and where business may have its most meaningful impact.

Within that broader business context, the AACSB and QAA documents highlight the centrality of the core disciplines that constitute a typical education in business. These core disciplines represent the critical activities in which all forms of business engage. Our work leverages what has already been identified in these documents (and others)[4] but pushes for more integration of the concepts across disciplinary boundaries and with consideration for the overarching development of the identified competencies.

Table 7.1 summarizes the key elements of business context and the core disciplines identified by the AACSB and UK QAA guidelines, and shows a relatively high level of agreement at this level of abstraction.

Competencies: Analytical and Personal Skills

As important, we believe, as the concepts business students learn are the underlying competencies they develop. We will broaden the existing work in this regard, and suggest the significant implications of doing so on our choice of ways to assess learning. In the prior work, there are two types of competencies highlighted: analytical and personal. One might readily argue that these underlying competencies are required in many fields other than business, and thus form a baseline body of skills, a topic to which we return later. Table 7.2 summarizes the analytical and personal competencies

---

[4] The 2009 Tuning Project report "Reference Points for the Design and Delivery of Degree Programmes in Business," supported by the European Commission through the Socrates and Tempus programmes (of the Directorate–General for Education and Culture) offers another thorough review of the learning outcomes for business that shows considerable agreement with much of the AASCB and QAA work as well as many of the arguments put forth here.

Table 7.1 High-level Concepts Identified by AACSB and UK QAA as Important to Business Students

		Included in AACSB	Included in UK QAA
Concept Area 1: Business Contexts	Economic	X	X
	Environmental	X	X
	Legal/Regulatory	X	X
	Political	X	X
	International/Global	X	X
	Social	X	X
	Technological	X	X
Concept Area 2: Core Disciplines	Accounting*		X
	Economics	X	
	Finance	X	X
	Information Systems	X	X
	Marketing	X	X
	Operations	X	X
	Organizations	X	X
	Strategy		X

*Accounting is not included in the AACSB's standards for business because AACSB has separate standards for business and accounting.

Table 7.2 Competencies Included in the AACSB and UK QAA guidelines

		Included in AACSB	Included in UK QAA
Analytical Competencies	Data analysis	X	X
	Statistics	X	
Personal Competencies	Communication	X	X
	Personal development	X	X
	Thinking	X	X

called out in the AACSB and UK QAA standards, again showing a great deal of agreement.

Although the strength of this prior work on learning outcomes is evident in its comprehensiveness, such comprehensiveness has a particular character. It is articulated within and remains strongly tied to established disciplinary silos (e.g., finance, marketing, strategy). Thus, it lacks the integration we see as crucial given the evolving nature of the contemporary business environment. There is also a need to clarify the distinction between concepts (what students need to know) and competencies (what they should be able to do). This is particularly important because some of the competencies we recommend, such as ethical judgment and cross-cultural management, involve not simply intellectual skills, but emotional and social development. Finally, the significant trends we have identified—from new business-and-society relationships, to globalization, to Big Data, to the integration of creative and critical thinking—will reframe and reconfigure some of the established functional areas in business. We attempt to capture this recalibration of business knowledge in the next section on essential concepts and competencies.

Essential Concepts and Competencies for the Business Major

We found in our discussions with the SSRC's assembled panel of business professors considerable overlap with earlier efforts, such as the AACSB curricular standards and the UK Quality Assurance Agency's Subject Benchmark Statement. In what follows, we draw heavily from such previous efforts, but reconceptualize and update them for the 21st century. In doing so, we strive to make more explicit our understanding of what it means to do business well in practice and to highlight the emerging trends in business that must now be incorporated into learning outcomes for the major.

Within our general schema, essential concepts are the models and frameworks business professionals draw upon in their problem framing and solving work. Essential competencies are the skills and dispositions required by individuals in business in making their professional choices.

Essential Concepts

Consensus around broad themes in the area of essential concepts emerged fairly readily. These themes represent the deep conceptual understanding we would expect to see in graduates of a business program. There are more specific learning outcomes one might associate with each concept, but they provide a broad sense as to what businesspeople must understand. Many of these concepts span the traditional disciplines of business. This was an intentional decision, reflecting our expectation and aspiration for business education to be a more richly integrative experience. Further, we hope that this broader angle of vision will provide an opportunity to reframe some of the underlying concepts to better match the needs of today's organizations as they strive to transform and innovate in a more complex, uncertain, and volatile business world. Here, in broad terms, are the things we expect business students to understand when they leave our programs.

Concept 1: Business in Society

The conception of business implicated in much of our discussion was the notion of business as *nested* or *embedded* in society. Rather than viewing business as a segregated activity, one in which choices can be readily justified as "just business," this nested conception of business contemplates a professional commitment to the view that business finds its normative grounding in a broad conception of service to society. In a world in which the roles of business, government, and civil society are changing and intertwined, this is becoming increasingly important. The notion of business as a world unto itself, subject only to its own disparate set of rules, is ill suited for the character of our increasingly dynamic and more interconnected lives.

The October 24, 2015, issue of *The Economist*, whose cover story is "Reinventing the Company," brings the discussion of business in society into the mainstream, opening with the assertion that "entrepreneurs are redesigning the basic building blocks of business" (9) and proceeding to describe the ways the entrepreneurial culture is not only changing the ways larger corporations think about how they do business but also the fundamental ways we structure, for example, consumption in our society. Business leaders today are designing a new world that promises to look radically different from the one in which we now live (Brynjolfsson and McAfee 2011). They need to understand their role in designing that world, the effects of their choices on others, and how their choices will play out through the variety of systems they are changing (Goleman 2013). One might simply look at the myriad issues surrounding the rollout of companies like Uber and Airbnb to see the need to appreciate what business leaders confront today.

Such a nested conception of business in society has significant import. For increasingly the relevant society in which business operates is an economically globalized environment embedded in a technologically integrated world. Thus, the commitment to a more richly nested conception of business entails three correlative notions. The first is a more robust and multidimensional understanding of globalization. The second is a more sophisticated and nuanced appreciation of business analytics in a new technological era. The third is the ability to see the various elements of business and their interactions with the broader society and the interactions among societal elements, as a system, and to understand the leverage points for change in that system (Meadows 2008). Thus, a more richly nested conception of business necessitates the mastery of two correlative concepts (globalization and system dynamics) and a correlative competency (informational and technological literacy).

Without this broader understanding, large global issues such as climate change and disparities in distribution of wealth cannot be addressed. At an industry level, the massive changes that will be wrought by new technologies such as self-driving cars will require considerations that go well beyond the bounds of an individual company to redesigning cities and ultimately how we live. As students learn the basic concepts of business outlined in prior work, they must see how those concepts can be more broadly framed to grapple with such problems and opportunities, and how the business choices they are making will affect our broader society as they are implemented.

Concept 2: Globalization

Globalization is defined as the worldwide movement toward economic, financial, trade, and communications integration resulting in an interconnected and interdependent world with free transfer of capital, goods, and services across national frontiers. The process of globalization has accelerated in recent years as the result of improved telecommunications and the penetration of the Internet into previously unreachable regions. Business schools have responded in a variety of ways. Traditional study abroad programs provided students with some exposure to other cultures but have given way to deeper global experiences. The schools that have delivered powerful intellectual experiences in the study of the global economy are those that have built curricula on interdisciplinarity, such as Harvard Business School's core MBA course on business and government in the international economy.

Globalization requires rethinking the underlying concepts identified in prior work with a critical eye to seeing them through a global lens. There is no doubt, for example, that global companies have to approach marketing with an eye to balancing global positioning and messaging along with local customization efforts.

Accounting practices vary widely based on different regulatory standards globally, requiring different accounting strategies. Strategy is no longer bounded by national or industry lines as implied in many strategy models. Beyond the need to rethink the basic concepts of business is the need to increase cultural awareness and enhance the ability to leverage differences (e.g., those involved in designing for the bottom of the pyramid), allowing a company to both thrive in and take advantage of different world perspectives.

Concept 3: Strategy

Within the global and rapidly changing business context, business leaders must quickly design and redesign strategies and determine the best way to implement those strategies, improvising and adapting as the environment continues to change. Emergence of the triple bottom line and subsequently the integrated bottom line[5] approaches to measuring an organization's performance is changing how corporate leaders make strategic choices. No longer is achieving profits the only measure of a company's success: In the face of increased complexity and change, the more mechanistic models of organizations through which strategy is enacted are giving way to models such as complex adaptive systems (Spiegel 2014). Students thus need to understand both the larger dynamics of business and the systems through which strategy is executed.

Business students will have to learn how to operate in a world of increasingly difficult and complex trade-offs (e.g., How can I

---

[5] The integrated bottom line is a process for integrating financial, environmental, and social costs and benefits into a unified measure of business activity. Conventional objectives of profitability, competitive advantage, efficiency, and economic growth are judged successful by their compatibility with biodiversity, ecological sustainability, equity, community support, and maximized well-being for a variety of stakeholders. The integrated bottom line differs from the triple bottom line in that all measures are combined into one balance sheet and income statement rather than being accounted for separately.

keep costs low and people employed but not exploit them?) that require evaluation across traditional disciplinary boundaries. Business students will have to learn more dynamic models of strategy making, such as dynamic capabilities models (Teece and Pisano 1994) and transient advantage frameworks (McGrath 2013), and to select from among a growing array of alternative business models, such as shared economy and multisided platform. Business students will have to understand more deeply the dynamics, thus leveraging the correlative system dynamics concept, of their own businesses, starting with the basics of the business model canvas (Osterwalder and Pigneur 2010). Widespread adoption of the canvas in a variety of businesses speaks to the desire to see strategy making as an integrated whole, and to understand the interactions among its elements. They will also have to learn new models of organizational design (e.g., complex adaptive systems, networked organizations, communities of practice) to understand how to go about implementing strategy.

Concept 4: System Dynamics

We have highlighted in the three prior concepts—business in society, globalization, and strategy—both the need to view businesses themselves as systems and the need to understand the dynamics of the systems in which they operate. Achieving organizational goals entails understanding, operating, and monitoring the execution systems that efficiently turn organizational inputs, such as materials and labor, into the organization's desired outputs, ranging from goods or services to experiences or transformations. Making and executing strategy requires appreciation of the dynamics of the systems that sit around the organization, from the supply chain or value chain in which it resides to the broader business context in which it operates and that it influences.

MIT has a long history of teaching system dynamics in a very explicit way to its business students, engaging them in modeling the systems they are studying, creating, or affecting. These systems modeling approaches have been widely used in, for example, assessing means of managing climate change and other such environmental impacts (Meadows 2008), understanding the dynamics of markets (e.g., modeling the ups and downs of the real estate market), and evaluating the effects of the implementation of governmental policies and regulations (e.g., health-care policy). They have also been used within organizations to diagnose a quality program (Repenning and Sterman 2001), to help improve the efficiency of the supply chain (Sterman 2000), or to evaluate the performance of the new product development process (Repenning, Gonçalves, and Black 2001). A set of archetypes for understanding system dynamics has made the field more tractable (Senge 1990).

Future business students need to be able to build dynamic models of the complex systems in which they are working, developing a better sense of how their actions will affect those systems and more readily identifying points of leverage for change in the system. Although the formal methods developed at MIT for understanding systems are extremely valuable, simpler approaches can help students as well. Simple visualizations of systems, such as flowcharts, customer journey maps, and information maps, help students grasp the complexities of the systems they are studying.

Concept 5: Consumer Engagement

Research at least as far back as the 1970s (e.g., Rothwell et al. 1974) has regularly shown that the primary failure mode of new products in the marketplace is lack of understanding of customer and user needs. Feigenbaum (1983) highlights:

> Quality is a customer determination, not an engineer's determination, not a marketing determination or a general management determination. It is based upon the customer's actual experience with the product or service, measured against his or her requirements—stated or unstated, conscious or merely sensed, technically

objective or entirely subjective—always representing a moving target in a competitive market.

Today, as consumers increase their expectations not only for products and services but also for experiences and transformations (Pine and Gilmore 1998), companies increasingly seek to become what some call customer-driven organizations.

Becoming customer focused, however, is not trivial for organizations long driven by efficiency and profitability goals. Identifying desirable goods, services, and overall customer experiences involves discerning, analyzing, and engaging consumer needs and preferences; defining the value to be delivered; and then communicating the value of the organization's outputs to the customers. Kimbell (2014) argues that value emerges in use, meaning that companies must increasingly see themselves as co-creating value with customers. This requires not only developing close relationships with customers and users through a variety of means but also fostering and sharing a fully developed sense of the experience the organization wants to deliver at all levels of the organization. Delivering the customer experience requires well-orchestrated execution across the organization. This requires understanding the job to be done through the experience created, all of the different ways customers and users want to access the organization, how to deliver and price to value, and how to educate customers and users about the solutions provided (Ettenson, Conrado, and Knowles 2013).

The current design thinking movement, like the quality movement before it, puts deep understanding of customers front and center in its approach. The lean start-up movement similarly emphasizes regular interaction with customers to design to their needs. All of these approaches, old and new, cut across traditional disciplines, integrating them with a focus on serving, or co-creating value with, customers and users.

Concept 6: Transparency, Disclosure, and Metrics

Business organizations must identify, measure, and allocate financial resources. Increasingly, they must do so around the integrated bottom line, examining not only financial performance but also environmental and social performance. Niche schools such as the Presidio School of Management and the Bainbridge Graduate Institute at Pinchot have placed integrated bottom line thinking at the center of their business programs.

Moreover, business organizations in the 21st century are encountering heightened demands for accountability and disclosure, and facing, somewhat paradoxically, growing expectations and skepticism. There is thus a need to define, share, and communicate more effectively the value of the work they do to a wider group of stakeholders. As yet another feature of the business and society concept, business organizations must be prepared to engage disparate conceptions of value in communicating with their constituencies. An employee fearful of losing his job, a consumer seeking lower prices, and a local government official committed to protecting his community's water supply may understand *value* in different ways.

In articulating these conceptual themes, we have been intentional in richly contextualizing and broadly framing around the established disciplinary silos of business. Our approach is aimed at rooting more fully the business disciplines in the underlying conceptual understandings that are central to business. As emerging trends require a recalibration of business knowledge, the traditional functional areas must remain attuned and responsive to the evolving practices that inform them, integrating with other functional areas as needed.

Essential Competencies

Along with having knowledge of theoretical models, concepts, and principles, the best business practitioners possess a number of practical competencies. Developing such competencies is thus a central part of the education a business major should provide. Our discussion of such practical competencies brought to the fore a range of intellectual, emotional, and social skills. The diversity of skills here arises from the complex and challenging nature of decision-making in today's dynamic business environment. In our discussion, we strove to articulate the combination of capacities and dispositions necessary for effective deliberation and wise judgment in the contemporary business world.

We offer the following four practical competencies not as generic skills, but as contextualized, field-specific capabilities needed and applicable to the distinctive character of business practices and their emerging environment. Particularly because of the way these four practical competencies overlap with transformative trends within the business environment, there is the need to integrate them fully into the essential concepts identified thematically in the previous section.

Competency 1: Select from and Deploy Diverse Thinking Skills

In the business world now emerging, business choices involve a complex mix of social, political, economic, and technological imperatives. The choices to be made in this dynamic and turbulent environment involve many actors and elements that interact with one another, and are non-linear, such that a minor change can have disproportionate effects (Kimbell 2014). Such a complex mix of disparate constraints and opportunities points to the need for greater cognitive diversity in business thinking.

More specifically, analytical thinking is by itself no longer adequate in a business environment in which the analytic schema to be employed is frequently up for grabs. In today's more complex and multifarious business world, business choices have multiple and even incommensurate framing possibilities: They are "wicked problems" (Rittel and Webber 1973, 155). Business students must thus become increasingly adept at working in and across multiple thinking styles. They require *critical and analytical thinking* to probe assumptions in any given schema; *integrative thinking* to "assess and balance conflicting ideas" and to seek "a creative resolution of the tension in the form of new models" (Rotman School of Management, "Integrative Thinking"); *systemic thinking* to see "how the thing being studied interacts with other constituents of the system" (Aronson 1996, 1); and *design thinking* (previously known as creative problem solving), a form of thinking that effectively integrates empathy and creativity with a focus on rapid experimentation.

In aggregate, simply said, there is a thirst for better and clearer thinking in the framing and solving of problems. One might argue that the ability to frame and solve problems has always been important in education, and indeed that is true. We believe, however, that in a world of increasingly rapid change (e.g., in technology and consumer expectations), and with increasing access to the content provided in a business education online, being able to digest information and frame and reframe the problems to be solved will become a more and more important skill in and of itself. Further, more explicit understanding of different approaches to framing and solving problems is needed. Although critical and analytical thinking methods in particular are implicit in many business courses, rarely are general approaches to framing and solving problems made explicit. Thus, we highlight thinking as an important part of business education.

Critical and analytical thinking: Critical and analytical thinking has been defined as follows:

> It is a complex process of deliberation which involves a wide range of skills and attitudes. It includes identifying other people's positions, arguments and conclusions; evaluating the evidence for alternative points of view; weighing up opposing arguments and evidence fairly; being able to read between the lines . . .; recognizing

techniques used to make certain positions more appeal-
ing than others . . .; reflecting on issues in a structured
way . . .; drawing conclusions about whether arguments
are valid and justifiable . . .; synthesizing information
. . .; [and] presenting a point of view. (Cottrell 2011, 2)

Business schools, and our education system more broadly, have
arguably focused a great deal of attention on the development
of critical and analytical thinking capabilities, even if implicitly,
through the means by which subjects are taught.

Integrative thinking: Integrative thinking underpins the development of the University of Toronto's Rotman School of Management's curriculum. Roger Martin, dean of the Rotman School
from 1998 to 2013, defined integrative thinking as the ability "to
assess and balance conflicting ideas, business models or strategies,
and instead of choosing one at the expense of the other, generate
a creative resolution of the tension in the form of new models,
new decisions or new ways of doing things" (Rotman School of
Management, "Integrative Thinking"; see also Martin 2007). The
University of Virginia's McEntire School of Commerce teaches
integrative thinking through its Integrated Core Experience, a
seven-course sequence that has been "carefully constructed to give
students a vantage into the world of business from multiple angles,
integrating the analytic, strategic, and behavioral skills they'll
need to tackle real-world problems, with projects from corporate
sponsors" (McEntire School of Commerce, "Integrated Core").

Systems thinking: "The approach of systems thinking is fundamentally different from that of traditional forms of analysis. Traditional analysis focuses on separating the individual pieces of what
is being studied . . . . Systems thinking, in contrast, focuses on how
the thing being studied interacts with the other constituents of
the system . . . of which it is a part" (Aronson 1996, 1). "Systems
thinking . . . is practiced . . . in a wide variety of fields, [but] it is
still a difficult subject to teach. This difficulty has in large part

been caused by the adoption of traditional teaching models that emphasize disciplinary analysis. These [traditional methods] are poorly suited to teaching the very different mindset that systems thinking entails" as they resist thinking across disciplinary boundaries (Kay and Foster 1999, 171). Systems thinking, particularly as embodied in system dynamics modeling (Sterman 2000), will require development of courses that integrate materials across the traditional business disciplines. MIT continues to lead in teaching system dynamics, including a variety of online courses in addition to those taught on campus (Sterman and Rahmandad 2013).

Design thinking (creative problem solving): Design thinking has come to be defined as combining empathy for the context of a problem, creativity in the generation of insights and solutions, and rationality in analyzing and fitting various solutions to the problem context (Visser 2006). According to Tim Brown, CEO and president of IDEO, the goal of design thinking is "matching people's needs with what is technologically feasible and viable as a business strategy" (Kelley and Kelley 2013, 19–20). Design thinking goes further than analytical thinking by acknowledging multiple points of view and different frames, by encouraging generative thought to explore multiple alternatives, and by focusing on learning through experimentation (Beckman and Barry 2007). As applied to business, design thinking implies being able to construct knowledge both within the organization (research) and about the users' world (data gathering and fieldwork) and at the same time generate alternative concepts both internal to the organization (in studio design work) as well as in co-creation with the customer (Kimbell 2014).

Business students in the future need to be explicitly taught how to think through framing and solving problems and how and when to select from the wide variety of approaches that are available to them.

Competency 2: Exercise Ethical Judgment

The same growing complexity of the contemporary business world that gives rise to the need for greater cognitive diversity in business thinking also brings to the fore the need for fostering in business students a more developed and sophisticated sense of ethical judgment. As an increasingly important dimension of the business-in-society concept in which *society* is an economically globalized environment embedded in a technologically integrated world, ethical judgment needs to be more thoroughly and intimately integrated into business education. Global society is increasing its expectations of business, asking that business pursue its aims in ways that are fair, equitable, and sustainable. Thus, rather than a curricular add-on or an ancillary component of business studies, ethics should be central to the study of business and transformative of its basic character. This transformation involves integrating critical perspectives with the more traditional instrumental orientations of business education. It also involves helping students find their inner focus, developing self-awareness and self-control, and tuning them into their own thoughts and feelings, as "a failure to focus inward leaves you rudderless" (Goleman 2013, 4). If we wish students to discover a renewed sense of their own agency in shaping their business environments, we must deepen the ethical development they engage in throughout the multiple experiences of their business education.

While the cognitive skills necessary for ethical reasoning in business are clearly important, ethical judgment here is more than an intellectual exercise. It involves a critical self-awareness, empathy for and understanding of others, and a disposition toward positive change in the world. It also requires the capacity to deliberate not simply in an ideal or static context, but in fast moving, pressured environments, subject to shifting economic, political, social, and technological restraints. Combining such emotional and social development with enhanced ethical reasoning skills is central to preparing today's business students for the personal complexities and professional challenges they will encounter in their working lives. Such development and enhanced skills should foster not an indoctrination into an externally imposed ethic, but rather should deepen the student's capacity for articulating and exercising independent ethical judgment.

Competency 3: Demonstrate Informational and Technological Literacy

The basic building blocks of technology have been improving in performance at an exponential rate for something like thirty years now (Brynjolfsson and McAfee 2011). This places us today at the knee of an exponential curve, at a tipping point where technology will facilitate unprecedented and in many ways unforeseeable changes. The evolution of technology will drive significant change in what businesses do, how they deliver it, and how they manage themselves, implying that business leaders will have to know enough about these evolving technologies to know in what ways they might be leveraged in their own businesses. Further, in an age of data and information, students will need the ability to understand, probe, interpret, and communicate business information using written, oral, visual, and quantitative means of doing so.

In response to these technological changes, business schools must make adjustments in how they educate their students. In particular, a substantive area that has significantly transformed business school curricula in the last two decades has been the rise of the field of business analytics, and it deserves special attention here. The field of decision sciences is certainly not new, but the ways it has reorganized around the analysis of Big Data has become a major substantive change for business education. Students will need to learn the fundamentals of working with data (e.g., from statistics and decision sciences) as well as what it means to conduct business in a Big Data environment (e.g., collecting data about consumers, using data to drive operational decisions).

Competency 4: Management, Teaming, and Cross-Cultural Competence

Achieving organizational goals entails engaging and coordinating the efforts of individuals within business enterprises. Teaming will be core within these systems, involving the rapid creation and disbanding of teams around tasks or activities to be done in the moment (Edmonson 2012). Teaming in organizations is the "engine of organizational learning . . . a way of working that brings people together to generate new ideas, find answers and solve problems" (chap. 1).

But, as Edmonson points out, "people have to learn to team; it doesn't come naturally" (Edmonson 2012, 24). In particular, diverse teams have been shown to either significantly underperform or overperform more homogeneous teams (Ely and Thomas 2001). As globalization increasingly brings together individuals from a variety of backgrounds, experiences, and understandings in business settings, this dynamic will have greater impact. Diverse teams underperform when they are either blind to the diversity present, or when they treat the diversity with stereotypes. They outperform when they have a learning perspective that allows them to acknowledge and leverage the multiple bodies of knowledge that are present on the team. Thus, learning to effectively leverage the diversity, cultural or otherwise, present on a team will be critical to the success of businesses.

More broadly, in a global business environment, understanding of different cultures and how best to operate within them will be core to succeeding in global markets. Students will not only have to learn appreciation of other cultures, but also how to use that appreciation in making both strategic and tactical business decisions.

Although we often ask students to work in teams (or groups) while they are in school, we rarely provide them with the tools they need while working in those teams to improve the performance of the team itself, and to improve their performance as team members and ultimately team leaders. Development of this competency requires more closely embedding teaming curriculum into the courses in which students participate in team activities, which provides the opportunity to teach teaming over time, across multiple courses. Thus students can practice teaming and leveraging diversity (cross-cultural competence) in the relatively safe confines of an educational environment, allowing them to grow those skills over time.

Essential Concepts and Competencies for the Introductory Course

Teaching essential concepts and competencies is, potentially at least, at stake at the introductory level of the business major. Our discussions with business faculty, however, took note of the way introductory business courses typically focus on economics, accounting, and math, thus giving primary emphasis to the teaching of a rather narrow set of concepts relative to the major as a whole. In our brainstorming about alternative possibilities, we turned to newer, more integrative approaches to an introductory-level course in business, such as incorporating start-up exercises or experiential learning opportunities into the introductory curriculum.

It is crucial to create, as Alfred North Whitehead (1929) put it, a state of romance in the beginning if we wish to engage students in learning business. Our desire to create a state of romance for the beginning business student dovetails nicely with the business-in-society framework as a core concept. A view of business that engages not only students' desires for professional advancement and financial gain but also their personal ideals and larger social aspirations will more powerfully motivate the kind of ethical leadership, creative and critical thinking, and perseverance that we wish to encourage.

Such a desire for an initial state of romance also favors a more richly contextualized approach to the introductory-level coursework for the business major. This is because such a deeper attraction arises out of not only being wholly engaged as a person, but also out of being engaged by the whole picture of business and importantly its connections to the broader societal agenda. A more richly contextual approach to introducing students to the study of

business allows students to appreciate more fully the value and significance of courses in economics, accounting, and math, exposing
the linkages of these subjects to the full range of business topics. It
also offers students critical opportunities to enter into and reflect
upon the larger questions of business's nature, purpose, and value.
Reflecting upon such larger questions will underscore the need for
the greater cognitive diversity within business thinking that we
have advocated.

Current and Future Assessments

Within our discussion of learning outcomes, questions of assessment frequently surfaced because of the intimate linkages between
the two domains. For instance, assessment that occurs not only
at the end of particular functional courses, but is woven throughout an experiential exercise is a form of assessment more fully
attuned to the notion of business as an integrated practice serving
its stakeholders. Thus, the emphasis on integration that charac-
terized much of our discussion regarding learning outcomes has
implications for our understanding of assessment. Advocating, for
instance, systemic thinking as a learning outcome requires a correlative approach of assessment.

Linkages such as these also raise another issue regarding the
relation of learning outcomes and assessment. Although the learning outcomes we desire should be the basis of the assessment forms
we devise, the reverse is also possible. The metrics of our assessment forms in practice may also subtly influence our aspirations
for learning. We must be mindful of conflating what is most easily
measurable with what is pedagogically most desirable.

Current Assessments

As with earlier efforts to articulate the concepts that business
students need to learn and the competencies they need to develop,

there is considerable previous work seeking to define appropriate assessment tools.

Some of the assessments aim to be comprehensive, evaluating students across most of the concepts and some of the competencies we earlier identified in our discussion of prior work to articulate learning outcomes. Such assessments include the Educational Testing Service (ETS) Major Field Test for business, the Business Assessment Test (BAT) developed by a consortium of California State University business schools in the early 2000s, and, for graduate students, the Graduate Management Admissions Test (GMAT). The ETS MFT and the BAT primarily employ multiple-choice style questions to assess student understanding of business contexts (legal and social environment, international issues), core disciplines (accounting, economics, information systems, marketing, and finance) and analytical competence (quantitative business analysis). The GMAT, although still primarily employing multiple-choice style questions, aims to assess competencies (analytical writing, integrated reasoning, quantitative skills, and verbal skills).

Other assessments are less comprehensive or in-depth in evaluating specific core concept knowledge but offer a better evaluation of the ability of students to integrate learning across the concept areas and to apply the competencies to their problem framing and solving work. Examples of these evaluation tools include the following:

- _Capstone Simulations_ (capsim.com): Widely considered the gold standard for strategy simulations, Capsim provides multiple simulations for both "regular" business and international business. Along with the simulations, they offer embedded assessment and assurance of learning tools (http://www.capsim .com/comp-xm/). The Capstone simulation is appropriate for senior capstone students, but the organization also offers Foundations, a simplified version of Capstone focused on baseline knowledge (http://www.capsim.com/foundation/) through which students can get an introduction and then build more specific and technical knowledge.

- *AAC&U VALUE Rubrics* (https://www.aacu.org/value-rubrics): This is a relatively new, wide-ranging effort to measure learning outcomes using faculty-designed grading rubrics. Some of the rubrics would be particularly well suited for measuring the kinds of learning outcomes we have emphasized in this white paper (e.g., cross-cultural competence and globalization).

- *Inbox exercises*: Inbox exercises have been used for many years as a competency assessment for assessing how potential candidates for a job might perform day-to-day. There are many of these types of exercises—some are openly available and some are proprietary, but all focus on evaluating competencies rather than concepts.

Prior assessment efforts also include tools that measure specific core knowledge deemed important not only for business students but also for college students at large. When major accreditors began including ethical reasoning and global orientation in their learning outcomes (e.g., as AACSB did in 2003), many business schools looked for validated instruments to use in these core areas, including the following examples:

- *Intercultural Development Inventory* (http://idiinventory.com/): This is a validated instrument that requires facilitators to be certified in administering it, much like the Myers Briggs Type Indicator (MBTI). Many schools use this to assess the global dimension of learning outcomes. There is research supporting its validation and usage.

- *Defining Issues Test (DIT)* (http://ethicaldevelopment.ua.edu/dit-and-dit-2/): The DIT, developed by psychologist James Rest in the 1970s, focuses on ethical learning. Though it is widely used, it has some significant limitations, namely, it makes significant assumptions about the cognitively heavy nature of individual moral reasoning, limiting the inclusion of social psychology and other significant perspectives.

We highlight only a few of the many current approaches to assessing business learning outcomes here, but we can discern the general contours of the character of such approaches. The major and most comprehensive assessments focus largely on the concepts and analytic competencies, thus lacking a richer attention to key personal competencies, such as creative thinking, emerging as critical in contemporary business trends. Assessment tools that are focused on competencies tend to be more narrowly focused, thus missing the broader and more encompassing integration we are calling for in the 21st-century business environment. New initiatives, such as the AAC&U VALUE rubrics project, are starting to address more fully such contemporary needs, though AAC&U does so from the perspective of general education, rather than providing contextualized, business-specific approaches.

Future Assessments

As our aspirations for student learning in undergraduate business education grow and evolve, so must the assessments we have at our disposal to measure students' progress toward those goals. Looking ahead, we see the need for the development and refinement of assessment tools and processes in five key areas.

Increased Use of Integrated Approaches

Along with recommending a more contextualized introductory course to the business major, we see a correlative need for more integrated assessment frameworks from the start. It is important that from the beginning students see the whole if they are to meaningfully engage the parts. Integrated assessment approaches are also crucial as students progress through the required functional areas (e.g., strategy, marketing, finance) of the business curriculum. If students are to embrace the creative possibilities of a dynamic business environment, they must transcend narrower siloed perspectives. The broader and more encompassing integration we envision should include both concepts and competencies and effectively incorporate personal competencies, such as ethical judgment and cross-cultural management that are at the core of emerging trends within the contemporary business environment.

More Continuous and Incremental Feedback During the Learning Process

As we are asking more of students' intellectual and personal development in the business major, we believe they deserve more real-time, individualized feedback to ensure the progressive mastery of content and skills during their engagement with course readings, exercises, and simulations. End-of-course assessment should complement, rather than substitute for, this ongoing assessment process. The growing popularity of badging systems such as that used by Khan Academy point to the interest in such incremental and real-time feedback.

Richer Infusion of Business and Society and Globalization Perspectives

In emphasizing the necessity to reframe and reconfigure established domains of business knowledge in light of contemporary trends, we see the need for integrating new perspectives into the content associated with the traditional functional business disciplines. Thus, there is a need for assessment tools to evaluate, for example, student competence in strategy within a business and society framework or marketing within a globalized economy.

Greater Incorporation of Technology-Enhanced Data Gathering Capabilities

Although we affirm the enduring value of personal mentoring, social learning environments, and face-to-face instruction, we urge the development of assessment tools that leverage technology's expanded data gathering capabilities to enhance instructors' awareness of students' academic strengths, struggles, and progress. We ask the following: What are the reoccurring and distinctive blind spots in the learning process that are not readily apparent to the instructor via traditional classroom interaction? How can technology illuminate such areas? Might we, for example, evaluate a student's performance on a team using some form of video analysis, or might we evaluate their communication skills with some form of semantic analysis? The technological capabilities we might leverage are far beyond the scope of this paper, but we are certain there are approaches yet untapped that would allow us to more deeply understand student comprehension and application of concepts. As a significant related benefit, immersing business students within such a data-rich educational setting will help prepare them for the technologically sophisticated business environment in which they will work.

Greater Attention to the Diversity of Cognitive Styles

In reviewing current assessment approaches, we saw a focus on critical and analytical thinking, but not a developed and sustained attention to other forms of thinking that we see as crucial in the emerging contemporary environment of business. Thus, we would recommend the development of assessment tools designed to more explicitly and fully evaluate integrative thinking, systemic thinking, and design (creative) thinking along with traditional analytical thinking. These approaches will focus less on having students identify a single correct answer to a specified problem, but will instead test their abilities to frame a problem in the first place, to generate alternative solutions, and to formulate tests of those solutions.

Conclusion

In examining the learning outcomes and assessment tools for the undergraduate business major, we have drawn upon current understandings and approaches, identifying what we see as key learning outcomes and salient needs for future assessment. Particularly in the current dynamics and trends we highlight, we see an underlying injunction, both for business students and the institutions that educate them: be at once more socially aspirational and self-aware. A critical corollary: use technology wisely to invent meaningful futures with a global perspective. With an integrated view of business and society and the recognition of our social arena as a globalized world, business students and their institutions must continue the process of expanding their horizons and engagements. In a wired world we will know more things, and if the promise of Big Data and business analytics holds true, know them more deeply and with greater certainty. Yet in an era of the customization and personalization of education, both students and business schools must also know themselves better. Self-knowledge in students is important because in an era with more educational choices, they must become more adept at reflecting upon and navigating their own learning and development. For the institutions that educate these students, self-knowledge is of equal importance. For unless they know what they are trying to do and can show they are doing it well, they will have missed the possibilities this new world will offer.

In contemplating this new world, it is prudent to look back as we go forward. The word *business* has its etymological roots in an Old English term meaning "busyness." There is wisdom here if we are willing to pause and discern it. For as Henry David Thoreau is sometimes misquoted, "It is not enough to be busy. So are the ants. The question is: What are we busy about?" In this new world we are entering, we in business education must ask anew: What are we busy about? We should be ready to be surprised by our answers.

References

Aronson, Daniel. 1996. "Overview of Systems Thinking." *Thinking Page*. http://www.thinking.net/Systems_Thinking/OverviewSTarticle.pdf.

Association to Advance Collegiate Schools of Business (AACSB).
    2013. "2013 Business Accreditation Standards." http://www.aacsb.
    edu/accreditation/standards/2013-business/learning-and-teaching/
    standard9.aspx.

Beckman, Sara L., and Michael R. Barry. 2007. "Innovation as a
    Learning Process: Embedding Design Thinking." *California
    Management Review* 50: 25–56.

Brynjolfsson, Erik, and Andrew McAfee. 2011. *Race Against the
    Machine: How the Digital Revolution Is Accelerating Innovation,
    Driving Productivity, and Irreversibly Transforming Employment and
    The Economy.* n.p.: Digital Frontier Press.

Colby, Anne, Thomas Erlich, William M. Sullivan, and Jonathan R.
    Dolle. 2011. *Rethinking Undergraduate Business Education: Liberal
    Learning for the Profession.* San Francisco: Jossey-Bass.

Cottrell, Stella. 2011. *Critical Thinking Skills: Developing Effective
    Analysis and Argument.* New York: Palgrave Macmillan.

The Economist. 2015. "Reinventing the Company." October 24. http://
    www.economist.com/news/leaders/21676767-entrepreneurs-are-
    redesigning-basic-building-block-capitalism-reinventing-company.

Edmondson, Amy C. 2012. *Teaming: How Organizations Learn, Innovate,
    and Compete in the Knowledge Economy.* San Francisco: Jossey-Bass.

Educational Testing Service (ETS). 2014. "Major Field Test in Business:
    Test Description." https://www.ets.org/s/mft/pdf/mft_testdesc_
    business.pdf.

Ely, Robin J., and David A. Thomas. 2001. "Cultural Diversity at
    Work: The Effects of Diversity Perspectives on Work Group."
    Administrative Science Quarterly 46, no. 2: 229–273.

Ettenson, Richard, Eduardo Conrado, and Jonathan Knowles. 2013.
    "Rethinking the 4 P's." *Harvard Business Review* 91, no. 1: 26–27.

Feigenbaum, Armand Vallin. 1983. *Total Quality Control.* New York:
    McGraw-Hill.

Goleman, Daniel. 2013. *Focus: The Hidden Driver of Excellence.* New
    York: Harper.

Kay, James J., and Jason A. Foster. 1999. "About Teaching Systems
    Thinking." In *Proceedings of the HKK Conference, 14–16 June*, edited
    by G. Savage and P. Roe, 165–172. Ontario: University of Waterloo.

Kelley, Tom, and David Kelley. 2013. *Creative Confidence: Unleashing the Creative Potential Within Us All*. New York: Crown Business.

Kimbell, Lucy. 2014. *The Service Innovation Handbook*. Amsterdam: BIS Publishers.

Martin, Roger. 2007. *The Opposable Mind: How Successful Leaders Win Through Integrative Thinking*. Boston, MA: Harvard Business School Press.

McEntire School of Commerce (University of Virginia). n.d. "Integrated Core Curriculum (ICE)." https://www.commerce. virginia.edu/undergrad/ice.

McGrath, Rita Gunther. 2013. "Transient Advantage." *Harvard Business Review* 91, no. 6: 62–70.

Meadows, Donella. 2008. *Thinking in Systems: A Primer*. White River Junction, VT: Chelsea Green Publishing.

Osterwalder, Alexander, and Yves Pigneur. 2010. *Business Model Generation*. Hoboken, NJ: John Wiley & Sons.

Pearlstein, Steven. 2012. "Can We Save American Capitalism?" *Washington Post*, August 31. http://www.washingtonpost.com/ opinions/can-we-save-american-capitalism/2012/08/31/800de6be-f04e-11e1-ba17-c7bb037a1d5b_story.html.

Pine, Joseph B., and James H. Gilmore. 1998. "Welcome to the Experience Economy." *Harvard Business Review* 76: 97–105.

Quality Assurance Agency for Higher Education (QAA). 2007. *Subject Benchmark Statement for General Business and Management*. Gloucester, UK: QAA. http://www.qaa.ac.uk/en/Publications/ Documents/Subject-benchmark-statement-General-business-and-management.pdf.

Repenning, Nelson, Paulo Gonçalves, and Laura J. Black. 2001. "Past the Tipping Point: The Persistence of Firefighting in Product Development." *California Management Review* 43: 44–63.

Repenning, Nelson and John D. Sterman. 2001. "Nobody Ever Gets Credit for Fixing Problems That Never Happened: Creating and Sustaining Process Improvement." *California Management Review* 43, no. 4: 64–88.

Rittel, Horst, and Melvin Webber. 1973. "Dilemmas in a General Theory of Planning." *Policy Sciences* 4: 155–169.

Rothwell, Roy, Christopher Freeman, Anthony Horlsey, V. T. P. Jervis, A. B. Robertson, and James Townsend. 1974. "SAPPHO Updated-Project SAPPHO Phase II." *Research Policy* 3, no. 3: 258–291.

Rotman School of Management (University of Toronto). n.d. "Rotman's Integrative Thinking Program." https://www.rotman.utoronto.ca/ ProfessionalDevelopment/Executive-Programs/CoursesWorkshops/ Programs/Integrative-Thinking.aspx.

Sandel, Michael. 2012. "What Isn't for Sale?" *The Atlantic*, April. http:// www.theatlantic.com/magazine/archive/2012/04/what-isnt-for-sale/308902/.

Senge, Peter. 1990. *The Fifth Discipline: The Art & Practice of The Learning Organization*. New York: Doubleday.

Spiegel, Markus. 2014. "Organizational Innovation and Change in a Dynamic and Complex World: 'Simplexification'—Towards a Complex Adaptive Systems Perspective." Doctoral Dissertation, University of Liechtenstein.

Sterman, John D. 2000. *Business Dynamics: Systems Thinking for a Complex World*. New York: McGraw-Hill.

Sterman, John, and Hazhir Rahmandad. 2013. "Introduction to System Dynamics." *Massachusetts Institute of Technology: MIT OpenCourseWare*. Cambridge, MA: Massachusetts Institute of Technology. http://ocw.mit.edu.

Teece, David, and Gary Pisano. 1994. "The Dynamic Capabilities of Firms: An Introduction." *Industrial and Corporate Change* 3, no. 3: 537–556.

Visser, Willemien. 2006. *The Cognitive Artifacts of Designing*. Mahwah, NJ: Lawrence Erlbaum Associates.

Whitehead, Alfred North. 1929. *The Aims of Education and Other Essays*. New York: Macmillan.

8

A Set of Further Reflections on Improving Teaching, Learning, and Assessment

Editors' Note

Reflecting our openness to critical commentary and reflection, we have invited a set of commentaries on the work from thought leaders in higher education: Peter Ewell (National Center for Higher Education Management Systems); Natasha Jankowski and George Kuh (National Institute for Learning Outcomes Assessment); Carol Geary Schneider (Association of American Colleges & Universities); and Charles Blaich and Kathleen Wise (Center of Inquiry at Wabash College).

A Promising Start and Some Way to Go: Some Reflections on the Measuring College Learning Project

Peter T. Ewell

National Center for Higher Education Management Systems

The SSRC's Measuring College Learning (MCL) project should be recognized as one of the most ambitious assessment efforts currently under way. In these brief reflections, I want to point out some positive features of the project, then outline some important challenges the project faces. In conclusion, I'd like to offer a few suggestions about possible ways forward for this interesting effort.

Noteworthy Features of MCL

Let me begin with three positive features of MCL. First, it is unambiguously centered on faculty. Most of the authors of the white papers in this volume are teaching faculty and understand from direct experience the challenges associated with improving instruction in their disciplines and the kinds of assessment information that will be needed to ground such efforts. Second, MCL is centered on learning in the disciplines, reflecting the insight that starting with disciplines will engage faculty best and that learning in the disciplines is what most academics consider legitimate *collegiate learning*. MCL has also involved disciplinary associations and communities much more actively than have most other assessment efforts. Third, the project's leaders have exhibited considerable openness to receiving input from the research and assessment communities. The fact that colleagues like George Kuh and Carol Geary Schneider who are skeptical of standardized tests are included as reactors in this volume provides strong testimony for the sincerity of this stance. The effort is also quite consciously incremental; few decisions are cast in stone and every step taken is conditioned by experience gained in the last. These are good qualities and I trust they will continue if the project moves forward.

Five Challenges

Despite these positive features, the MCL project faces at least five major challenges. First, one of its long-term objectives is to produce valid and reliable standardized assessment instruments within each of the six chosen disciplines. But decades of experience with free-standing instruments of this kind—including generic skills tests like the Collegiate Learning Assessment (CLA) and discipline-specific assessments like those in economics and engineering in the Assessing Higher Education Learning Outcomes (AHELO) Feasibility Study—is that student effort is, at best, uncertain when these examinations do not count. MCL project leaders are aware of this challenge and have thought about ways to address it. These include administering these assessments as part of required capstone courses in their respective disciplines and rewarding students with certificates or monetary payments if they perform well. The effectiveness of these remedies, nevertheless, remains untested.

A second challenge is that the central purpose of the enterprise is still not entirely clear. Much of the project's rhetoric admirably emphasizes instructional improvement, but improvement does not necessarily require standardized assessments based on common content or, with the exception of benchmarking, the ability to compare performance across contexts. One claimed potential application is to assess aspiring transfer students, but the central question for most transfers is about their mastery of generic skills like writing or quantitative fluency, not disciplinary content. As Sam Messick of ETS explained some two decades ago, the validity of any assessment rests substantially on the uses to which its results will be put. Yet the MCL project has not yet given sufficient consideration to the practical utility of the kinds of assessments it advocates.

Establishing a central purpose will also help govern decisions about the most important technical features of the instruments envisioned. One of the most important is the balance in coverage between subject-matter content and skills elements that may, in part, cross disciplines. The competencies described in this volume are a mix of these: some are unique to the discipline, while others represent more generic proficiencies, like locating or analyzing information, that are set in the context of the discipline. If one outcome of the MCL project is to support generalizations about the latter across subject areas, as I believe it should be, instruments will have to be designed and administered to ensure this is possible. And the real demand from key stakeholders outside the academy like employers and policymakers is for measures of generic skills.

Two related practical challenges round out my list of five. The first is that MCL is bucking the current trend away from test-based assessment in American higher education. According to the National Institute for Learning Outcomes Assessment's (NILOA) survey on the conduct of assessment in academic programs, the modal forms of assessment at the department level are performance assessments and rubric-based ratings of student assignments and other artifacts; only about 30 percent of academic programs use standardized examinations. Admittedly, the current lack of use may be due to a dearth of suitable instruments—a condition that MCL hopes to alleviate. But the fact remains that its stance on assessment technology puts the project out of the mainstream of current assessment practice at the program level. The final related challenge is that the MCL project appears to lack a business plan that ensures its long-term sustainability. Up to now, the project has been generously supported by the Bill and Melinda Gates Foundation, but this will not continue indefinitely. There are many potential business models from which to choose to make the project sustainable: SSRC could market the instruments directly or work through the appropriate disciplinary associations to do so; alternatively, a major testing organization could offer the instruments. But marketing, pricing, and the ongoing availability of alternate forms of the instruments would be continuing challenges.

The Way Forward

Given this situation, I offer three suggestions to consider if the project is to move forward, none of which will be surprising to the project's leaders. First, continue to take every opportunity to communicate with stakeholders and the academic community. MCL participants' work has necessarily proceeded largely in private to date, but the publication of this volume represents an inescapable coming out. Communicating effectively will require greater clarity about the purpose of the enterprise and full transparency with respect to how assessments will be designed, created, and made available to the academy. Second, roll out assessments and other products when they are ready without waiting to release everything at once. With six suites of instruments to build, there will undoubtedly be uneven development. Early release of measures that are ready—perhaps in a pilot form—will help build a user community quickly, which is particularly important in a new venture. Similarly, don't hesitate to create intermediate products that add value to the overall strategy well before draft assessments are created. The six competency frameworks, for example, could easily be used to create curriculum maps to determine how and where particular programs address each element and, more importantly, to identify where they do not. They could also inform the development of faculty guides for creating aligned classroom assignments and examinations, in much the same way as the Degree Qualifications Profile (DQP) has done. Finally, don't stop developing. As soon as actual assessments are created from competency frameworks, experience suggests, there is a tendency to stop looking at the latter. In contrast, as Tuning has demonstrated, such frameworks are living entities, always subject to rethinking because of new knowledge and the evolution of new ways to organize and teach these proficiencies.

The MCL project constitutes a fresh departure on the age-old quest to improve instruction in an important collection of disciplines. I wish it luck and urge its leaders to continue to call on fellow members of the assessment community to advise them on this journey.

MCL and Disciplinary Discourses: A Promising Step toward Assuring Collegiate Quality

Natasha Jankowski and George Kuh

National Institute for Learning Outcomes Assessment

The Measuring College Learning (MCL) project brought together groups of faculty from six disciplines to identify concepts and competencies fundamental to their respective fields and reflect on related assessment practices. Encouraged and supported by disciplinary associations and some specialized accreditors, the goal was to ensure that today's students are getting from the undergraduate experience what they need to survive and thrive during and after college in an era of dynamic economic and social change. Toward this end, participating faculty devoted considerable time and energy to fleshing out core concepts and competencies, which were then presented in a series of discipline-specific white papers. Although much was accomplished, much remains to be done for MCL to realize its promise. In this essay, we summarize some of the project's salient contributions with an eye toward the challenges that must be addressed to achieve its goal.

Contributions

To its credit, MCL engaged faculty members in meaningful conversations about what is essential for students to know and be able to do as a result of studying a particular field, thereby serving several important purposes. For example, the discussions addressed how to intentionally sequence educational experiences over time to scaffold and deepen student learning. This process is similar to what we observed faculty and staff typically do at institutions using Tuning and the Degree Qualifications Profile (DQP) to reach agreement about the core concepts, appropriate inquiry approaches, and desired competencies expected of general education as well as different fields of study.

Identifying the necessary concepts and competencies relevant for their respective disciplines brought to light the need for curriculum mapping, alignment, and assignment design as critical steps for assuring disciplinary proficiency and building coherent pathways to student success. These outcomes are consistent with and extend the current work of the National Institute for Learning Outcomes Assessment (e.g., Hutchings, Jankowski, and Ewell 2014; Jankowski and Marshall 2014).

The faculty authors made it clear that the essential concepts and competencies they identified are not intended to stand independent one from another, but must be integrated and applied by students. Especially important to efforts to implement coherent, learning-rich guided pathways to certificate or degree completion is finding ways to help students perceive and acknowledge the connections between their experiences inside and outside of class, the outcomes the educational program is designed to elicit, and the outcomes they have attained. Indeed, the authors of the MCL white papers found that their discernment process helped to generate answers to such questions as why certain elements are foundational to a particular discipline, but not necessarily others. It also shed light on why and how to design assignments and other educational experiences to induce students to practice the essential tasks of reflection and integration that will enable them to transfer their learning to settings beyond the current classroom, laboratory, or studio. Much like what we found with the DQP and Tuning projects, when faculty talk together and reflect on the essential elements of their discipline in combination with what matters in terms of expected student learning outcomes, they more readily reach consensus about the importance of pedagogical approaches, curricular designs, and assessment frameworks that are congenial with an institution's stated desired outcomes of college and the expectations of a variety of stakeholders external to the campus.

Each of the MCL white papers builds on prior work in their field to reach consensus about desired outcomes and how to assess them. They each refer to the importance of engaging students in introductory courses and designing tasks requiring students to demonstrate they have integrated core concepts and competencies across the program of study. They also emphasize the need to use assessment approaches that align with the desired outcomes and yield actionable evidence, ensuring that students actively participate in the process.

For example, the MCL in Business paper focuses on the future of the field, expressing a keen desire to define explicitly the core elements of a strong business program. At the same time, the authors caution that because the field is complex and nuanced, certain of these elements may be contestable because of a program's particular purposes and local circumstances, including institutional culture and employer needs. Biology faculty emphasized the need to connect this work with instructional enhancement efforts to increase the likelihood that faculty would use pedagogical approaches consistent with desired outcomes. The economics paper underscored the role of classroom assessment to encourage faculty to be more explicit about what they are teaching and why. The communication paper echoed many of these same ideas while pointing to the need for a larger collaborative effort to enhance student success. The history paper argued for more frequent use of assessments of authentic student learning. The sociology presentation emphasized what was implicit in all the papers—that what makes a discipline unique is that the whole is greater than the sum of its individual parts (e.g., courses, papers, internships). Helping faculty to recognize, celebrate, and innovate based on acknowledging what makes their discipline distinctive is one of the more promising contributions of the MCL project.

Challenges

Taken together, the MCL white papers are understandably long on fleshing out what constitute core concepts and competencies but short on the kinds of discipline-specific standardized assessments that can point to what is needed to improve student performance. True enough, a field must first agree on what is worth knowing and being able to do along with appropriate pedagogical strategies that will help students attain those outcomes before it can determine how best to document whether students have achieved those outcomes. But assuming the MCL papers have adequately captured these essential elements, the next necessary step is to describe what constitutes a coherent educational experience bolstered by ongoing multiple formative feedback processes for students and programs. Any effort to develop summative tests of discipline-specific knowledge, proficiencies, and dispositions must assume that students have experienced the educational program in a manner consistent with the program's espoused intended design. Of course, no single test can determine whether the enacted or delivered program and students' actual experiences are aligned with the field's foundational elements and preferred pedagogical approaches, curricular components, and assessments.

Another challenge is appropriately situating the MCL project in the national dialogue about improving and assessing student learning. NILOA's work in this arena shows a recent spike in the use of rubrics, portfolios, and scaffolded learning experiences that build over time. Indeed, when asked which of the sources of information on student learning are most useful to inform decisions, the number one response was classroom-based assessments (Kuh, Jankowski, Ikenberry, and Kinzie 2014). Common to these tools and approaches are frequent feedback and reflection experiences. Although the white papers reference the need for measures of authentic student learning, the major goal of the project—identifying what students should know and be able to do after obtaining a baccalaureate degree in a given field—may well evolve into the search for standardized tests that will inevitably be used to compare programs and institutions. Whether such an eventuality can also serve to enhance the quality of student learning and institutional performance remains to be seen. Indeed, experience shows that it is difficult for institutions or programs to use the results from standardized tests to inform curricular improvements; in part, this is because such tools are often designed and employed for the purpose of accountability as contrasted with improvement (Jankowski et al. 2012).

So it appears that the MCL project is at a crossroads, given that the set of white papers opine for assessment tools and approaches that could potentially serve formative needs—providing feedback to both instructors and students for how to improve learning outcomes and curriculum design—while also providing summative indicators of quality. Clarifying the assessment ends valued by the

MCL project would help focus the next stage of work. It would also be instructive to determine what role, if any, the work could play in encouraging appropriate levels of transparency (i.e., how to communicate program and student performance to those with a need or interest in knowing, including students). For example, employers today are less interested in transcripts and test scores and more interested in evidence that a student can use what they have learned to deal with complex, unscripted problems in different settings (Hart Research Associates 2013). How the MCL project could better prepare students and assist institutions and employers in meeting this complicated set of challenges warrants further discussion.

References

Hart Research Associates. 2013. *It Takes More Than a Major: Employer Priorities for College Learning and Student Success*. Washington, DC: Association of American Colleges & Universities.

Hutchings, Pat, Natasha A. Jankowski, and Peter T. Ewell. 2014. *Catalyzing Assignment Design Activity on Your Campus: Lessons from NILOA's Assignment Library Initiative*. Urbana: University of Illinois and Indiana University, National Institute for Learning Outcomes Assessment (NILOA).

Jankowski, Natasha A., and David W. Marshall. 2014. *Roadmap to Enhanced Student Learning: Implementing the DQP and Tuning*. Urbana: National Institute for Learning Outcomes Assessment (NILOA) and Institute for Evidence-Based Change (IEBC).

Jankowski, Natasha A., Stan O. Ikenberry, Jillian Kinzie, George D. Kuh, Gloria F. Shenoy, and Gianina R. Baker. 2012. *Transparency and Accountability: An Evaluation of the VSA College Portrait Pilot*. Urbana: University of Illinois and Indiana University, National Institute for Learning Outcomes Assessment (NILOA).

Kuh, George D., Natasha Jankowski, Stan O. Ikenberry, and Jillian Kinzie. 2014. *Knowing What Students Know and Can Do: The Current State of Student Learning Outcomes Assessment in US Colleges and*

Universities. Urbana: University of Illinois and Indiana University, National Institute for Learning Outcomes Assessment (NILOA).

How MCL Can Make a Lasting Difference

Carol Geary Schneider

Association of American Colleges and Universities

The work initiated through Measuring College Learning (MCL) is an important marker in the ongoing effort to make visible what students are supposed to achieve through their college majors and to help document what, in fact, they have achieved. The reports developed by the several task forces are illuminating, and I suggest in the second part of this essay some ways that they can be put immediately to very important use. But first, a few words on the MCL assessment strategy itself.

MCL was, of course, envisioned as part of a multipronged toolkit for assessing student learning in major fields that would complement other assessments of general education and cross-cutting learning outcomes or proficiencies such as critical thinking or communication skills. As of this writing, it remains unclear whether the intended tests will be developed. Moreover, the papers produced for this volume provide only the most general guidelines for psychometricians. So the test development effort remains something of an unknown, and may not happen.

I do, however, want to echo Peter Ewell's caution, expressed in this volume, that it's extremely challenging to get students to show up and do their best on standardized tests that are voluntary, rather than required. We know this from over a decade of field-testing the Collegiate Learning Assessment (CLA). The performance task aspects of the CLA were (and still are) a significant step forward in assessment strategy. For this reason, the Association of American Colleges and Universities (AAC&U) initially was a partner in the CLA effort. But as a former member of the CLA board,

I came to doubt that tests with high stakes for the institution and no stakes for the students taking them are an appropriate index of students' learning gains in college. The same concern would apply to a department's adoption of voluntary tests of learning in the disciplines. Without a stake in the results of an assessment, students have no real incentive to make sure those results embody their best work. This is especially true for seniors, whose attention is usually split in many compelling directions during their final year. We may learn what they can do on the run, but surely what we'd like to know is what students can do when they give their entire effort to a complex problem or set of problems.

It's plausible, of course, to require that all students take a standardized test to complete their major or degree programs. But because that would likely be far more expensive than simply testing a representative sample of students, requiring new disciplinary tests of all students in a department may not be an affordable option.

Believing that assessments of college learning should show what students can do when they know the work counts, AAC&U has recommended a quite different assessment strategy, one that uses validated scoring guides—the VALUE rubrics developed for cross-cutting learning outcomes[1]—to assess samples of work that students originally created as graded course assignments.

With ample funding from federal and private philanthropic sources, AAC&U, nine state systems, and over eighty diverse colleges, universities, and community colleges have demonstrated

---

[1] Through AAC&U's Valid Assessment of Learning in Undergraduate Education (VALUE) project, teams of faculty and other educational professionals from over a hundred higher education institutions developed rubrics based on the most frequently identified characteristics or criteria of learning for each of sixteen cross-cutting college learning outcomes. To learn more about the project or to download the VALUE rubrics, visit www.aacu.org/value.

that the VALUE rubrics can be used in an organized way, across multiple disciplines and multiple years of study, to provide evidence on strengths and weaknesses in students' achievement of such essential learning outcomes as critical thinking, quantitative reasoning, and communication. In 2016, that demonstration is expanding to include additional learning outcomes such as ethical reasoning, intercultural competence, and integrative learning.

A VALUE Assessment Strategy for the Disciplines

As the opening essay in this volume makes clear, MCL leaders have been generous from the outset in proposing that the MCL disciplinary assessments can and should be viewed as complementary to AAC&U's focus on assessing cross-cutting learning outcomes (a term I prefer, incidentally, to *generic competencies*). But, in fact, the VALUE strategy for assessing students' learning gains in college could be adapted for disciplinary fields as well.

If developed, discipline-specific scoring guides or rubrics ("Major VALUE") could enable faculty to assess the intellectual skills or competencies that the disciplinary task forces have articulated for the six disciplines included in the initial MCL analysis of learning goals. Scoring guides also could address the concepts the task forces consider essential. I believe it would be highly useful to the relevant fields to develop discipline-specific scoring rubrics for the concepts outlined in the opening chapter and in the various task force white papers.

As a historian looking at the historians' recommended concepts, for example, I know it would be challenging but well worth the effort to articulate scoring guides for history as an interpretive account, the relationship of past and present, historical evidence, complex causality, and significance. But if I were a student—and this is my core point—I am quite certain that I would be far better able to demonstrate my understanding of such concepts in the context of a well-researched paper completed for a course grade than in the context of an optional test I took on the run, with only a few minutes to think through the questions asked, to analyze the documentary artifacts provided, and to consider the argument I wanted to make. Moreover, if ETS or another testing agency moves to develop standardized tests for such concepts, psychometricians and historians are going to have to work together anyway to translate the past into actual testable concepts. It would be far better, in my judgment, for them to work together instead on the development of scoring guides or rubrics for such concepts that faculty can apply to samples of students' course-related writing and research. The rubrics could then be used both by departmental faculty in assessing their students' progress toward degree-level mastery and also in national studies of learning in the discipline, organized along the lines of AAC&U and SHEEO's current VALUE demonstration project.

Discipline-related scoring guides would enable evidence of students' learning to be drawn from the required curriculum and from work students have already completed for a grade. This approach would build confidence that the student work being assessed represents, at least for most students, what they can do when they are actively trying to get the assignment right because the assignment actually counts, for the course and for their progress toward a degree.

It really is time to break that reflexive connection educators developed over the past century between the concept of assessing students' learning and the assumption that we absolutely must use standardized tests to produce accurate results. I am mindful that the VALUE strategy AAC&U is advancing marks only the beginning of that longer term shift. But we could make huge progress if MCL and the disciplinary societies were to band together to insist that the use of student work and validated rubrics is a preferable approach to demonstrating the value and worth of college study.

But Before We Assess, Let's Attend to the Curriculum!

With all that said, however, I want to point toward a complementary, yet different, use of the significant intellectual work that the MCL project has elicited.

This volume begins with the argument that we need new measures to show that college really is worth it. But as Arum and Roksa know very well, there is broad agreement across many forms of assessment that our colleges, universities, and community colleges are significantly *underperforming* when it comes to the development of the cross-cutting capacities currently being assessed. Students' highly uneven achievement on key cross-cutting learning outcomes has already been documented through the VALUE national demonstration projects, through studies by the Wabash Center for Inquiry in the Liberal Arts, and by Arum and Roksa themselves.

Moreover, as the abundant research on novice–expert thinking demonstrates, students achieve their highest levels of critical inquiry and other cross-cutting skills in their disciplines, not in foundational general education studies. Critical inquiry is always about something, and the major, when well organized, provides guided practice in applying particular analytical and inquiry strategies to the content areas that field explores. Optimally, as AAC&U has recommended repeatedly for a quarter century, the major also provides guided practice in connecting its own interpretations with those of other communities—other disciplinary communities and real-world communities in which students hope to take their place (AAC 1991; AAC&U 2008, 2015). One of the great strengths of the MCI disciplinary papers is that their authors see the value of connecting learning in a discipline with the larger society and with other fields of inquiry.

If the major is the context in which students are developing their most advanced cross-cutting capacities, and if large numbers of students are demonstrably underperforming on many different measures of those capacities, then—to my mind—the needed next step is to redesign students' pathways through their majors in ways that make it more likely that students will both achieve the goals of the major and develop the cross-cutting capacities that faculty have identified and that students will need to participate effectively in the economy and in our democracy (Hart Research Associates 2006, 2008, 2010, 2013, 2015; National Task Force 2012).

As educators, everyone involved in MCL and related initiatives, such as Tuning or VALUE, needs to focus on helping far more students successfully achieve the specific goals for the liberal and liberating education that the MCL and Tuning studies have articulated.

Today, I would argue, there is a well-established consensus on the core components of a quality college education. This well-established consensus reaffirms the importance of a strong liberal education that combines broad and specialized learning. But it also adds new components to our contemporary conception of liberal learning. These components include specific intellectual skills or cross-cutting capacities that need to be practiced in general education and in majors. They also include opportunities for students to integrate and apply their learning in the context of both disciplinary problems and real-world problems of the kind they will face in the workplace and in civil society (AAC&U 2007; Hart Research Associates 2016; Lumina Foundation 2014).

Along with reports from disciplinary Tuning efforts across multiple states, the MCL reports provide contemporary maps and markers for ensuring that students' learning in specialized fields contributes robustly to their preparation for a complex world. But there is a yawning chasm between reading a report on intended learning goals for a discipline and mobilizing to ensure that a program of study is well designed to help all students actually work toward those goals.

My hope, therefore, and my strong recommendation, is that MCL leaders will band together with leaders from Tuning efforts and from the relevant disciplinary communities in order to advance far-reaching curricular redesign in their fields. Higher education will never successfully fulfill its most ambitious goals for student accomplishment until faculty agree they have a communal responsibility to design programs and courses that ensure students reliably encounter the intended core concepts and frequently practice the necessary cross-cutting capacities.

AAC&U already is moving in exactly this direction with its contemporary LEAP Challenge, which argues that all students should be well prepared to produce significant projects—what we call *signature work*—in the final phase of college.[2] These projects optimally connect students' learning in their majors with their learning from other fields of inquiry related to their interests. Over fifty institutions already are working on LEAP Challenge projects, and we expect others to join this effort soon. This recommended addition of meaningful culminating work to the expected curriculum is a reform already demonstrably in the making. Today, according to the National Survey of Student Engagement, 47 percent of graduating seniors say they are doing (or have done) culminating projects (NSSE 2014, 41). The vast majority of these are completed in majors.

But why only 47 percent? Why not all students?

A senior project could—and should—be assessed to see whether it demonstrates mastery of the concepts important to the student's major as well as development of cross-cutting capacities needed for the world beyond college. It could further be assessed for evidence of the student's ability to employ approaches from more than one field—that is, to see whether the student can combine general and disciplinary studies effectively.

Before we can assess culminating work, however, we need to ensure that senior projects are well designed to help students take their conceptual learning and their cross-cutting inquiry capacities to a high level of achievement. And, crucially, we need to ensure that students have had ample preparation and practice in their prior

---

[2] Part of AAC&U's ongoing Liberal Education and America's Promise (LEAP) initiative, the LEAP Challenge calls on colleges and universities to engage students in signature work that will prepare them to integrate and apply their learning to a significant project with meaning to the student and to society. For more information, see http://www.aacu.org/leap-challenge.

studies to tackle a senior project successfully. If the Major VALUE rubrics recommended above are developed, faculty in departments could use those rubrics in setting criteria for senior projects and back-mapping the curriculum so students are well prepared.

The MCL reports provide a strong point of departure to create those high-quality learning pathways through the multiyear college curriculum—and across two-year and four-year transfer. What we need next, and what I warmly encourage MCL leaders and partners to move rapidly to help create, are curricular maps that our students and faculty can follow.

References

Association of American Colleges (AAC). 1991. *The Challenge of Connecting Learning: Project on Liberal Learning, Study-in-Depth, and the Arts and Sciences Major.* Washington, DC: Association of American Colleges.

Association of American Colleges & Universities (AAC&U). 2008. *Our Students' Best Work: A Framework for Accountability Worthy of Our Mission*, 2nd ed. Washington, DC: AAC&U.

Association of American Colleges & Universities (AAC&U). 2015. *The LEAP Challenge: Education for a World of Unscripted Problems.* Washington, DC: AAC&U.

Association of American Colleges & Universities (AAC&U). 2016. *College Learning for the New Global Century: A Report from the National Leadership Council for Liberal Education and America's Promise.* Washington, DC: AAC&U.

Hart Research Associates. 2006. *How Should Colleges Prepare Students to Succeed in Today's Global Economy?* Washington, DC: AAC&U.

Hart Research Associates. 2008. *How Should Colleges Assess and Improve Student Learning? Employers' Views on the Accountability Challenge* Washington, DC: AAC&U.

Hart Research Associates. 2010. *Raising the Bar: Employers' Views on College Learning in the Wake of the Economic Downturn.* Washington, DC: AAC&U.

Hart Research Associates. 2013. *It Takes More Than a Major: Employer Priorities for College Learning and Student Success*. Washington, DC: AAC&U.

Hart Research Associates. 2015. *Falling Short? College Learning and Career Success*. Washington, DC: AAC&U.

Hart Research Associates. 2016. *Recent Trends in General Education Design* Washington, DC: AAC&U.

Lumina Foundation. 2014. *The Degree Qualifications Profile*. Indianapolis, IN: Lumina Foundation.

National Survey of Student Engagement (NSSE). 2014. *Bringing the Institution into Focus: Annual Results 2014*. Bloomington, IN: Indiana University Center for Postsecondary Research.

National Task Force on Civic Learning and Democratic Engagement. 2012. *A Crucible Moment: College Learning & Democracy's Future*. Washington, DC: AAC&U.

Don't Let the Promise of Better Measures Tomorrow Excuse Inaction Today

Charles Bluich and Kathleen Wise

Center of Inquiry at Wabash College

We are grateful to the seventy faculty from six disciplines who worked hard over the last two years to identify a concise set of core concepts and competencies for their disciplines. Faculty who have struggled to identify learning outcomes for their own departments will appreciate how difficult it would be to identify a succinct set of learning outcomes that would be relevant for an entire field as it is represented across hundreds of colleges and universities. Whatever happens next in the Measuring College Learning Project (MCL), the papers in this volume provide faculty in these six disciplines across the country with relevant background information about measures and outcomes that they can use to kick-start the development or refinement of their departmental assessment plans.

One consistent thread through the papers is the need for better measures of the core concepts and competencies that the committees identified for their disciplines. Indeed, one of the Social Science Research Council's (SSRC) goals for this project is to "develop a new faculty-informed field-specific instrument and field test it alongside existing instruments of generic collegiate skills and measures of instructional practices."[3] Unfortunately, if experience is a guide, even with hard and well-funded work, it will take five to ten years before new and better tools are available for the disciplines represented in this project. The question for us, then, is beyond the guidance that this excellent collection of reviews may give to faculty who are working on their departmental learning goals, what should we do now to prepare for the time when better measures are available? This is an important question because measures on their own do not promote student learning, and the lack of better measures is not the main obstacle that currently prevents faculty from using evidence to improve student learning.

Fulcher and his colleagues (2014) nicely summed up the problem of seeing better measures as the path to improving student learning:

> A pig never fattened up only because it was weighed. A racehorse never ran faster because a stopwatch was clicked. A fevered dog's temperature never dropped as a result of reading a thermometer. . . . Nevertheless, some infer that student learning will automatically improve as a result of assessment. Indeed, test vendors often convince administrators that new instruments X and Y will bring about student learning. Such tools have not, do not, and will not by themselves improve learning.

We have been here before. In the early 2000s, the lack of modern critical thinking tests led to the development of the

---

[3] http://www.ssrc.org/programs/measuring-college-learning/

performance-based Collegiate Learning Assessment (CLA). The increased popularity of this measure along with the advocacy of higher education associations that supported the Voluntary System of Accountability led to revisions in the ACT CAAP Critical Thinking Test and the ETS Proficiency Profile so that they could be administered using roughly the same value-added method that the CLA used to assess institutional contributions to improved critical thinking. Subsequently, the Association of American Colleges and Universities (AAC&U) developed and promoted the use of its VALUE rubrics as an advance over these standardized measures that would permit faculty to use students' own work to measure how much they were developing on a range of learning goals, including critical thinking. Although none of these measures is perfect, we think they provide useful information about student learning, and that the evolutions of these and other measures shows that our ability to measure critical thinking continues to improve. But to what extent has the development, refinement, and expanded use of these measures at colleges and universities across the country resulted in demonstrable improvements in students' critical thinking? The evidence suggests not very much (Kuh et al. 2015).

We are not arguing that better measures would not help faculty develop a more precise sense of how much their students are learning. Of course they will. However, it is also true that evidence from students' performance on papers, exams, presentations, and departmental and institutional surveys, as well as information from student transcripts and faculty evaluations, among other things, already provide information that is more than good enough to help faculty identify, develop, and test changes in their majors that might improve student learning. The evidence we currently have could be better, but it's not useless. The fact that many departments, if they are using this information at all, are using it to write obligatory annual assessment reports rather than developing and testing changes to their majors means that there are other obstacles we need to address in the time before better standardized measures arrive so that these measures have a chance of helping us improve student learning.

In our experience, an important step that many departments could take *now* is to approach assessment as something more than a bureaucratic exercise to be completed with as little effort, interruption, or pain as possible. Effective, faculty-led assessment is grounded in ongoing conversations among faculty about the collective and developmental impact their work has on their students. It focuses on conversations that foster agreement on the concepts and competencies that faculty in the department hope to develop; reflections on whether the structure of the department's curriculum is consistent with these goals and research findings on student learning; questions about patterns that faculty notice in student work on assignments and considerations about whether these assignments really test, and foster, the departments' learning goals; and experiments in pedagogy that are aimed at improving students' in- and out-of-class experiences. In essence, assessment is an ongoing conversation about faculty development informed by evidence from students that promotes experiments in curricula, pedagogy, and experiences aimed at improving student learning. These conversations, experiments, and reviews of the impact of these experiments can only happen if the faculty in a department are willing to talk with one another, change what they are doing in response to these conversations, and communicate what they learn from these changes to their colleagues. Quality measurements are important, but the willingness of faculty to work together, including the willingness of individual faculty to give up things they want to do in their particular courses to improve how well students learn shared departmental goals, is even more important. Improving education is more about collective action than measurement.

We are encouraged by the careful work of the MCL panels. But we are also both mindful of and impatient with the fact that after so many years of working on assessment, we are still focusing on the first stage of the multistage assessment loop—defining learning outcomes. We can do much better for our students with what we have in hand.

References

Fulcher, Keston H., Megan R. Good, Chris M. Coleman, and Kristen L. Smith. 2014. *A Simple Model for Learning Improvement: Weigh Pig, Feed Pig, Weigh Pig*. Urbana: University of Illinois and Indiana University, National Institute for Learning Outcomes Assessment (NILOA).

Kuh, George D., Stan O. Ikenberry, Natasha A. Jankowski, Timothy Reese Caine, Peter T. Ewell, Pat Hutchings, and Jillian Kinzie. 2015. "Beyond Compliance. Making Assessment Matter." *Change Magazine* 47: 8–16.

Index